Disruptive Behaviour in schools!

Causes, Treatment and Prevention

Dr Portia G Holman
Dr Nelson F Coghill

Chartwell-Bratt   **Studentlitteratur**

© Portia, Holman, Nelson Coghill, and Chartwell-Bratt (Publishing and Training) Limited, 1987

Chartwell-Bratt Ltd, Old Orchard, Bickley Road, Bromley, Kent BR1 2NE, England
ISBN 0-86238-118-5

Studentlitteratur, Box 141, S-221 00 Lund, Sweden
ISBN 91-44-26411-9

Printed in Sweden by Studentlitteratur, Lund

Contents

Preface

To put right what begins to fail, whether a car or a marriage, one must understand how it works and why it is failing; and to understand what one is doing, it is essential to define what one regards as failure. Thus, to get from this book all it can give us, we must be sure what a school is — and the behaviour of its children will tell us a lot about that. We can then decide what we ought personally to do if that behaviour needs changing.

The authors are well qualified to study human response to experience. Both qualified and practising doctors, to them sickness and disruption call for investigation as the prelude to correction. But, since the organism holding our attention is now a school, its signals of distress cannot be read in terms of biology and its related sciences alone. They have their social and economic overtones. In a school, issues of authority may lead more readily to breakdown than may accident or infection; child and teacher may dislike each other, teacher may dislike the head, and the head may quarrel with the education office, or be cool towards the parents. The staff as a whole may resent others among the social services; some children are rebellious and unhappy because they are tormented by their classmates, perhaps because they are badly clothed and rarely bathed, their miseries exacerbated by hunger and deprivation. Premises and equipment may be inadequate, career prospects poor, police already harrassed and unsympathetic, community resources deficient. Thus, to ask why things go wrong with children at school raises many questions and calls up many views. It is the wealth and variety of these within this book that we shall find instructive.

There was, over and above the personal values and beliefs of the authors, every administrative reason for them to have teamed up as they did, devoting their time and energy to the common cause:

> "Why do so many children find themselves straying — or getting shoved — to the wrong side of life, and in the very schools appointed to lead them somewhere else altogether? If we can discover why, how do we then set about helping them, and their schools — and, if we can, the shovers, as well?"

I believe this book, without setting a fashion likely to threaten its own standards, will inspire several others; Western society, wherever one looks at it, is breathing heavily. We must study very carefully what, in the here-and-now, is said to be going wrong; when we do that we start to discover what is wrong with ourselves and those who are said to be in charge. We may then learn something quite new, just as we do by reading this book.

Reg Revans
Altrincham

Foreword

This significant book has its roots in local workshop and group activity concerned with behaviour problems in mainstream schools. The people involved encompassed a wide range of experience and perspectives in education and associated disciplines.

In acknowledging the stress experienced by teachers, in particular over difficult behaviour, their puzzlement as to how to respond and their frustration when 'expert' help seems lacking, the task must nevertheless be grasped by mainstream schools in which behaviour problems frequently occur. The first step is the sometimes painful recognition that social contexts have a significant influence upon children's experience, perceptions and reactions and that, whatever the suspected aetiology of a child's difficulties, the environment may be analysed and modified to bring about some reduction of a child's negative feelings about himself and other people, and so of the unacceptable behaviour.

Within the constraints of the many and increasing demands upon the school's available time, any school community of serious intent, led by the headteacher and all senior staff, including those with specific responsibilities for children with special needs, will be striving to improve its understanding and practice, within an appropriate framework. Because of the varied aetiology of difficulties and of professional responsibilities the framework must be wide and sophisticated. It covers awareness of relationships, not only in the home but within the school and between school and home. It embraces the issue of authoritarian or democratic management and the associated issues of power, control, cooperation and participation; equal opportunities for all operated through 'reward' rather than 'punishment'; high expectations and the laying aside of stereotyping and labelling; the maximising of internal and external resources, in particular the human resources — in the interests of the many children in manifest need of specific understanding and relatively greater support.

The principle of cooperative relationships between school, parents and pupils, and between professionals is fundamental, as is vigorously advocated by the authors. Whatever the constraints of time and skills, resources can be husbanded to the end of listening, the better to understand the experience and attitudes of others. The authors are adept at presenting arguments from different perspectives. They are not prescriptive as to solutions but emphasize the role of responsive relationships with advisory services in the continuous development of staff. Experts may help in this but only as an adjunct to the self-development of the school's strength and confidence.

In charting so thoroughly the complexities of the collective needs of carers and cared for, the authors have provided a valuable source book for teachers with senior responsibilities, and for others from relevant disciplines.

Maria C Roe BA, PhD
Formerly Senior Staff Inspector for Special Schools, ILEA.

Acknowledgements

We acknowledge our debt to the Disruptive Behaviour in Schools (DBIS) Group which acted as a stimulus to write this book. We are grateful to the many people who devoted time, energy and thought to help the group. The following members attended regularly: Dr Robin Benians, Dr Nelson Coghill, Muriel Colley, Toni Hertenstein, Dr Portia Holman, Allen James, David Jobson, Margaret Lorde, Stephen Novy, Sandra Ormerod, Walter Phipps, Janet Prince, Margaret Roberts and Jean Simpson. The following attended some of the group's meetings: Shirley Goodwin, Richard Heathcote, Jenny Jeffries, Kathy Markovich, Graham Nelson, Marion Stern JP, Michael Stone, Roy Willis and Nancy Zinkin.

We are grateful to the following who contributed information and/or critical comments: Reg Hartles CBE, Chief Education Officer, the London Borough of Ealing; Gill Brandon, Harry Clarke, Evelyn Davies, Shelagh Garvey, M B Gilbey, Christopher Harvey, Geoff Hartnall, Elizabeth Hopkinson, Edward Korel, Hans Lobstein, Anita Loring, Rowland Lowe, Mary Marsh, Bill Moody, Graham Munn, Don Perry, Joyce Shepherd and Pamela White. We thank Dr Annette Rawson and A B Cooper, of the DHSS, for help with factual and statistical information.

Ken Anderson, lately Director of Social Services in the London Borough of Ealing, has given great help with successive drafts of the chapter on social services. We are grateful to Margaret Roberts, Dr Robin Benians, Sandra Ormerod, Kathy Johnson, Sallie Withers and Bill Huddleston for their comments and contributions; and to Gill Libretto for making available to us unpublished data on withdrawal units. Muriel Colley and Robert Laslett have given invaluable help in the publication of this book.

The original initiative to look at the communication systems of schools and relevant agencies was inspired by the work of Prof R W Revans with whom one of us (NFC) had worked for many years. We are grateful to him for his help in setting up the action learning project referred to in the book.

We have received useful information from the London Branch of the Association of Workers for Maladjusted Children, the National Children's Bureau, the National Foundation for Educational Research, the National Society for the Prevention of Cruelty to Children and the Spastics Society.

We owe much to Helen Coghill for her support during the preparation and writing of this book, and for help in reading and commenting on the manuscript. We are grateful to Marie Munn for her patient typing of drafts of the manuscript.

Abbreviations

ACE	Advisory Centre for Education
AIMS	Association for Improvements in the Maternity Services
ALP	Action Learning Projects
AO	Attendance Officer
ATD	Aide à Toute Ditresse
AWMC	Association of Workers for Maladjusted Children
AWMCTE	Association of Workers for Maladjusted Children and Therapeutic Education
BASW	British Association of Social Workers
BBC	British Broadcasting Corporation
CASE	Confederation for the Advancement of State Education
CCETSW	Central Council for Education and Training in Social Work
CG	Child Guidance
CGC	Child Guidance Clinic
CQSW	Certificate of Qualification in Social Work
CSV	Community Service Volunteers
DBIS	Disruptive Behaviour in Schools (Group)
DES	Department of Education and Science
DHSS	Department of Health and Social Services
ECT	Electro-convulsive Therapy
EHV	Educational Home Visiting
ENT	Ear, Nose and Throat
EWO	Education Welfare Officer
FE	Further Education
FSU	Family Service Unit
GP	General (medical) Practitioner
HMI	Her Majesty's Inspector(s)
HMSO	Her Majesty's Stationery Office
IFAL	International Foundation for Action Learning
ILEA	Inner London Education Authority
IT	Intermediate Treatment
·LEA	Local Education Authority
MIT	Massachusetts Institute of Technology
MP	Member of Parliament

viii

MSC	Manpower Services Commission
NACRO	National Association for Care and Resettlement of Offenders
NAGM	National Association of (school) Governors and Managers
NALGO	National Association of Local Government Officers
NAS/UWT	National Association of Schoolmasters/Union of Women Teachers
NAWCH	National Association for the Welfare of Children in Hospital
NAYPIC	National Association of Young People in Care
NCB	National Children's Bureau
NCOPF	National Council for One Parent Families
NCPTA	National Confederation of Parent Teacher Associations
NCVO	National Council for Voluntary Organisations
NFER	National Foundation for Educational Research
NHS	National Health Service
NIPPERS	National Information for Parents of Prematures: Education, Resources and Support
NISW	National Institute for Social Work
NPEU	National Perinatal Epidemiology Unit
NSPCC	National Society for the Prevention of Cruelty to Children
NUSS	National Union of School Students
NUT	National Union of Teachers
OED	Oxford English Dictionary
OPCS	Office of Population Censuses and Surveys
PE	Physical Education
PPA	Preschool Playgroups Association
PTA	Parent Teacher Association
ROSLA	Raising of the School Leaving Age
STOPP	Society of Teachers Opposed to Physical Punishment
TV	Television
UK	United Kingdom
UN	United Nations
USA	United States of America

For troubled children
and those who care for them

Introduction

How is it that little children are so intelligent and
men so stupid? It must be education that does it.

Alexandre Dumas, fils, quoted in L Treich's
L'Esprit d'Alexandre Dumas

This book is the somewhat unexpected outcome of discussions of the
governors of a mixed comprehensive high school in the London Borough
of Ealing. On succeeding occasions the head reported on unacceptable
behaviour of some of the boys. Delinquency was a secondary problem,
confined to a few children, some of whom were also disruptive in class.
The morale and work of pupils and staff were adversely affected, directly
by the behaviour of the children and indirectly by the apparent inability
of the school to get help with its problems.

One of the governors (NFC) had studied methods of improving operational relationships in the management of a hospital. It was clear that
when people were able to learn from their own and others' experience at
work by free communication, problems could be better defined and were
more likely to be solved (Revans, 1972, 1976; Coghill, 1976; Coghill,
Mohey, Steffens and Stewart, 1977). It was apparent that many problems
of behaviour in schools were multifactorial in origin. The behavioural
problems in this school were unrelieved because the relevant agencies
(Table 1) had little or no contact with each other. Human problems are
insoluble if the people concerned do not discuss them together.

We suffer two broad consequences of children's disruptive behaviour.
Repairing vandalism and caring for disturbing children and adolescents
is expensive to the tune of many millions of pounds a year (1); and it is
costly in social terms — dealing with the distress of children and parents,
and the disturbance of schools and communities. Disturbing behaviour (2)
may be a threat to our way of life, not only directly by its assault on our
values, but also by an exclusive 'law and order' reaction to it. The
consequence of *not* caring properly for disturbing children is the cost of
the antisocial and mentally ill adults they become. When the measures
taken (or available), for example putting children (so expensively) into
care, not only fail to 'cure' the 'disorder' but actually confirm young
persons in their antisocial courses, there is a strong case — well argued
by Taylor, Lacey and Bracken (1979) — for us to examine what we are
doing. If social workers, teachers, doctors and indeed all of us were to
become more aware of the steps that lead inexorably to adolescent and
adult unwanted behaviour it might stimulate us to provide better care for

1

our troubled children. As the National Children's Bureau (NCB) has shown in its 'Who Cares?' project (Page and Clarke, 1977) the children themselves would be a valuable source of information and opinion in this exercise.

The governors of the school in question realised that this problem was not confined to one school. They thought that discussions between professional groups concerned would create a temperate atmosphere in which difficulties could be analysed, and professional attitudes defined. They asked the Education Committee to hold a conference as a first step, to bring together teachers and others concerned with the children or their families. The Education Committee set up a working party jointly with the Social Services Committee, consisting of councillors and senior officers to consider the nature and scope of a conference as one of a number of initiatives that might be taken. Although the working party sought the views of a number of organisations, the views of staff at basic levels, and of parents, were not solicited. Its interim report (London Borough of Ealing, 1977) — no final report is available — gave useful information about educational and other relevant facilities in the borough, but no coherent strategy of intra- and inter-professional communications emerged.

The other author of this book (PGH) had worked with Dr Maxwell Jones, pioneer of the 'therapeutic community' (Jones, 1952, 1962). We decided to set up a multidisciplinary group of professional people to examine disruptive behaviour in schools (DBIS group). The group included child psychiatrists, the head of a special school for maladjusted children, teachers from comprehensive high schools, a school counsellor, social workers, a play leader from a borough Parks and Amenities Department, school governors, a member of a police juvenile bureau, a borough councillor and a consultant physician. Contributions were made by a health visitor, a juvenile court magistrate, a director of a community centre and a health educationist. The group met 17 times over a period of some 20 months.

Disruptive children are currently dealt with by using one or more disjointed family/educational/social/medical (including psychiatric)/legal measures, too often with little or no communication between the parties. Those involved may not know what to do, and they may not be aware of what others are doing; worse, they may be in conflict (Watkins and Derrick, 1977). Schools are upset by the common practice of magistrates putting off judgements by repeated remands (3) while waiting for social reports and for other reasons. In the meantime, the child may fail to attend school and commit more offences, or may continue to attend, perhaps

2

intermittently, and cause more disturbance. Schools feel that neither social workers nor magistrates understand their difficulties. A sense of isolation and lack of support, and unawareness of other services or how to use them, are among the reasons for teachers feeling helpless in dealing with disruptive pupils.

The matter is complex because of the number and diversity of individuals and agencies who may be concerned with disruptive behaviour of school children (Table 1). Two or more agencies will mostly be involved. If such agencies work in isolation then neither the individual case nor the problem in general will be resolved. Locally the basic defect in communication was recognised (London Borough of Ealing, 1977) and it appears to be nationwide (FitzHerbert, 1977). The DBIS group was struck by the differing attitudes of teachers and social workers to the needs of the child.

The child with disruptive behaviour, while he may be an intolerable trial to the adults involved with him, is usually unhappy in himself. A child is governed for his first 16 years by adults many of whom have forgotten much of their own youth, and are largely motivated by self-interest. Many adults have difficulty in understanding and managing childhood aggression and violence. Rejection, the common response, compounds the child's difficulties. In all this we recognise that the *adult* predicament may be agonising. Even when the adult has personal resources for coping with life's difficulties, these may need bolstering by outside help — which may not be available even when it is desperately needed.

A report of the DBIS group's transactions, incorporating matters of definition, communication and attribution, and with references to studies and reports of work elsewhere, was submitted to the local authority. Much of the thought and material in this book are derived from the group's discussions.

Apart from the number of different people needed to help with disruptive behaviour the matter is complex in terms of the numerous strands of causation, treatment and prevention. Complexity is compounded by the natural dependency of children, the inadequacy of some parents and the multifarious relationships required for teachers to deal with behaviour problems.

This is not a book primarily about methods of education. Its purpose is to show how freer communications between professionals, and changes in their attitudes and practices, may help to modify behaviour in both children and teachers that has undesired consequences. Our aim is to increase mutual awareness of the roles of all professionals caring for

3

children so as to facilitate their working together. In Part I of the book we define the problem of disruptive behaviour and its causes, and mention how it affects teachers particularly. In Part II we suggest ways of dealing with it at an early age at relatively small cost. We discuss ways in which teachers and school policies may influence children's behaviour. We believe that preventive measures would reduce the frequency and the financial and social costs of disruptive children.

In Part III we discuss the value of training both for staff caring for children with disturbing behaviour, and as an aid to earlier recognition of the problem and its prevention. In Part IV we examine the purpose and nature of education; and the promotion of communications and relationships between professionals and agencies. Many local and national initiatives and bodies designed to help with the difficulties of children, schools and parents, blush relatively unheard of. To promote dissemination among people in the field, we provide information about a number of them (Appendix 1) (4).

We hope that the book will be helpful to teachers, social workers, child guidance staff, educational administrators (and inspectors and advisers), education welfare officers, doctors, nurses, health visitors, health educationists, clergy, parents, police and older pupils.

The motif of obligations to children is taken up in publications such as those of the National Council for Civil Liberties (Rae, Hewitt and Hugill, 1979). The UN has issued a list of ten 'Rights of the Child'. 1979 was the International Year of the Child, 1981 the Year of the Disabled and 1985 International Youth Year. Let these be a spur to adults to examine their attitudes to children, and their care of them. Children's interests should be paramount.

In many areas of the country education is provided in first, middle and high schools; in others schools are classed as primary and secondary. We have used terminology which we hope will avoid confusion about children's age ranges.

We have eschewed use of the term 'misbehaviour' because it implies judgement about deviation from the 'normal'. It is better to speak of behaviour which people find 'disturbing'. The word 'stress' is often used in relation to people in difficulties. Attempts to define it (Galloway, 1985a) are not entirely successful. The Shorter OED suggests that the word is an aphetic form of 'distress'. In this book we speak of adults and children being under stress when they suffer experiences they cannot endure, using the word to denote not the burden so much as its effects upon the person. Throughout we use the male pronoun for simplicity, rather than 'he/she' etc.

4

Table 1: Individuals and agencies who may be concerned at appropriate times with difficult children and their families

1. **Children**

    The child concerned

    Other children, in or outside the school, and/or their parents

2. **Parent(s) or parent substitutes of the child concerned**

3. **Teachers**

    Form teacher (first or middle school)

    Head teacher and deputies

    Counsellor, housemaster(s), tutors, remedial teachers, other specialist teachers (withdrawal units), any other teacher particularly affected by the problem

4. **Other members of the school staff**

    School nurses or matrons

    School caretaker

    School secretaries

    School welfare workers

    Kitchen staff

5. **Others concerned with the school or the child**

    School Governors

    School council

    The LEA

    The Social Services Department

    Child guidance team

    Police

    Magistrates

    Doctors (eg, school doctor, GP or consultant)

    Education welfare officers

    Health visitor

    Youth services

    Representatives of religious bodies

6. **Special schools or special units** for difficult children

Notes

1. The peak age of offending is 15 years (Secretary of State for Education and Science, 1985).

It is impossible to obtain accurate and up to date information about the cost of vandalism. The Department of Education and Science (DES) keeps no records of its cost in schools. It was reported in *Parents and Schools*, a CASE publication, in Nov 1976 that vandalism and arson in schools was costing over £15m per annum. One third of school vandalism was done by children under 12. It was estimated that in Glasgow alone the cost of repairing vandalism would build two new primary schools a year. The DES (1985) reported that one local education authority (LEA) in 1984 spent £1.3m making good damage from vandalism, and another LEA £300,000 simply repairing broken windows. The DES (1986a) reported that vandalism and arson cost 60 LEAs nearly £60m in 1984/85. The newspapers contain almost daily accounts of vandalism to telephone kiosks, shop windows, cars, railways, football grounds, and public and private property.

The average cost of children in care per child per week in England and Wales for 1981-82 (the latest years available) are as follows: Department of Health and Social Security (DHSS) (1984): boarded out £29.52; in community homes £201.01; in registered voluntary homes £160.51; in other accommodation £49.07. There is great variation between different parts of the country. According to 1985-86 estimates for England and Wales (Personal social services statistics available from the Chartered Institute of Public Finance and Accountancy) the cost (excluding capital charges) per child per week in a hostel or community home (without education) averaged £214.96 in non-metropolitan counties; £196.87 in metropolitan districts; and £351.48 in London. The same source gives the cost per child per week in an observation or assessment centre as averaging £336.25 in non-metropolitan counties; £242.62 in metropolitan districts; and £987.55 in London.

In 1979 it cost over £100 a week to keep a young offender in a detention centre (National Association for Care and Resettlement of Offenders (NACRO), 1979a). Incarceration of young people is ineffective as a preventive and it is expensive — £10 000 a year (in 1979) to keep one young person in a secure establishment (Tutt, 1979). The cost in 1982 of detaining one child in such a unit had risen to between £20 000 and £45 000 a year (Hencke, 1982a). It costs about £10 000 a year to keep someone in prison.

2. *Observer* 9/9/1979. Picture and caption — 'Young hooligans beat the boredom of late-night travelling by discharging a fire extinguisher at a cowering passenger. Sometimes the violence is worse. One passenger has died and others have been stabbed in a series of motiveless attacks during recent months. London Transport workers have also been victims of the thugs.'

   Scobie W. Murder is child's play in the cities. *Observer* 9/9/1979. — A description of gang warfare and killings by young people (aged 12 to 26), in the USA. Many of the killings were wanton.

3. Claimed as a virtue in Leeds where repeated remands are used with avowed punitive purposes, to induce truants to attend school. Although this practice is moderately effective, it is merely symptomatic treatment. How much do such unwilling pupils learn at school? Repeated adjournment of court cases presumably 'works' by incorporating the parents who have to attend each time with their child; this is helpful, but there is little institutional learning where it is also needed: the school (Hersov and Berg, 1981).

4. And see *Someone to talk to directory* (Eds) Thompson D, Webb P, Pudney M. (See references.)

Part I: The nature of the problem

Chapter 1 — The children

The beginning of health is to know the disease

— *Cervantes.*

Many people, while they have little difficulty in recognising physical handicap, seem reluctant or unable to accept the reality of psychological handicap in disturbed children. Such children are in double jeopardy: unable to cope with their feelings they at best get no sympathy and at worst, and all too commonly, are repulsed by adults lacking understanding of their disability and put off by their behaviour (Colley, 1976). Children under the age of 12 tend to be easier to control; they are more likely to rebel when they are older. Primary schools may be able to deal with most behaviour problems because of smaller school size, and the way they organise the time-table and curriculum. Bright children may be upset because of dull parents, or homes that do not facilitate their school work. In middle class homes there may be undue parental pressure upon a dull child. If the peer group has a stronger influence than parents, children who stay at home to do homework may be despised and so give up doing it.

Young people send messages about their feelings of alienation or lack of engagement, for example T-shirts reading: 'No future', and 'Damned'. Punk styles of hair, clothing and body decoration illustrate young people's feelings about how society regards them, and are an attempt to develop a personal identity in an unaccommodating environment. There are still too few outlets, both in and out of school, for the less well endowed children. They compare unfavourably with those for the intelligent, the athletic, or the child with creative gifts. To be 'bad' may be the sole means by which relatively deprived children gain attention. Any attention, for a child who craves it, however painful or unpleasant, is better than none.

The terms disruptive, delinquent, disturbed, maladjusted

The label 'problem children', much used earlier in this century has been dropped both because it is too vague and because it can be replaced by any number of words, each describing a particular type of behaviour such as, for example, disruptive, disturbed, delinquent. Yet in 1945, the Ministry of Education, as it then was, searching for a general term to cover these and similar problems brought into use and imposed on psychologists and psychiatrists, the term 'maladjusted' (1). If 'problem' as an adjective is vague, 'maladjusted' is equally so. While the term may be useful to psychiatrists who can apply it to any child whom they believe to have special 'educational, social or personal' needs, it almost defies definition (Holman, 1973). As for 'disturbed', this is a hypothetical attribute, inferred by psychiatrists from behaviour which is 'disturbing'. Although 'delinquent' and 'disruptive' give a better clue to the nature of a child's problem, each covers a variety of behaviour that is disapproved of. 'Disruptive' is applied to a spectrum ranging from mild tiresomeness to violence that may threaten health or life, the child's own, or others' (Cook, 1975; Goldacre, 1977).

Deliberately absent pupils (truants), and nuisances whose presence is all too obvious, can both be regarded as disruptive but since the motivation and the effect on others are different in the two cases, it is not unreasonable to keep the word disruptive for the nuisances. The term disruptive is, then, not entirely an exception to the vagueness that besets all the labels attached to non-conforming and non-compliant behaviour. The definition is subjective, depending on attitude, reaction and degree of tolerance of the observer. Most people would agree that children who are delinquent in or out of school, noisy, uncontrollable or violent, exhibit features characteristic of disruptive behaviour. Many factors, such as the point in the spectrum from mild to severe of any of these characteristics, the teacher's value systems and personality, and his ability to control turbulent children, account for the considerable variation in the number designated disruptive by different teachers.

It has been suggested (Evans, 1981) that two types of disruptive behaviour may be recognised. There is 'a low-key and insidious form of disruption which may run through a school and be very destructive of the teacher-learning process.' This is characterised by non-cooperation, mild dis-obedience, lateness for lessons, failure to bring equipment or to produce homework, open boredom, clowning, chattering and so on. Secondly there is a small number of alienated pupils with aggressive behaviour of varying degrees. But there is a spectrum for all categories of behaviour. Difficulties in defining disruptive behaviour are discussed by Badger (1985).

We suggest that the prime factor in defining delinquency in young children is the planned and deliberate nature of anti-social activities. Although many children commit what might appear to be delinquent acts, these may in fact be impulsive and unplanned, and due to immaturity;

14

they are acts usually resulting from opportunities taken at random with inability to foresee the consequences. In younger children delinquent behaviour outside school usually takes the form of stealing or breaking and entering, and in the teenager a common offence is taking and driving other people's cars. Such children often truant for long periods. According to Metropolitan Police statistics a quarter of all serious crimes in Greater London are committed by children. Although many delinquent acts do not directly affect teachers or schools, they may nevertheless affect other pupils. Some pupils admire delinquents and derive vicarious excitement from their exploits: a few are encouraged to emulate them. It hardly needs saying that all this has an unsettling effect on the life, discipline and morale of the school, making learning less effective for many other children.

Although disruptive children are usually maladjusted, not all maladjusted children are disruptive. Maladjustment is less an attribute of the child than, on the one hand, a short-hand description of his total situation (his capacity to bear pressures imposed on him) and, on the other, an administrative label without which he cannot (or could not until very recently) be provided with the help of a special school (1) (Holman, 1973). Among children to whom this designation is often applied there are three main groups.

1. Children with psycho-social problems. In this group are children who have suffered to excess from strains imposed by their families or social environment. Among them are those described as 'difficult', 'beyond control', 'destructive', 'delinquent' or 'violent'. 'Conduct disorder' is the term often applied to their behaviour. However, because of overlaps with other groups, and because of the traumata to which they have been exposed, we prefer to describe these children as showing 'protest behaviour'.

2. Children with a pathological disorder. The behaviour of children in this group may be bizarre. The underlying cause is often some organic disorder, either congenital or acquired in early life. These children include the psychotic or autistic, those with brain damage, those with various forms of epilepsy and those with certain kinds of metabolic, endocrine or postencephalitic abnormality. Their behaviour ranges from the withdrawn to the overactive and uncontrollable.

3. Children with behaviour disorders secondary to other handicaps. These may be regarded as exhibiting protest behaviour at the frustrations imposed by the primary sensory or motor handicap, or even by seemingly

15

trivial handicaps such as birthmarks, speech defects or other minor physical disability. The behaviour may be aggravated by the way these are treated, or it may co-exist with psycho-social handicap.

A number of people have written about maladjustment from different professional standpoints (Tutt, 1983; Burland, 1983; Reeves, 1983; Shuttleworth, 1983; Griffiths, 1983). Laslett (1983) discusses the terms 'maladjustment' and 'emotional disturbance'. With so many differing views further study will be necessary to reach a better understanding of childhood emotions and behaviour, and of children's reactions to their environment.

The teacher's view of troublesome children

Passive children. This usually small group is not strictly speaking our concern, but deserves a brief mention because of the amount of time and attention these children need and the extent to which they call on the school's resources of pastoral care. It is customary to distinguish two types. There are the 'withdrawn' (2) who may not be discovered unless they are looked for and who may be, to a greater or lesser degree, depressed. Withdrawal is their form of protest and, if they are not helped, they may swing over to more active and violent behaviour. Teachers may be alarmed by children who suddenly change and 'blow up'.

The other type, the school refusers (sufferers from school phobia) are also withdrawn and they are to be regarded as on the borderline of mental sickness, torn by an insoluble conflict which makes it impossible for them to get themselves to school. They should be clearly distinguished from truants who make conscious voluntary decisions not to go to school as a gesture of revolt against adult authority. Truants are neither at home nor at school, but often time their return home as if at school all day. School phobics not only fail to get to school, they never go anywhere (Hersov, 1972). Children who stay away from school may be overlooked and, therefore, estimates of their numbers are not always accurate. 'Psychological truancy', when a pupil is physically present but emotionally and motivationally absent — 'switched off' — is also a serious problem (Hamblin, 1978).

Active troublesome children. While some children simply stay away from school, some are always there because school is important to them if they have horrid home lives. In general, teachers find the most troublesome children are those who have a difficult relationship with their parents. Some truants are to be numbered among actively troublesome children; when they are at school they may be disruptive and have a high nuisance value for their teachers. There is a tendency for the milder cases to become more severe. Their behaviour can be seen as a 'cry for help' but it is often answered, if at all, after much damage has occurred. They need to be helped from the moment of their arrival in school, or even earlier. Given the right sort of help, some at least may come to identify themselves with the school, feel some obligation towards it, and gain something from the years spent in it.

There seems to be a tendency to put difficult pupils with less experienced teachers. In the classroom disorders of behaviour may be catching, with the result that even some well-motivated children may join a gang. This may be either for fear of being thought milksops, or getting 'picked on' by their peers and becoming friendless. Children find it exciting to play up teachers, or witness others do it, and it may become uncontrollable. Unless disruption is contained, most members of the class stop learning (what the teacher would like them to learn), and the effect on the teacher may be devastating. Children may disrupt the life of the school by unacceptable behaviour outside it, for what a pupil does elsewhere influences other children; and it affects parents' opinions about which school they would like their children to go to.

A single theft in a school will often take some hours of one or more senior teachers' time to investigate. Vandalism is also a common occurrence. Apart from its cost it depresses morale and fortifies incipient pupil alienation. A fire in a school may take a sizeable part of it out of use for months with adverse effects on the work of pupils and teachers. Crime and vandalism may affect elderly people's health (Coakley and Woodford-Williams, 1979). There is a close relationship between vandalism and failure to meet children's basic emotional needs (Pringle, 1973).

Extent

> Pauvreté fait gens méprendre et faim saillir le loup
> des bois
> — *François Villon*

To many people it seems that nowadays there are more aggressive dis-ruptive schoolchildren than formerly. This may be so but we believe that this feeling is mainly due to greater awareness, and of changes in society's view of what is acceptable. After all vandalism by public schoolboys, usually ascribed to 'high spirits', and described as 'horseplay', has not been unknown (Honey, 1977), and there is much anecdotal evidence of

17

behaviour in public schools that would at best be called undesirable and at worst frankly delinquent (Chandos, 1984). Biographies (Connolly, 1938) give accounts of the bullying and ill-treatment of younger boys by older pupils, and of drunken, disorderly and destructive behaviour on special occasions such as the Eton-Harrow match. A Cambridge professor, now dead, told us how, at his public school, a group of boys on their free half day would visit the village shop. One would ask for something known to be kept at the back of the shop and in the absence of the shopkeeper the rest would seize and make off with everything within easy reach. This went on weekly for several years until they left school. More recently boys from Westminster School made door to door collections of money for mythical charities, until rumbled by a parent.

Rutter (1979a) did not think that the general pattern of adolescent development and disorder had altered to any substantial extent in this country in recent years. Periodically there are accounts of violent behaviour in schools in other countries even Japan, often thought of as the home of conforming behaviour (Williams, 1983).

Disruptive children have always been with us (Lawrence, Steed and Young, 1984). Whether or not there are more of them, we are certainly now more aware of them. In any school, between 10 and 15 per cent of the pupils have emotional problems (Kolvin, Garside and Nicol, 1976; Laslett, 1977a), *but not all are disruptive*. The figures given by Kolvin and Laslett tally with those in the Warnock Report (Department of Education and Science (DES), 1978b). Laslett has stressed that the actual number of children who are disruptive is small, even taking the maximum estimate made by any large school. Boys commonly do more damage than girls but third-year secondary school girls may be among the most difficult. In a school of about 1000 children there will be 20-30 hard-core disruptive pupils, supported by a larger number of 'part-timers' mostly inside the school, but some outside (ex-pupils with old scores to repay). The ordinary law-abiding adult may not appreciate the widespread turmoil a few disruptive pupils can cause in a school, though teachers and the media sometimes exaggerate. Not all senior educationists believe that the problem of disruptive behaviour is worsening: London's late Education Officer, Peter Newsam, believed that disruptive behaviour in Inner London Education Authority (ILEA) schools was getting less. Bolton (1981) concluded that there was no firm evidence that disruptive behaviour in schools was becoming worse or more frequent.

There is a great excess of boys in all categories of disturbed or disruptive children. In special schools for maladjusted children the ratio of boys to girls is about 7:1. Some pathological conditions and handicaps other than maladjustment are commoner in males than females, and so, for different reasons, is the tendency to protest, that is, to have a high nuisance value for others. While some forms of maladjustment are precursors of mental illness in adult life, this is not true of all. In every psychiatric service for adults, at all ages, women are more numerous than men. This may be because in adulthood, patients, with few exceptions, tend to refer themselves, whereas in childhood referral is usually made by some adult for whom nuisance is probably the most frequent criterion. It may well be that many actually or potentially mentally ill children are overlooked, particularly girls. The sex ratio in schools for the maladjusted is very close to the adult sex ratio if the populations of psychiatric and penal institutions are combined.

The proportion of the total population at school has been considerably increased by the raising of the school leaving age, from 13 years in 1944 to 16 in 1976. Moreover the increase has almost all been of older, bigger, more mature young persons. 'Gangs' are part of the culture of the mid-teens; and today's teenagers, being still at school, have more leisure in which to form them. Some gangs are constructive, for example pop groups, or groups working with younger children, the aged, the handicapped etc, but children with low self-esteem tend to congregate in anti-social gangs.

The media give rapid and wide dissemination of anti-social and violent activity and often magnify it. The delinquent may be seen as a 'hero' and violence taken as a model. Such tendencies are reinforced by equivocal differentiation between the behaviour of goodies and baddies in films. The media have given prominence to disruption and disturbance in comprehensive schools without supplying hard statistics to prove that it is a new phenomenon. Why there should be so much antagonism to comprehensive schools is an interesting question but not relevant here except that it seems to be part of a labelling process used merely for denigration.

Drug taking

This problem is reported to be affecting many more children, at ever earlier ages. Teachers find any increase in behavioural uncertainty in children bewildering and upsetting.

The special problem of the violent child or parent

Disruptive children may be violent. In gang violence there tends to be a self-perpetuating element so that often, when once begun, there is no stopping until there is nothing left to destroy. The violence of the troublesome individual child may be symbolic or token — broken pencils, torn paper, books thrown on the floor. Fighting children are a more disturbing sight but most disturbing of all is violence directed at the teacher. School children, as they get older, reveal a good deal of hostility towards teachers. We hear from the United States of violent attacks by large and powerful teenagers on teachers, sometimes resulting in murder. We have heard of only one case of a pupil murdering a teacher in this country — evidently backed by his parents who, when interviewed by a psychiatrist, said 'Why all this fuss, anyone would think our son had committed a crime?' *(Personal communication.)*

In this country there is reason to believe that teachers are attacked less often than some reports suggest. The National Association of Schoolmasters, at its 1977 conference published its first survey on its members' experience of school violence in the early 1970s. It showed that personal violence was rarely experienced by teachers in schools. However, this may be changing (Boseley, 1986). Scott (1982) pointed out that not only is violence directed at teachers rare, but in the ILEA it has notably declined since the decision was made to ban corporal punishment in its schools.

Occasionally a parent attacks a teacher. Teachers are not the only professional group justly to feel anxiety about aggression from clients. Mental nurses have adopted precautionary, at times restrictive, measures because of it. They have two advantages that teachers lack: they are given specific training in the handling of violent patients and they are seldom alone in charge of potentially violent persons. What the teacher really needs is help before such disasters occur. It is a historical accident that leaves a teacher facing one or more violent pupils single-handed.

Notes

1. Ministry of Education. School and Health Regulations, 1945: 'Maladjusted pupils are pupils who show evidence of emotional instability or psychological disturbance and require special educational treatment in order to effect their personal, social and educational re-adjustment.'

2. 'Withdrawn' is a word used in psychiatry to designate persons who shrink from making relationships with others. This is unfortunate since the word is, in common use, virtually synonymous with 'removed'. 'Mr. A decided to withdraw from school his withdrawn son' would make sense to a psychiatrist but must seem nonsense to the ordinary reader. Teachers do not ask for the withdrawal from their class or school of withdrawn children. On the contrary, it is the child at the other end of the spectrum whom they would like to see withdrawn from their presence.

Chapter 2 — The secondary school and the teacher

The 1944 Education Act embodied two main principles: 1) that all children should have a secondary education; 2) that it should be of more than one type, namely 'grammar', 'technical' and 'secondary modern'; the 'technical' was soon dropped. That there should be a distinction between the smaller group of children likely to profit from the 'abstract approach to education' and the larger group for whom a 'practical approach' would be suitable was due to theories of psychologists that a person's 'intelligence' was innate and unchangeable. It also had to do with the separation of learning from doing that is such a feature of our educational system. In effect children were classified on the results of standardised tests into first and second class citizens. It was not foreseen that this division would also apply, for the most part, to schools and their teachers.

Social class and educational opportunity

Parents and teachers became unhappy with the 1944 system. The attack on it was many pronged. On the one hand, a number of the children in second-class schools got as good or better results in public examinations than the supposed intellectual elite. On the other, studies indicated that psychologists' theories were based on insufficient evidence. It was shown that those with a privileged home or school environment tended to get test results better than the national average; while those in under-privilged circumstances scored below it. Furthermore the intelligence of emotionally disturbed children often improves *pari passu* with their mental state when this is appropriately treated. Studies such as those of Floud, Halsey and Martin (1956) and Fraser (1959) pointed to a number of features of under-privilege and paved the way for the detailed consideration of home, school and neighbourhood undertaken by the Plowden Committee (DES, 1966).

Comprehensive secondary education

There were divisions of opinion about the value of comprehensive education; doubts afflicted all political parties, and the educational and social service professions. Pedley (1956, 1963) among others argued powerfully against the selective system and in favour of comprehensive secondary schooling for all. Eventually a Labour Government became firmly committed to it though it was rather slow to implement it (Marsden, 1971), and the comprehensive principle was not generally adopted until 1974. By that time the 1944 system had had time to congeal, and the reorganisation was bedevilled by the cost of new buildings, and feelings of threat and insecurity among teachers — common concomitants of changes in work styles and privileges. A grammar school regarded itself as socially superior and tended to look down upon the secondary modern, particularly perhaps the one with which it became linked in the re-organisation for comprehensive education.

Professor Harry Rée (1981) has pointed out that the comprehensive school is an 'entirely new animal' which people both inside and outside the school have tried 'to turn into something they have been more familiar with when they were young.' Secondary modern children in comprehensives were taught by grammar school teachers, who although regarded in the early days after reorganisation as superior to the others, had little experience, or indeed aptitude, for the task, and the children often reacted in ways that nonplussed them. Now, in most secondary schools, there are teachers who understand the nature of the 'new animal'. However, teachers are faced with great obstacles to the development of comprehensive education because of severe financial stringency and anxiety about their own future.

Furthermore there are still people who try to show that comprehensive schools are inferior to those they replaced. We certainly need properly conducted comparative research to provide better education for young people — our future citizens, but this has hardly yet been undertaken. A good account of the working of a large mixed comprehensive secondary school has been given by Davies (1976). He disposes of some of the associated myths.

The school scene

The school cannot escape the effects of child distress '. . . whatever happens in the future, whatever legislation may be passed, whatever improvements may be made in our welfare services, it will still be the schools who will bear the brunt of whatever child distress exists: their normal purposes and endeavours will continue to be impaired by its effects' (Clegg and Megson, 1973). For a teacher to describe a child as aggressive, insolent, rude, disobedient, turbulent or violent is to delineate a threatening kind of person. It also tells us something about the very real anxieties of the teacher well described by Kyriacou (1980), Lawrence et al (1984), Laslett and Smith (1984) and Kloska and Ramasut (1985). Such epithets do not tell the whole story. If children who wish to work for examinations have their learning time and facilities upset and curtailed because of the behaviour of other children, tensions arise within themselves, in their parents (especially those with academic ambitions for their children) and in the school. Teachers will feel frustrated if, for any reason, their more promising pupils are impeded.

Teachers regard schools as places in which 'work' is done, defining work as the acquisition of knowledge and skills that will lead to some form of examination success. It is recognised that children of a low level of ability may not take any examination but it is thought that they should do work of a similar sort though at a slower pace. Such things as sport, drama, art, music and other creative activities, discussions of personal relationships, and of the material, social and emotional experiences of adult life tend to be regarded as of less importance, though this is changing. If teachers see their job as simply to 'teach', bound by the rigours of examination syllabi, there will be conflict with children who have little capacity to function academically or socially, and are likely to have a low self-image which cannot always be upgraded in the ordinary classroom. There is evidence that teachers may have a partial and selective understanding of pupils, underestimating the wide range of thoughts, feelings, ideas and acts that pupils hide from them (Hargreaves, 1978).

The secondary school. Behaviour problems are usually less severe in primary schools. In secondary schools the child may be experiencing the physiological and psychological changes of puberty; the first serious wish to become independent of parents, to prefer the company of the peer group to that of adults. In short, we have an adolescent crisis of contradictory feelings: on the one hand, the wish to grow up and, on the other, anxieties about the process. It is an age of swings of mood, resentment at being 'treated like a child', and at the same time a great need for the caring support that is shown to small children. The ideal is care without authoritarianism. Adults tend to give the opposite of what the young person wants: for example, Mum ceases to cuddle and kiss but she and/or Dad lay down rules about dress, length of hair, and time of coming in at night. People who would not use corporal punishment for a primary school age child may begin to do so when he is 11 or 13. If the school reinforces or outdoes the parents in harshness it will receive a blast of adolescent rebelliousness. 'Action and reaction are equal and opposite.' Fortunately, the majority have sensible parents who discuss, consult and treat with respect. Habits of compliance acquired earlier will then persist. With luck the child really wants to learn and will tolerate a good deal from teachers who are teaching him something he regards as useful. But the few who are or have been under excessive stress at home have two main ways of reacting at school: they will either stay away, or make nuisances of themselves. They may do both. These are the disruptives, the truants or the delinquents. They are in effect protesting against the way society has treated them, but society has the big battalions and will win, though it may be a pyrrhic victory, turning the rebels into enemies of society.

The teacher's burden

> The school as prison: the headmaster is the prison governor; the teachers are warders (one of the two things for which they can be dismissed is failing to check the list of the prisoners); the prisoners are the pupils, in the obvious instance, but the teachers are prisoners too.
>
> — Ian Lister (1974b)

The child is not the only person 'locked in' at school. Cultural, professional and traditional forces ensure that the teacher in the classroom is also placed where there is seldom any escape except by leaving the job, and perhaps the profession. Teachers deserve all the support their colleagues, their employers, the ancillary professions and society in general, can give them and this they do not always get. A warm relationship with parents and other professionals can prove helpful and supportive.

On the whole teachers in a grammar school had to make few decisions. Pupils were selected and streamed by the 11+ examinations; the curriculum was decided by the requirements of the examination boards. In comprehensive schools teachers have to take part in complex decisions. Some changes in schools (Table 2) have been helpful but others have created difficulties for teachers and children. Secondary schools are large and teachers and pupils may not know each other. Some children aged over 16 are obliged to remain in school despite their wishes. Pupils are becoming more independent in their attitudes to teachers and to notions of punishment. Respect for those in authority has to be earned. Some teachers feel their powers of adaptation are under strain and they emphasize the stresses of classroom teaching. Nevertheless some people think that too little has changed in our educational system.

There is no doubt that many heads feel powerless to influence events affecting the work of their school. The education office may be felt to be distant if not dismissive, unsupportive or otherwise unhelpful. Governors are uninvolved. Child Guidance (CG) staff and social workers are busy, difficult to get hold of and chary of working closely over problems arising from pupils' behaviour. Professional isolation makes it difficult for heads to get help to deal with their problems.

Ann Jones (1980), a headteacher, believed that difficulties have arisen because society has expected too much of its schools. Teachers have to act as counsellors, friends and father-figures in addition to their traditional role. Although teachers' pride in their ability may make them reluctant to ask for advice, Ann Jones believes that the main fault lies in a lack of communication between schools and welfare agencies. No effective 'early warning' screening system identifies children with difficulties. Few schools try to tackle the problem before children reach crisis point, and primary and secondary schools do not liaise well. In spite of the pastoral work done in most schools now, teachers may not know where to find advice. Case conferences including social workers and educational psychologists too easily become exercises in buck-passing.

Another head, Audrey Jackson (1976), began a study of headteachers' attitudes that became a study of the stresses and strains they faced because of changes in their roles, and the reorganisation of their schools into comprehensives. Many heads felt overtaxed by their work and under-trained for it. She found herself involuntarily in a counselling role because the heads knew of no other source of help for their difficulties. What is seldom appreciated are the personal problems that many teachers have, like other people (Jones NJ, 1977). A survey of teachers by Kyriacou and Sutcliffe (1978) revealed four main sources of stress: pupil misbehaviour, poor working conditions, time pressures and poor school ethos.

Teachers receive little training in the causes of disturbing behaviour in children or in the joint action required for its prevention and treatment. Many teachers finally develop an attitude towards disruptive pupils expressed as: 'Get these children off the school premises'. Children cannot be put into watertight compartments for parts of the day, so there seems to be no escape from pastoral duties for teachers. Some accept this role partly or wholly, but others, while deploring anything that gets in the way of 'teaching', feel no duty to resolve situations arising from incidents that impede their work, and are resentful at receiving what seems inadequate help. Many parents forget that schools do not provide the only learning forum for life; after all they have the care of the child from birth until he goes to school. The best learning provision for children will be supplied by parents, teachers and other professionals working together.

We have been told that many gifted experienced teachers spend too much time as administrators when they are badly needed in the classroom, yet junior teachers complain that they have too little influence in running the school. Often much time is spent by highly qualified people on one child, taken up with reports, meetings, discussions, case conferences etc, and all too frequently it is some relatively inexperienced person who spends time, and not a great deal of it, *with* the child.

Teachers have a number of other problems nowadays. The shortened high school day, achieved by 'integrating' the lunch hour, may reduce thieving from local shops and other undesirable behaviour, but the practice greatly reduces extracurricular activities. Some parents even opt for such schools so that children who leave school at 3.0 pm can act as minders for younger children at home. Teachers complain that younger children come tired to school after watching television (TV) until late at night. It must depress teachers that fewer young people are going on to higher education (DES, 1983a).

Relationships between teachers and other agencies

Schools have traditionally regarded themselves as rather closed and self-sufficient communities. They seldom talk to each other. Only comparatively recently have we begun to appreciate the impact of social and environmental factors on the behaviour of pupils, and their ability to learn. This may explain why many teachers still do not seek help from agencies outside the school, do not even know of their existence, or when they do, do not know how to use them, or complain of the difficulty of making referrals. Apart from emphasis on academic excellence that motivates teachers' work and helps to form their attitudes, there tends to be the feeling that to seek help over classroom difficulties would indicate incompetence, and be detrimental to a teacher's career. Pressures from parents for their children to succeed, and from teachers' own professional standards should not be underestimated. All these are component strains in teachers' work which they are often unable to control. Feelings of helplessness may cause anxiety.

Schools may delay in asking other agencies for help with these children because it may have taken a long time to get it in the past; when it arrives it may be of little use, and agencies sometimes appear frankly unhelpful. A secondary school head referred a disruptive child to the child guidance centre as being likely to be 'maladjusted'; he received a brief report to the effect that the child was in fact *well* adjusted — to his life of crime and other disruptive activities. A high school boy who had been expelled from another school, whose mother suffered from agoraphobia and whose father was mentally unwell, was found kicking the ribs of a smaller boy on the ground. The father agreed with referral to the child guidance clinic who were informed about the parents' problems. The school received a short report that the boy said he had been unjustly accused and had not been kicking anyone. When agencies nominally there to provide help appear unresponsive, even uncaring, teachers do not react by reconstructing their own definitions of deviance, they counter-challenge the official definitions, and psychologists' legitimacy and competence to make them. Teachers re-assert their own — 'everybody knows this kid is maladjusted', and 'psychologists are fools' (Hargreaves, 1978). If there is foolishness we suggest it is the failure of both parties to enter into dialogue to try to understand the reasons for discrepant definitions and attitudes, and to reconcile them, though for many reasons it may be difficult to establish a dialogue.

A feature of such reconciliation is awareness by professionals working together, of the roles of each. For example a deputy head gave up hours of her off-duty time to the care of a child who was in a state of acute mental disturbance. The police were helpful but this caring senior teacher was at first unaware of the function of a child guidance psychiatrist in such a case. When contacted, the psychiatrist responded at once. In work with such problems even good care and practice are not sufficient if undertaken without knowledge of what others can contribute.

While we may sympathise with the school, nevertheless psychologists and psychiatrists have no access to magic. Only if all the agencies concerned, including the Education Office, ask fresh questions about the intractable problems that disruptive behaviour gives rise to will advance be made towards solving them. This cannot happen without a well developed, actively used, communication network. The inertia of authorities and agencies slow to question and respond will inhibit schools from seeking help with their children's difficulties.

There is no doubt about the divergence of views many teachers and social workers entertain about each other and their roles. Although some schools have a close and effective relationship with social workers, many teachers feel that social workers see the child only in the family context, more concerned for the parent than for the child. The needs of the teacher seem to come some way after that. Teachers, because they work with the child, tend to be more child oriented. It is bound to be a cause of concern to a teacher when a social worker considers it good practice to restore a child to parents who appear to be injuring him, and pay no attention to the teacher's evidence that this is so. However, the teacher must not assume that any alternative will be better. It may harm the child as much to be put in a children's home, or with uncongenial foster parents. The social worker may sometimes seem to be not very good at choosing substitute homes but if the situation is critical the social worker has to act quickly and the only 'place of safety' available may, in the long run, prove unsuitable.

It upsets teachers that some social workers consider schools to be pillars of reaction.

> Two West Indian brothers were disruptive in a first school, and were the greatest problem the school had ever had. The younger was impossible to contain, always wandering about, with no concentration, sometimes violent, terrorising other children. The two boys had different fathers, the mother being in and out of hospital. The boys used to be sent out shopping without money, and were beaten if they returned empty handed. Both were intelligent. A social worker accused the teacher of trying to convert the children into 'nice white middle class boys'. Rapid improvement in the boys' behaviour occurred after one term in care.

Teachers will give examples of other experiences with the social services:

> N, a West Indian boy of 12+ in a mixed comprehensive school, was aggressive, uncooperative, disruptive; threatened staff and pupils with violence, and came in late. Outside school he was in trouble with the police for thieving, and stayed out all night without explanation. His parents, who found him 'out of control', were seen several times by the head, and asked for his help. The school knew little about the family or rearing pattern (we may ask why?). N was seen at the child guidance clinic and reported to be 'normal'. The parents said they would welcome help from the Social Services Department who, when contacted by the head, said they would see the mother if she would call in. The mother was not very bright or much educated, and seemed unlikely to have the confidence or initiative to do this. End of term intervened: no knowledge of whether the mother was helped. Next term the news was that N and his elder brother had been charged by the police with mugging and were in a detention centre.

Attitudes and adaptation

We have already touched on some aspects of teachers' professional attitudes. A group of head teachers considered the problem of school disruption caused by the delinquent child. They expressed exasperation at the effects of the behaviour of these children on schools, and their own powerlessness to control it. In their recommendations for action emphasis was almost entirely on what they thought others should do to help them. The only ways the heads could see of dealing with the problem were by the application of bureaucratic procedures, and by punitive measures directed at children and parents. However, we must look behind schools' expressions of frustration if we are to understand their sense of isolation and helplessness. Alongside this sympathetic approach schools will, it is hoped, develop their own commitment to solving their problems.

Many teachers take the view that the disruptive pupil should be removed from the group he is disturbing. Many disrupters disrupt only a few classes; indeed some who disrupt one class may be the star turns of another. Thus disruption depends in part on the relationship between pupils and teacher, and it may be either party who bears the greater responsibility for the problem. While difficulties can sometimes be solved by a head of house or tutor, usually the child is regarded as the culprit and he is cautioned, warned, subjected to some sanction and expected to conform to the teacher's expectations. If not, he may be suspended, moved to another school or sent for a period to the school withdrawal unit, 'private studies area' or 'sin bin' where he continues to do the same work in circumstances in which he may feel penalised.

Teachers seem to think that disruption should be treated by punishment, if not by barbaric methods, nevertheless by humiliation. They are seldom aware of the home circumstances or background of the child, or, if they concede the need of help, believe that it should be given by somebody else. We would urge teachers to accept the view that the majority of disrupters are suffering, or have suffered, from their family circumstances and are in need of help. Pupils who don't work may not be able to, and in most cases of disruption much fuller investigation of the child's home environment is called for than usually takes place.

Teachers may suffer from role conflict, having authority over their pupils but at the same time being under the authority of the head or the inspector. On the one hand the teacher tries to behave as parents and teachers used to behave towards him; on the other, he behaves in the way he as a child behaved towards authority figures. A teacher of 35, 15 years in the profession, when told by the head to get her hair cut, saw this as a threat to her identity. The ideas behind modern schooling make role conflicts even more complex (Wragg, 1978). Roles are in flux, changing with society's needs. Yet many teachers do feel ready to accept new functions, though they are unhappy when pressed into roles for which they have neither bent nor training. Many teachers are now front-line social workers, the first to see a bruised child, hear a family hard-luck story, or give a cold and hungry youngster food and clothing. While it is reasonable to expect teachers, as professional people, to examine their roles from time to time, not everyone can fulfil all roles. There must be a degree of specialisation.

33

Change, and its acceleration, is a current force that makes demands on most professions and callings. It is a difficult and painful process for professions, no less than for individuals, to undergo changes of attitude and self-image. Despite teachers' feelings of being hard-pressed in a changing educational culture, many schools and teachers are learning to cope with society's changing demands upon them and child education is becoming more child-centred. Adaptation will be helped by regarding their work as a service, pupils and parents as clients, and change as a challenge, worthy of colleague support.

Many schools have little or no tradition of internal discussion of problems and too often possess a thoroughly authoritarian structure, with a generation gap between heads and the bulk of teachers in their schools.

We end this chapter with a quotation from Alistair Mant (1977), working in the field of management:

> Whatever the educational structure — school, university or business school — one can state two simple truths with some confidence:
>
> **1.** That the throughput of an educational establishment is complex; more, that is, than the students themselves. For example the secondary school will process incipient delinquency and some will do it much more effectively than others. Teachers have so little grasp of this as a *throughput*, as opposed to a burden, that they are largely unaware that some schools do handle it much better than others . . .
>
> **2.** That, irrespective of the curriculum, the experience of simply taking up a student role in an educational establishment 'teaches', through the skin, about authority and authority structures. Often, it teaches no more than simple distrust of 'authority' as a vague idea and, thus, a concomitant reliance on personal power for survival. Most teachers would accept this proposition at an intellectual level with very little idea of how their own behaviour may reinforce such prejudices.

Table 2: Some of the changes that teachers have had to assimilate in the last 20 years.

- Comprehensive education, with disappearance of familiar grammar and secondary modern schools
- Increases in school size
- Changes in curricula
- Changes in teaching methods
- Raising of the school leaving age (ROSLA)
- Role conflicts
- Greater parent, pupil and teacher involvement (governors and PTAs)
- Reduction of the powers of the head
- Mixed ability teaching, with teachers experiencing pupil behaviour, attitudes and abilities outside their range of teaching skills; some teachers shying away from the extra work entailed that is without financial recompense
- Cuts in educational spending
- Special problems of heads
- Increased expectations from parents and pupils
- Increased administrative responsibilities
- The 'permissive society'

Chapter 3 — The origins of disruptive behaviour

Different approaches put varying emphasis on different factors in the causation of disruptive behaviour in children. There are few people who now believe that behaviour is determined entirely by genetic factors, though these are bound to play a part in the growth of personality and character. With the development of the theory and practice of behaviour modification, especially in the US, has come great emphasis on dealing with the child's current behaviour, seemingly to the virtual exclusion of its underlying causes. An American professor of psychiatry, well known for his practical views of child management, has even said: 'A new professional discipline has emerged: child psychiatry. It is based on an assumption we cannot share, that children who need help are "emotionally sick". Few of them are really sick; most are misguided' (Dreikurs, 1968). In fact not many child psychiatrists see child psychiatry in terms of 'emotional sickness'. They see children's problems in terms of disordered ways of relating to people and/or immaturity (poor emotional development).

Most of those concerned with the subject would agree that milder forms of disturbing behaviour can be dealt with by one or other of the methods suggested by the proponents of behaviour modification though it is seldom claimed that more than 50-75 per cent of a child's behaviour is adequately modified by their methods. In most forms of disturbing behaviour, short perhaps of the 'normal stroppiness' of teenagers, or the mild attention-seeking of the young child, there are aetiological elements that have to be considered if the child's behaviour is to be permanently changed and if we are to understand how to prevent such behaviour. Therefore, in dealing with these problems, we prefer an eclectic approach, with emphasis on emotional deprivation and its origins. Use of the word 'deprivation' has been criticized on the grounds that it has been devalued. But as Rutter and Madge (1976) say, behind the word lie people who suffer various forms of personal and social disadvantage. 'The term may generate semantic confusion but the human predicament is real enough'. We do not have strong feelings about the word, though agree that 'disadvantaged' would sometimes be more appropriate. Rutter (1979a) emphasizes the multivariate 'causes' of childhood disadvantage.

Stresses and strains, it hardly needs saying, vary in severity, and people differ in their capacity to withstand them. Everyone has his breaking point — even Job. The combination of severe stress and high vulnerability is particularly disastrous and this is the lot of those young children who are materially and emotionally deprived. One result is behaviour that society finds unacceptable. Many things interfere with a person's capacity to develop, ranging from the manner of rearing and parental values, to family and other trials. Rejection in various forms that may be explicit or implicit, can adversely affect a child's emotional stability. Physical separation may be harmful, but the quality of the relationships that develop between adults and child, and the way these are sustained or broken, are probably equally important (Rutter, 1979b). Some need much support when meeting stress, others little. In this chapter we discuss the basic needs of the child and look at many of the causes of disruptive behaviour, as steps in the complex process of diagnosis and therapy, and of prevention.

The basic needs of the child

The family that is 'good enough'

Only in the present century has bringing up children been recognised as a difficult task. Only in the last thirty years has it been realised that many children are harmed while being reared and that this affects their future behaviour. Only recently has thought been directed to detecting and preventing this harm (Bowlby, 1951; Fry, 1965; Rutter and Madge, 1976; Rutter, 1981).

Disruptive children, however many people may be affected by them, constitute only a small number of secondary school children. It follows that the vast majority of parents, and others concerned with the care of young children, find ways of preventing the development of disturbing behaviour in teenagers. Children who cause little or no trouble in schools have mostly had a secure infancy because of a warm, continuous and intimate relationship with loving, responsible and responsive parents. They have been allowed to learn by making mistakes in a predictable and caring environment, and they are able to make good relationships with peers and adults. They have developed an identity and a satisfactory self-image. We are speaking here of children who are free from any significant handicap and do not live with disabled parents.

In spite of the physiological and psychological turmoil of adolescence, most young people are able to show genuine concern about the needs of others and at no other time in their lives are they more anxious to help solve society's problems. Parents have two conflicting roles to play in bringing up their children. On the one hand they need to give love and to be seen to give it; on the other they have to 'socialise' the young, help them to see what is approved and disapproved of by the adult world, and prevail on the child to have regard for these standards. To combine these two functions is by no means easy and the best of parents will sometimes err; in spite of this the majority succeed. Unfortunately it is those who fail whose teenage children make problems for their teachers and it is with these that we are concerned.

Most of those who are entrusted with the care of young people are neither saints nor angels but ordinary, reasonably well-meaning people with problems of their own but who are, as the late Donald Winnicott (1957, 1965) used to say, 'good enough'. There are exceptions: some children are so handicapped from birth or from an early age that they need a degree of understanding beyond the capacity of the well-intentioned person who lacks special training; but most of those who become 'difficult' in adolescence do so because the care they have had in their early lives has been far from 'good enough'.

A child starts life as part of his mother and only slowly becomes ready for short separations from her. Unlike other mammals, after birth humans remain immature and dependent for a long time, the biological period being prolonged in our society by some additional years of socially determined dependence. The task undertaken by parents, later supplemented by teachers, is to help the child through from dependence to independence, from ignorance to knowledge, and from selfishness to an appreciation of the needs of others. The minimum time given to this is 16 years, frequently several years longer, and in that time the child is undergoing changes both biological and social. At the same time his parents may be experiencing vicissitudes in themselves or in their environment with consequent physical and emotional manifestations. The child may experience illness or loss of relatives who matter to him, parental separation or divorce, parental unemployment or other calamities in the family. The manner in which the child reacts to such events will be determined in large measure by his previous upbringing.

We turn now to the origins of rebellion and hostility in teenagers who are potentially normal at birth.

Environment

Antisocial attitudes in children leading to disruptive behaviour may be attributable to specific traumatic events or more commonly to a long period of adverse circumstances such as ill-treatment, neglect, emotional deprivation and socio-economic disadvantage. Some children seem predestined to disruptiveness either by innate or early acquired personal handicaps, or by the circumstances of their family or social environment. The likelihood of trouble in adolescence could probably be predicted in some families before birth or even before conception. The role of the school environment in the genesis of behaviour problems is considered later.

The less than 'good enough' family

The 'typical family' (Winnicott, 1957, 1965) has 'good enough' parents who are able to transmit cultural values to their children, but there are seemingly minor disasters that may make them less proficient in this. Even for a husband and wife whose home life is to all appearances satisfactory: good material conditions, reasonable income, adequate educational background and fair agreement about the needs of children and the technique of rearing — the change from being a mutually absorbed couple to being parents may impose a greater strain than they can easily adjust to. For parents often have unrealistic expectations of parenthood, and do not foresee the demands their children will make upon them. Neither mother, father nor older child may have experience of new babies. One or both parents may have insufficient emotional resources to develop and maintain simultaneous emotional relationships with spouse and child, or may be in other ways unready for parenthood, and these are factors in marital breakdown.

In our society the mother bears a disproportionate amount of the responsibility of rearing children. After the birth of a child a mother may be deprived of adult companionship and feel lonely: she may feel tired and depressed, even to the borderline of mental illness. If the mother suffers from unrecognised depression after childbirth, this may be interpreted by her husband as a change in her attitude towards him, and may lead to marital conflict just when the wife needs loving support. If seeds of misunderstanding and resentment are sown in the adults the child is often the unwitting victim, expected to carry an emotional burden beyond his strength. The child is then likely to react in one or more ways described as neurotic, or he may develop a 'conduct disorder'.

When growing up every child inevitably has to relinquish his need for immediate satisfaction. Although this may be in his long-term interests, at the time it may seem to a young child that it is merely to defer to the wishes of others. Even in the best households children vary in their ability to mature and become less demanding. If, in the process of growing away from his parents, the child feels that he is not loved, he may, for example, take to stealing. In the 'good enough' family the prevailing emotion is love which strengthens the child's wish to please the parents. If there is parental or parent-child conflict and resentment prevails, the child will have conflicting feelings of love, hate and guilt. The wish to oppose and defy tends to set the pattern of his behaviour. These feelings will colour his attitude to other adult authority figures. The more adverse the environment, and the longer he has to endure it, the more likely will his behaviour be determined by hostility. Such children tend to have little self-esteem and little trust in their parents. When a child is difficult in school he is probably saying: 'I don't know how to deal with all these hostile feelings and impulses.' He is leaving it to the school to cope, asking it to set limits to his behaviour. Angry feelings in a child may be triggered by a teacher's anger directed at another child. The best teacher, in his relationships with children, thinks not only of control; he also tries to fathom reasons for children's behaviour. He avoids responding aggressively and tries to forestall aggression in the child.

It is fair to say that many disruptive children are the product of generations of family rearing patterns. In this country about one-third of families, irrespective of social class, bring up their children with the use of physical punishment. People usually follow their own childhood patterns of experience when as adults they rear their offspring. Children from 'hitting', punitive homes are often filled with aggressive feelings. If they have difficulty in controlling them their behaviour in school may be disturbing. Parents who over-react from their own upbringing may 'spoil' the child, but what the onlooker may regard as 'spoiling' is often no more than a way of assuaging guilt and a substitute for true parental love.

Very young children tend to react to frustration with aggressive language or behaviour and, even when there is a secure home giving care and love, the child's show of violence may bring out violence in the adult who may justify punishment or vengeance as a necessary form of training. It is not easy for adults to assimilate children's aggression. The adult with really violent proclivities may react to it by becoming a child batterer. To be good and kind in the face of infantile provocation is to set an example and children learn much by imitation. It is always difficult to know how children have been treated in their early days, but there is evidence to suggest that gentle handling safeguards the child from the worst effects of the pressures of the environment or from exposure to the portrayal of violence by the media. There is, however, evidence suggesting that high exposure to TV violence increases the degree to which boys engage in serious violence (British Medical Journal, 1976; Belson, 1978; Rutter, 1979a). We shall not list all the factors that may adversely affect the child and his family. We give many of them in Tables 3 and 4, and mention a few below.

Parental role and provision. These are diminished in many families as a consequence of socio-economic circumstances. If father is unemployed or earns a wage near subsistence level as surprisingly large numbers in work do, mother may go to work to bring the family above the poverty line; some fathers have to work away from home. So, in some families, for various reasons, parents may be away from their children. Loss of the extended family tends to isolate parents. Even those interested in their children's education may find difficulties, real or imagined, in making contact with teachers.

Parental aspirations — the young (new) father. The problems in changing from being a couple to becoming parents with the responsibility for one or several children present themselves most intensely with the coming of the first child. The mother has a profound biological relationship with the child who is part of her for the nine months before its birth, and indeed, to have a child or children may be one of the strongest forces motivating her to marry. The father may strongly wish to have a family but his reasons will be different and not usually as intense as his wife's. A well-known mathematician dreamt, while his wife was still pregnant, that he was teaching his child about infinitesimal series; others look forward to the day when they will be teaching their son about cricket or taking him to football matches. Fathers may secretly look forward to a beautiful and devoted daughter and, even when forewarned, are not prepared for the years in which the baby is only an egocentric demanding creature, a threat because it takes up so much of its mother's (his wife's) time and gets so much admiration from relatives and friends. Parents who attempt to realise their own frustrated aspirations through their children may cause problems for the whole family.

One-parent families. Since the publication of the Finer Report (Department of Health and Social Security (DHSS), 1974) there has been more interest in the circumstances of one-parent families. In Great Britain today there are about 920 000 one-parent families and over 1½m one-parent children, with a 6 per cent annual growth rate; that is, one family in eight has only one parent, of whom 90 per cent or more have only mothers (*Where*, 1978b; *Lancet*, 1978; Richards, 1979). In its Barclay Report, the National Institute for Social Work (1982) estimated that with divorces escalating from 27 000 in 1961 to 148 000 in 1980, one-parent families would exceed one million by the mid-1980s. However, it is not very common to have one parent only throughout childhood. Even 'unmarried' mothers may marry and many of them, though technically unmarried, are living in a stable relationship with a partner. Even so, a

44

few years of life as a one-parent family may be stressful and it is particularly unfortunate if this experience comes at the beginning of a child's life. Some reasons for being a member of a one-parent family put the child at a greater disadvantage than others.

As with other adverse conditions the greatest concentration is in the lowest socio-economic groups. 50 per cent of all one-parent families, compared with 20 per cent of two-parent families, are in the lowest income group. Two-thirds of families on supplementary benefit are one-parent families, and they tend to remain recipients of this benefit nearly three times longer than other families (National Council for One Parent Families, 1977-80). One-parent families are often, indeed, locked in the 'poverty trap' (Child Poverty Action Group, 1975).

We should not underrate the distress caused to older children by parental break-up, nor ignore the consequences. Children more often suffer from bed-wetting, and spend more time in care, when they have experienced marital break-up. Three-quarters of all children in care now come from one-parent families (Ferri, 1976). The increasing numbers of divorces, remarriages, and single-parent families are creating new dimensions to family life: one-third of all new marriages now involve re-marriage for one or both partners (Popay, 1980). When there are arguments by separated parents about custody of a child, probation officers may play a useful role as conciliators. Some solicitors and barristers try to work together with their opposite numbers for the welfare of the child and may settle out of court, a practice favoured by judges.

The unsupported mother, even the mature woman of good previous personality, may go into a state of apathy or depression when she loses her partner, as was found with women who lost their husbands during the last war. In these states of mind mothers have difficulty in loving their new baby and if 'attachment' is to occur they need a degree of support that social workers may not have time to give. Teenagers and the immature who have been deserted by their partners before or after the birth of their child may feel resentment and transfer it to the child, who is then at risk of physical or emotional abuse or both.

Separation of child from parents. Attachment to the parents is a basic human mechanism of great biological and social significance. Interfering with it may lead to profoundly disturbing feelings of rejection (Dartington, Henry and Lyth, 1976). Young children have little sense of time, and this is one reason why they have great difficulty in coping with separations. Separation from parents tends to make a child less able to cope with life (Bowlby, 1978). Even short separations such as the mother going into hospital for a second baby may have a devastating effect on a susceptible child under the age of three, who will also be facing some loss of attention because of the new baby (Dunn and Kendrick, 1980; Kendrick and Dunn, 1980). A mother has told us of her son who, from the age of six months, was kept in hospital for about four months (unnecessarily we would think nowadays) where the nursing care was excellent and where she herself was at his bedside from before he awoke in the morning until after he had gone to sleep at night. Even so, after his return home, he wakened in the night screaming for her and still sometimes awoke in terror at the age of eight years.

The problem may be greater if the child is admitted to a hospital where visiting is limited (Belson, 1976) (1). Such separations arouse destructive, even murderous feelings in some children. Limitations on visiting of children in hospital are in spite of: (a) repeated adjurations for open visiting by the DHSS, (b) the practice of unrestricted visiting in many hospitals without harm resulting; and are due entirely to attitudes of doctors and nurses.

Statistics and classifications can relate only to the objective and measurable, but data on family rupture collected by one of us (PGH) over a ten-year period (Table 5), may be useful if the reader can augment the figures with all that they imply in emotional inadequacy and failure over many years.

Health. Handicap or chronic physical or mental ill-health in parents may result in emotional deprivation in the children. On the other hand, parents may find it an intolerable burden if a child suffers from a disability such as enuresis, encopresis, or bronchial asthma with attacks occurring in the night; or even if, for no obvious reason, he tends to be wakeful at night. The father or mother who goes out to work will find interruption of sleep hard to bear. The burden of night care has usually been the mother's and must be so when the child is breast fed. Whether in or out of the home she also will have worked all day, often looking after other children in the family, a job whose responsibilities are certainly no less imperative and constraining than those of most men. These commitments coming perhaps on top of chronic tiredness and depression, may lead, as we have said, to inter-spouse resentments. One of us (NFC) had a patient, a man of 40 with a severe heart disorder, whose condition was aggravated by loss of sleep due to nightly wakefulness of his youngest child aged about 18 months. A small dose of a children's preparation of chloral given for a short time helped the child to develop a new sleep pattern. The father's condition greatly improved.

Neighbourhood. Young children living in upper storeys of tower blocks have limited opportunities to play outside, and youthful restlessness bears hardly on the mother who may become repressive. The seemingly aimless activity of childhood is a physiological phenomenon with a sound biological purpose. Its restriction is likely to result, as it does in other mammals, in disturbed behaviour. Too often, as children get older, they find no socially acceptable forms of excitement and adventure, and this is one reason they form gangs.

Seriously damaging upbringing

'Child abuse', a term denoting nonaccidental physical and emotional injury to the child, is committed at any time from birth onwards, usually by parents or guardians. It is among the causes of subsequent behaviour disorder. Child abuse is probably much commoner than was thought. Though the evidence is inadequate it seems likely that in Britain about 50 000 children are severely abused in some manner each year and of these it has been thought that about 60 die (DHSS, 1970; Baldwin and Oliver, 1975; *Select Committee on Violence in the Family*, 1977 (2); ADM Jackson, 1982; Oliver, 1983; Diamond and Jaudes, 1983). The most recent estimates indicate that parents or care givers cause the death of 150-160 children each year (Creighton, 1985). The brain of a young child may be damaged by merely shaking him. He may then cry more and behave in a way that parents with a low tolerance cannot endure. They further reject the child with more battering and severe mental handicap may result.

Since Kempe's pioneering work (Kempe, Silverman, Stele, Droegemueller and Silver, 1962) the subject is becoming better understood (Creighton, 1976; Franklin, 1977; Smith, 1978). Child abuse is strongly correlated with unemployment and financial difficulties, and with alcoholism, all of which are increasing (*British Medical Journal*, 1980). Child and possibly wife abuse are higher in army camps than elsewhere (3). Lynch and Roberts (1982) have reviewed the subject and added material from their own studies. Court cases of adults harming and killing young children have aroused public concern. The DHSS has issued two critical reports on the subject (Social Services Inspectorate, 1986; DHSS, 1986). Many child abuse cases are identified in school and teachers need help in diagnosis and over what to do. Social workers seldom draw teachers into consultation over them (See Part II, Chapter 5).

Incest, which is another form of child abuse, seems much more frequent than was realised (Kempe and Kempe, 1978; Ward, 1984; Porter, 1984). Girls are the main sufferers. Even if there is no sexual contact, awareness of parental incestuous attitude may be damaging to the child. We are only on the verge of understanding the emotional damage this may cause in the adult female and how this in turn may affect her ability to develop a secure emotional relationship with her husband and to rear her children with affection. Sexual abuse is now being more fully investigated (Wild, 1986). It presents special problems for teachers.

Childhood in care

Admission into the care system may be a recipe for personal destruction.
— Taylor et al (1979)

A child cannot survive without support and if the parents are unable to give it, some substitute must be found. If, for instance, one parent dies, the other often remarries. Loss of a parent by death is only one reason among many for looking for a substitute parent or family: some children may be adopted, some go to relatives, some to foster parents, others to children's homes. While these solutions are inevitably second-best there is reason to believe that a good proportion of adoptive and foster parents provide something fairly close to 'normal home care'. There is a lack of research into the feelings of children with substitute parents.

The child in care tends to belong to no one; several people may be responsible for him and no one of them may have this responsibility for long. 'She who writes the school report does not liaise with he who visits the uninhabitable home, he who chases up the truant does not compare notes with she who administers ECT to the parent. Sometimes it all smacks of the child presenting a problem to society, rather than society presenting insurmountable and undefinable difficulties to the child. All these bits and pieces come together in the children's home files like so much flotsam on a beach . . .' (Vincent, 1979). Deprived of the mother-child relationship so essential for the development of a sense of his own identity and of the capacity for 'socialisation' — the ability to respond to other people's needs and demands — the child is likely to be shallow, emotionless and puppet-like. If a child is injured by the parents (and many have died as a result), it is nevertheless better for the child to be in care. However, when children have had such dreadful experiences the least we should do is to ensure that conditions in foster homes, or council, voluntary or private children's homes, are as caring and loving as possible, for the child is doubly in jeopardy: rejected as he sees it by his parents (whatever the circumstances); and trying to grow up in strange surroundings (Cawson, 1978). Residential care still tends to reinforce, rather than reverse, delinquent proclivities. The complaint is often made that many community homes do not provide, as they are supposed to, remedial education for under-achieving children. But there are many greater deficiencies about which less is heard. It is particularly disturbing to hear reports of aggressive or violent attitudes shown in the way staff speak to children in residential care and indeed, of unauthorised violence inflicted on them.

Having regard to the needs of children deprived of normal home life and reared in institutions, it is inappropriate that some Authorities allow corporal punishment for such children (4). How shall we define the nature of caring? The DES (for special schools) and the DHSS (for community homes) keep no records of children suffering corporal punishment. The Residential Care Association, the professional body for staff of residential homes, has called for a ban on it. Violent adults increase children's difficulties and they are a poor model for behaviour. This may be one reason why residential care often fails with juvenile offenders (Cornish and Clarke, 1975). Much that happens to young people in residential care has not been common knowledge. When the facts are unearthed they are unbelievable. Until they had the evidence the National Council for Civil Liberties found it hard to believe that quite a number of young women were incarcerated as 'moral defectives' for no other reason than having given birth to an illegitimate child (Taylor et al, 1979; Hewitt, 1980; Smythe, 1985).

Each member of staff in a children's home has to look after more children than the average parent. The majority are untrained. They work a shift system and their work is done in relative isolation (Page, 1977). Many homes have a high staff turnover, so it is difficult for children to establish relationships with the adults looking after them. While it is fair to pay tribute to the many members of children's homes who do all in their power for the children entrusted to them, Holman (1976) and Page and Clarke (1977) describe shortcomings in the treatment of children in care. At best, since leaving home means parental loss to a child, he begins with a serious handicap (Moss, 1968). Such a child may want to know about his past, but be uncertain if he can bear the pain of exploring his feelings. Children who go early in life into long-term care tend to show major defects of personality in later life. A high proportion of adolescents or adults who become problems to society, come from second-best environments rather than 'good enough' natural families.

Currently about 96 000 children spend much of their lives between birth and the age of 16 in care. Of these over 55 000 are in residential establishments, the rest fostered. The number of children in care nearly doubled in the ten years 1970-80 but is now falling as more children are fostered. Data about the numbers of children in institutional care are available from various sources (Rowe and Lambert, 1973; The National Children's Home, 1983; DHSS, 1984). In 1982 over 29 000 had spent five years or more in care (DHSS, 1984). Vernon and Fruin (1986) found that social work decisions about children in care were more often reactive than proactive, and that many children thus remain in care not because of reasoned decision that this would be best for them, but by default. Case reviews were often perfunctory and case conferences unhelpful to the child. The DHSS (1985), commenting on this and eight other reports on social work decisions in child care, found the scene 'generally quite disturbing and depressing'. Vernon and Fruin (1986) suggest that social workers behave like this because they have not the skills for planning and decision making, and lack support from their seniors. The power of social workers is often commented on, yet they themselves feel *powerless* (DHSS, 1985). Who cares for the carers?

The Curtis Committee (Home Office, 1946) found so much physical misery in children's homes that it concentrated a great deal of its attention on that. Admirable as were its recommendations, they were made by people many of whom lacked understanding of children's emotional needs and so their report paid less attention to this aspect of child care. Until 1948, apart from the provision made by some of the more forward-looking voluntary organisations, and establishments set up by devoted and dedicated individuals, the long-term placement of children tended to be in orphanages that were large, barrack-like institutions run with great rigidity and little or no understanding of modern views on child development and children's needs. The Children Act of 1948 was intended to alter all that. Two of the main changes were to put greater emphasis on foster home care; and to make children's homes much smaller and to remove, as far as possible, their institutional character. The hoped-for improvement has only sometimes been achieved. Consequently children who went into care even in the 1950s found themselves in an environment that was no substitute for a warm and loving family. Many of those who are today parents have so lacked the essential experience of a close warm relationship with a parent or parent-substitute, that they have few inner resources to enable them to be caring parents to their own children, who in turn suffer emotional deprivation. Thus is the condition transmitted down the generations.

Children in care feel isolated and stigmatised. They notice that ordinary people and professional workers alike think that if they are removed from their parents they must have done something 'wrong'. In fact only about a fifth of the children are in care for this reason (Taylor et al, 1979).

Being in care seems to be seen by most people, including the 'caring staff', as a punishment rather than a remedy. This sense of being different and apart intensifies the difficulties of disadvantaged children (Page, 1977).

There has been little study of the ways that communal living affect children. The National Children's Bureau thought that children's own descriptions of their feelings about life in residential care — 'the voice of the child' — would provide an 'enlightening dimension' to the future development of child services. It instituted its 'Who Cares?' project (Page, 1976, 1977; Page and Clarke, 1977) which brought to light much suffering. The NCB held a national one day event — 'Who Cares?' — in 1975 for 100 young people growing up in homes scattered over the country. They were joined by 5 adults who had themselves grown up in residential care, and for the second part of the programme by residential and field social workers. All who attended the conference were enthusiastically responsive. As a result the NCB set in train further conferences and a mixed working group that met regularly.

This project showed (Page, 1977) that the educational and vocational needs of children in long-term care were met in a haphazard way. The children and young people were seldom brought into discussions about their future. Although local authorities had powers to assist, befriend and advise young adults who have been in care, and to support them in higher education and vocational training, few did so.

Many children in long-term care first came into it because they had been ill-treated or seriously neglected. Experience of pain rather than pleasure will condition such children's responses so that they make their needs and feelings known by aggressive or violent behaviour. The Who Cares? project found that corporal punishment and physical ill-treatment were accepted by many children as natural and inevitable, a necessary trial of childhood. Children were reluctant to confide in adults about ill-treatment, mutely accepting physical and emotional cruelty as the norm, and feeling that adults in authority did not take them seriously. Yet some of the young people appreciated the skill and patience of those who cared for them. Some local authorities have adopted some of the recommendations arising from this project. Many members of the groups have experienced personal growth and development (Niblett, 1980). The project is now being run by the National Association of Young People in Care (NAYPIC) composed of people who are or have been in care.

Young people have a capacity for absorbing shocks, provided they are not extreme, and for assimilating their environment. Given an opportunity they will talk about their life experiences, feelings and attitudes. Nurses, barely 18 years old, less than three months after starting their training were able to analyse the workings and shortcomings of their hospital with insight and precision, speaking in a forbearing and understanding manner of unpleasant vicissitudes and showing sympathy for the difficulties of people in authority (Coghill, 1976). It is easy to underestimate young people.

'X', a black social worker of mixed parentage, then aged 27 and studying at college for a Certificate of Qualification in Social Work (CQSW), told the DBIS group about his history as a child in care. He experienced numerous different foster and residential homes. Muriel Colley told the group the history of Mrs. 'Y', then aged 30, who was the mother of a child at her school for maladjusted children. The accounts illustrated the difficulties that children meet in developing human relationships and in maturing emotionally when they have had an insecure upbringing. A constant theme in the lives of 'X', and of 'Y', and of other children separated from their parents, is the question of identity. They yearn for proper own parents and often fantasize about them, imagining their mothers to be princesses. A child whom 'X' was taking about Liverpool believed his mother had golden hair. He wanted to welcome every fair-haired woman he saw in the street as his lost mum. Mrs. 'Y' had not known her mother. She asked 'was she my mother?' She perpetually asked questions about her family. Had she parents, or siblings? Everyone was evasive.

Harm may ensue to children from disruption of relationships when social workers leave their job, more so if there is a gap before successors are appointed. But there are many reasons why children aged around eight are already cynical about the possibility of establishing lasting relationships with adults. Continuity of care is a problem that needs more consideration in the caring professions generally.

Conclusions regarding children in care. While we cannot expect social workers to have true parental feelings for other peoples' children, and must accept that life in care is inevitably a 'second best', it need not be as bad as it often seems to be. It would help the child in care to be told more about himself and his background. These children, struggling to achieve emotional maturity desperately need the help they can derive from a clearer sense of identity. There is no doubt that children in care are upset when told about their parents or shown photographs of them and this may daunt social workers. Children in care usually have some contact with one parent. It is important that he/she and the staff co-operate in what children are told about their background.

The following are the points that those brought up in residential homes tend to emphasise:

1. The institutional nature of the establishment, less though it is than in the days before the Children Act of 1948.

2. The quality of the staff; it is a matter of luck whether members of staff are good or bad.

3. Failure of staff of all grades to understand the child's search for identity; and of the urgency of his need to know who his parents are, and why he was taken into and remains in care.

4. His lack of control over what happens to him.

5. The lack of adequate criteria for selecting foster homes, or monitoring in any effective way the quality of the one in which the child is placed. Contract fostering of teenagers with supportive discussion groups goes some way to meet this criticism (see Part II, Chapter 5).

6. The vicissitudes he may undergo because: (a) different establishments cater for different age groups; (b) changes from one place to another may be abrupt and all contact with a previous home lost; (c) parents may take a child home for a time and later have him placed back in care: frequently he then goes to a new school and possibly a new environment with a different culture pattern. Other interruptions, for example a period in hospital, in a convalescent home or a community home, may have the same results. Sometimes the change may be for the good, the child leaving an environment where he is unhappy for a better one; but usually the change is from a place where he has made some relationships and had some good experiences, to one which seems to him to be worse. It is in any case different and so, whether or not he is already emotionally handicapped, he is expected to start all over again laboriously making new relationships, a task that may be beyond his powers.

In these, and other ways, it is felt by those who have experienced it that, however well intentioned, little is done by child-care staff at any level to understand the magnitude of the emotional disability with which the child goes into care, or to develop qualities of their own that might go some way to compensate for it.

Prisons and secure units. 'Short, sharp shock' regimes for older adolescents convicted of minor crimes, are apparently used because of the ineffectiveness of penal institutions. 75-85 per cent of juveniles released from borstals (now called youth custody centres) and detention centres re-offend within two years although many of these young people would have had two or less previous convictions. There is the practice of remanding young people, mostly boys, aged 14-16 to adult prisons while awaiting trial or sentencing, though legally people under 21 (previously 17) cannot be sentenced to imprisonment, and many of these young persons are found not guilty at their trial. The Government excluded 14-year-olds from prison remands in 1981 (Home Office, 1980). Specially built secure places for children were due to rise eventually to 550 in number (DHSS, 1981). For humanitarian reasons as well as cost many local authorities appear unwilling to put children in these places, and instead they have been locked up in prisons and remand centres. However, courts may be misusing an amendment to the 1980 Child Care Act that came into force in 1983 so that more, not less, children are being locked up (5). There are 7000 youngsters locked up in what are now called youth custody centres and detention centres. In addition thousands of children in care are each year put into secure accommodation, for no crime, merely for being 'unruly'. Taylor *et al* (1979) found that one-fifth of girls in secure units were not taken to court following an offence. There are also children locked up in prisons or secure mental hospitals often for relatively trivial reasons, and for indefinite lengths of time; bizarre expressions of adult 'caring'. Perhaps it is as Tutt (1985) says we just do not like children in this country. There was the publicised case of 'Christine' who, beaten and rejected by her mother, was locked up in Holloway Prison by a crown court judge at the age of 14 without term to her imprisonment ('for the period of your life') for setting fire to some curtains in a community home. She was moved through a variety of prisons and other secure institutions, treated with tranquilisers, and ended up in a maximum security wing of a special mental hospital. Her case was taken up by MIND and became the subject of a TV documentary. After this, now aged 20, she was released from the special hospital.

We contrast how the authors were able to help 'Dorothy' many years ago. Then aged 15 she came under the care of one of us (PGH). She was thought to be in need of care when found outside a pub where her widowed mother was drinking. The only available place was in a remand home. 'Dorothy' had never done anything unlawful and resented her 'treatment'; she damaged the home — she was 'unruly' — and so was 'punished' by closer confinement. After consultation, she was admitted into a bed in the general medical ward of the other of us (NFC). There, after some initial forthright expressions of resentment — 'unruly' again — requiring counselling of the nursing staff, she settled down, and nine months later, aged 16, she was found a useful niche in society into which she fitted well. Secure units do not reduce aggression but foster it.

There are still impressive numbers of children, documented by NAYPIC and the Children's Legal Centre, sometimes as young as 10 years old, being harshly treated in care: locked up for weeks at a time for running away to go home, forcibly treated with tranquilising drugs, lacking participation in discussions about their future, their letters censored, not allowed phone calls, their parents denied access (Taylor *et al*, 1979; Tate and Breslin, 1983). These continuing actions indicate that social workers have too much power, that they do not always use it sensibly, that the courts collude and that politicians behave feebly when they could end these scandals. In English law the child has very few rights. A code of legal rights for children in secure units is much overdue (DHSS, 1981) and the Government is being urged to introduce legal safeguards for such children (Children's Legal Centre, 1982). Restrictions on locking up children in care were introduced in 1983, but they do not go far enough.

It is proposed to introduce residential care orders through the criminal process (Home Office, 1980). The British Association of Social Workers (BASW) would prefer separate care proceedings when there is sufficient evidence to warrant them, and would like to see an expansion of the probation service, with the development of intermediate treatment (6).

Secondary school organisation

The inescapable school situation

The nature of the day in most secondary schools is such that when the bell rings children have to move quickly to another class with no time allowed for the changeover. Though some schools are more flexible than others, all children, whether capable of coping or not, must fit into the pattern of the timetable. The main cause of rigidity in the system is emphasis on academic attainment so non-academic children or emotionally disturbed children tend to feel second-class pupils. Many teachers, under pressure to train children to pass exams, their skills being evaluated in these terms, find problem children a distraction and dislike having to deal with them.

When children have no classroom of their own, conflicts between child and teacher cannot be easily resolved. However much the teacher and the pupil might wish to talk over matters of any kind quietly together, it is difficult to find a time and place to do it. The competitive pressures of the average school environment, such as ranking in order, using marks, and publishing examination results, aggravate or generate insecurity in some children. For some older pupils' schools are little more than 'keepers of children' until they go to work. Teachers face undoubted difficulties with children who are not motivated to learning, and have no goals in life. Highly intelligent children are sometimes bored, perhaps because of the way subjects are taught. Older children who are not taught what they believe they need for their future, may become frustrated, bored and restive (Holt, 1969; Hemming, 1980). As they approach leaving age many teenage children are distressed at the thought of having to cope with the outside world still unable to read properly. The child's failure to learn for whatever reason, causes him to fall behind his peers. Nothing fails like failure.

Are teachers still tending to teach subjects not children, and failing to relate methods of teaching sufficiently to 'growing up kids'? Does schooling help children to mature by embracing a wide enough definition of education and the teacher's task? Although the advances that have taken place in pastoral care in many schools will help children to benefit from their schooling, they do not compensate for unsatisfactory curricula. Comprehensive education, whatever its not inconsiderable achievements, is failing to meet some needs of pupils and society (Hargreaves, 1982).

School policies

The structure of authority in state schools is laid down in the 1944 Education Act: 'Responsibility for the whole internal organisation, management and discipline of the school is vested in the head, together with the control of both teaching and non-teaching staff'. There is a trend for teachers with posts of responsibility to take more part in the organisation of their schools (Welsh Office, 1978). Many school policies arise from decisions taken by the staff, and some will be influenced by the prevailing ethos of the LEA and the community. The school can hardly escape from the social and emotional problems affecting the children who go to it and so will discharge its function better if its policies take account of them.

The way schools are organised, and the curriculum they offer, have an effect on children's behaviour and ability to learn (Rutter, Maughan, Mortimore, Ouston and Smith, 1979). We know that in similar contiguous demographic areas one school may have many delinquent pupils and another relatively few. Galloway (1985a&b) discusses the school's role in the causation of children's disturbing behaviour. The school, like other social institutions, is no more than a group of people collected together for one main, and several subsidiary, purposes. As in all organisations the institution, operating as a collective group, has effects not only on its employees but also on its clients. Much that a child learns from school, adult behaviour and attitudes, and life in general, is 'through the skin' (the 'hidden curriculum'). Children are impressionable and teachers, by the way they behave, are in a position to exert an effect upon them. Children develop strategies in school to protect themselves, just as 'subject peoples' (even inmates of concentration camps) consciously behave to preserve some dignity and personal integrity. 'To a very great degree school is a place where children learn to be stupid' (Holt, 1969). The hidden curriculum may have far more pervasive effects than has been realised. Hargreaves (1982) argues that many pupils feel its impact as an assault on their dignity; that working class pupils in particular are its victims; and that the children's counter-culture can be interpreted as a form of resistance. He suggests that many changes that have occurred in the way of life of the working class bear on children's behaviour, and that they are not easily comprehended by people like teachers, psychologists and doctors, who are predominantly middle-class. It is a reflection upon our educational system that proportionately no more working class children are going to university now than before the first world war (Halsey, Heath and Ridge, 1980).

All teachers tend to construct systems incorporating their current values and principles, and working hypotheses. They may distinguish an attachment group of pupils, those who are successful, rewarding to teach, giving plenty of feedback and making the teacher feel successful. These children get much of the teacher's attention and praise, and may be credited with higher attainments and intelligence quotient than objective tests warrant. Thus teachers formulate standards by which they judge all children. Those who do not reach them may become a 'concern group' and if these are unresponsive they tend to be described in even more negative terms (Silberman, 1969). Teachers, by the methods they adopt, get themselves on hooks (Rist, 1970). Then, to get unhooked, they have to say children are ineducable, delinquent, etc and must go elsewhere, thus defining a 'rejected group' (Silberman, 1969). Such children are credited with fewer virtues than they possess and are heavily criticised for their shortcomings. In an American study (Rist, 1970) the teacher arranged the children at three tables in the classroom. At table 1, located nearest the teacher, were those closest to the teacher's construct of the ideal: bright, rewarding and odour-free (!). At tables 2 and 3 were children progressively removed from this ideal. Table 1 made adverse comments about tables 2 and 3, and the last about themselves. Only those at table 1 made satisfactory academic progress.

Badly administered schools may encourage disorderly behaviour in the pupils. The authoritarian hierarchical form of traditional school management itself causes the children to think and behave in the same way (Hemming, 1980), and aggravates the difficulties some children have in developing relationships. Children bring patterns of behaviour with them but an individual teacher or the school as a whole may affect a child's develor..aent. The utterances and actions of some heads would be amusing did they not betray out of date attitudes of mind; like the head of a boy's grammar school who said 'I have no teachers in my school, only masters' (Where, 1972). In some first schools we have seen a line painted on the playground beyond which parents were forbidden to go when bringing or collecting their children. A refinement of hierarchical organisation at one such school was a rule that allowed junior teachers half a bun at coffee break while the seniors got a whole one. On the other hand we know of a first school which gives new parents a booklet, attractively illustrated by the children beginning with 'Welcome' and after a brief description of the activities of the school and staff (including the caretaker and kitchen workers) who are described as approachable and willing to help in any way they can, ends by saying that parents, sisters, brothers and friends are invited to come to 'family assembly' on Friday afternoons and to take part in the annual day's outing.

While many head teachers do attach importance to the views of their staff, few are prepared to be influenced by their pupils. They may respond favourably to the occasional piece of constructive criticism but are unwilling regularly to seek pupils' thoughts on the school and are dismissive of pupil opposition. The free flow of information and ideas between pupils and authorities is impeded by two aspects of the British system — the variety of petty rules to which most pupils are subject, and corporal punishment until lately commonplace in parts of the country.

Hamblin (1978) believes that devices like 'setting' have fragmented the teaching group, making it almost impossible for the teacher to maintain a consistent relationship with a pupil. He quotes Bazalgette who found that in commerce and industry young people worked in small, relatively stable task groups, which allowed supervisors to get to know them reasonably well, whereas secondary school procedures prevented form tutors gaining much knowledge of a pupil. The system of options and setting could result in fifth-year pupils having to relate to 12 different teachers besides their form tutor.

Disruptive behaviour may begin in the secondary school without it being known at an earlier stage in a pupil's life. So, it may be asked, is it due to the policy of the school, the nature of the discipline, the curricula offered, the fragmented nature of the high school day, the personalities of the head teacher or staff, or the lack of regard for the opinions of the teachers or the children, in helping to run the school? It seems unlikely that unexpected behaviour in the secondary school could always be put down to puberty or the secondary school environment. We believe that primary schools have more children with behaviour disorders than they admit to. At a conference, not one primary school teacher would admit to problems with disturbed children in his school; yet the secondary school teachers present gave evidence of disturbance among twelve year olds, coming to them from those same primary schools. Some younger children show signs of disturbance outside school, but provided the child gives no trouble in school the head does nothing about it. Indeed, as things are, why should he? In fact referrals to the child guidance service reach a peak from 8-12. It looks as if teachers struggle on, unwilling to admit 'failure' until, when they are facing the child's move onwards they desperately ask for 'something to be done'.

Successive reports by Her Majesty's Inspectors (HMI) (Welsh Office, 1978; DES, 1979, 1980, 1984a) despite much to praise, have criticized the curricula and teaching methods of many secondary schools. They found unvarying regimens of lectures and dictated notes, inadequate choice of courses, curricula dominated by examinations, much dull repetition and lack of purpose in the work, shortage of resources and of subject teachers, deficient in-service teacher training and old-fashioned buildings. There was insufficient attempt to encourage intellectual curiosity. 'Where children are rude or lethargic, it may well be a consequence . . . of the work they are being offered' (DES, 1980). The clear inference was that many pupils were underachieving because so many secondary schools expected too little from their pupils at all ages and whatever their ability. Secondary schools seemed reluctant to examine critically their own performance. However much the inspectorate may encourage self-evaluation, it will not be advanced when education authorities, for whatever reason, stop research into the effects of schools on children's behaviour (Power, Benn and Morris, 1972; Morris and Power, 1972; Mortimore, 1978).

Secondary schools have catered mainly for the 50 per cent or so of pupils with academic aspirations, and not for the rest who are dubbed 'failures'. The introduction of comprehensive education may have reduced the proportion of second-class pupils to around 50 per cent of the school compared to the 80 per cent or so who comprised the secondary modern schools' population. We look to teachers to change a system that classifies the non-academic child as inferior. The sense of failure in the less academically able is a factor in producing antisocial attitudes by denying achievement and self-respect: 'Until we . . . embark . . . on the task of developing young people as civilised human beings, we shall continue to break the hearts of thousands of adolescents, converting not a few . . . into hostile barbarians' (Hemming, 1981).

Schools should, and many do, provide a happy life for their pupils and a gateway to a fuller life later on. But for many 'Is there a life after school?' is all too good a question. Its cynicism derives from the difficulty young people experience in getting worthwhile jobs when they leave school, or indeed any jobs at all. In the 1980s cynicism may be justified by the state of the adult world they are entering, but what we may hope is a temporary misfortune should not distort the way in which schools prepare adolescents for the future. In examining what we are trying to do *for* our children, we find it is often to satisfy adults' own failed aspirations. Recognising this may help us to understand what we are actually doing *to* them.

Discipline

Studies in Yorkshire (Clegg and Megson, 1973) showed that schools with high use of the cane had high rates of court appearances of their children, the reverse being true when the cane was little used. These correlations stood regardless of various social factors. In many homes there may be no true discipline, that is teaching of self-discipline, although, as is often the case in West Indian families, there may be corporal punishment. Finlayson and Loughran (1976) showed that in schools with high delinquency rates pupils were significantly more likely to see teachers as authoritarian and arbitrary. It has been observed (Rabinowitz, 1981a) that the lesson in which disruptive behaviour tends to be most marked is that immediately following the physical education period, perhaps as a reaction to the relatively authoritarian figure of the PE teacher.

Motivation

In his earlier years, at home or at school, the child uses his brain to solve problems relevant to his life. He is optimistic and has fun. He learns to use his brain for one of its most important functions — thinking. Most children in primary schools are keen and able to learn, and are pleased to do things ('work') with mother or father. Most enjoy the school they attend. Most primary schools are not only child centred, but thoughtful in their attitudes to the family just as much as to the child. But in the later stages of primary education even those staff concerned about the children's family background and the emotional development of their children, put more emphasis on the academic side of education. Part of their task is to prepare children for the demands of the secondary school, and if they fail in this, they will be criticized. So there is a steady progression from the caring child-centred atmosphere of the nursery and first schools to the more or less impersonal secondary school. At the time of school transfer many children experience anxiety from internal problems unrecognised by teachers, and with which parents may be ill-equipped to deal. As the child ascends the educational ladder he is asked to learn more and more facts about matters he may perceive as having less and less relevance to his present or future life. His motivation for schooling may begin to fail, with resulting boredom if not alienation, and behaviour may be affected.

Labelling

People have a tendency to characterise others with attributes that fit more with their own attitudes and prejudices than with the reality of those reviewed. People have more sympathy with some physical handicaps such as blindness than others, for example deafness or skin blemishes (Bull, 1978; Bull and Stevens, 1980).

Labelling has dangers. Most of us readily apply epithets to the discreditable and the discredited. Doing so may relieve anxiety and frustration and give the labeller a sense of superiority. This contributes nothing at all to understanding why the discredited has behaved as he did and may have disastrous effects on a client. There is nothing charitable or compassionate about it; no help is offered to the stigmatized and often little to those affected by his behaviour. In fact the act of labelling closes the mind of the name-caller and actively inhibits converting the occasion into a learning exercise that might help the discredited to behave differently in future and give insight into the causes of his behaviour.

Labelling the child takes place at home, in the community and at school where it may do the most harm. It may be difficult to shake off as it is automatically accepted and used by courts, police, teachers and social workers. Stigma is a burden for anyone (Goffman, 1963), and particularly for a child who has to cope with problems in himself. When attached to children in care simply because they are in care, it is one more burden for the child. It is an indication of adults' unawareness of the insidious way labels are applied and communicated that whereas children in care are primarily the responsibility of social workers, it is they who criticize teachers for labelling children, and give this as one reason for reluctance to tell teachers all they know about a child. Teachers complain about this lack of communication. So the child is caught in adult crossfire. A more subtle form of labelling is a consequence of the hidden curricula of schools (Upton and Gobell, 1980).

A hostel for maladjusted girls sent 12 of them to the nearby secondary school. The head teacher complained to some visiting HMIs that these girls stood out and could be seen to be 'different' from the rest. The HMIs asked to visit the classes to spot these deviants. At the end of their tour they named 12 girls as likely to be the hostel girls, but, in fact, not one of them was.

Many young people with minor disabilities have been teased by other children throughout their school lives without adults being aware of the fact. Such defects include hare-lips, protruding ears, unsightly scars or birthmarks, and disabilities such as stammering, peculiarities of gait and so forth (Bull and Stevens, 1980; Rumsey, Bull and Gahagan, 1982). Remedying these defects and disabilities makes a significant contribution to rehabilitation. One of us (PGH) had as patients in a child guidance clinic two children, a brother and sister, whose minor disability was to have been born without thumbs. This had been the cause of unmerciful teasing from their first day at school and at the ages of eleven and nine they were on the way to becoming school phobics. They were normally intelligent and, in other respects, physically attractive children. Concerned parents and caring teachers knew that 'there was something wrong' but were amazed to be told what it was.

We explore the subject of labelling further in Part IV, Chapter 12, as a form of malcommunication. It is sufficient to emphasize here that attaching a label to a child may add to the problems he already cannot cope with, and will probably exacerbate his difficult behaviour. Help with disfigurement may be obtained from the Disfigurement Guidance Centre, pioneered by Doreen Trust.

Table 3: First causes of emotional disturbance in children

   1. Emotionally disturbed parents

* **2.** Pathological anxiety in parents: effects transmitted from one generation to the next within the family

* **3.** Deprivation: lack of parental love
                         inadequate play — high rise flats
                         parental systems of child rearing

        ● use of physical force as discipline

        ● excessive use of ineffective anger

        ● childhood in care

* **4.** Violence between parents

* **5.** Poverty

* **6.** Unemployment, possibly caused by poor work record resulting from chronic ill-health

* **7.** Effects upon parents of illness or behaviour in child's infancy or when young, such as:

    ● bronchial asthma

    ● encopresis

    ● enuresis

    ● wakefulness; hyperactivity; crying (*Select Committee on Violence in the Family*, 1977. Vol II, paras 583-775)

* **8.** Separation from parents in infancy and early childhood:
parent(s) in gaol
child in hospital (Dartington *et al*, 1976)
homelessness splitting family, sometimes with children in care
death of parent(s); strains in one-parent families

* **9.** Parent-child relationships disturbed by:
external vicissitudes
personal inadequacies of one or both parents
inadequacies of child
alien culture pattern
social isolation
family psycho-pathology
mental illness

***10.** Physical handicap in child.

*Constitute no 6 in Table 4.

Table 4: Factors aggravating pre-existing conditions, or acting as prime causes of behaviour disorder

1. Difficult living conditions:

    ● cramped quarters

    ● noise

    ● nowhere for privacy, or to do homework

    ● dismissive parental attitudes to learning and book work

2. Undernutrition

3. No conversation ⎱

    ⎰ leading to poor vocabulary and self-

4. No reading of books ⎰ expression, and to lack of ideas

5. Too much television; effect of viewing violence (Belson, 1978; Rutter, 1979a)

6. Other factors — *in Table 3

7. Effect of school upon the child:

    a. direct through school's policies (Rutter *et al*, 1979)

    b. indirect through school's reactions

        ● inadequate parental care; child smelly, illkempt and poorly clothed so that he is unpopular with peers

        ● chronic lateness at school and absenteeism so that the child misses school and health inspections, leading to unidentified and untreated defective vision and hearing, in turn leading to disaffection with school followed by behaviour disorders.

Table 5: Categories of family rupture found in referrals to Ealing child guidance clinic in a ten-year period

Category of family rupture	Number of referrals
Separation of parents	52
Divorce	17
Remarriage/cohabitation	31
Violence/cruelty	35
Neglect	15
Friction: mother/father	42
other — family	25
Death of parent	22
Physical illness	36
Mental illness of parents or parent substitute	37
Attempted suicide: mother/father etc.	12
Substitute parents (other than step-parents)	17
Disruptions in the childhood of the parents	31
Father absent — seeking work elsewhere	13

School population about 40 000; annual referral rate to the clinic: 300; approximately 3000 cases seen in ten years.

Notes

1. The National Association for the Welfare of Children in Hospital has conducted surveys of facilities for visiting children in hospital, the latest in 1982. Facilities have improved but are not yet ideal. At present about half of all children's wards allow 24-hour visiting. Only 40 per cent of adult wards containing children allow unrestricted visiting. Ear, nose and throat (ENT) wards lag behind all others, only 32 per cent having unrestricted visiting. 25 per cent of ENT wards still do not allow visiting on the day of operation, and a further 17 per cent restrict it severely. Accommodation for parents to sleep (often primitive) is available in an average of about 90 per cent of all wards.

2. *First Report.* Vol I, paras 24 and 31.

3. We are indebted to RD Ackerly, principal coordinating officer of the North Yorkshire County Council; and to JM Harrison, information officer of the Warwickshire County Council, for information about child abuse in army camps mentioned by A Fry in the *Observer* of 18/5/1980. The Yorkshire figures were compiled in 1978.

4. Nottinghamshire County Council banned corporal punishment from its children's homes in 1975, reintroduced it in six community homes in 1977, and banned it again in 1981.

5. Information obtained from the Children's Legal Centre in 1984.

6. The British Association of Social Workers' comments (Baldwin, Thorpe and Brown, 1981) on the Government White Paper on young offenders (Home Office, 1980).

Part II: Remedies and intervention

Chapter 4 — Introduction

Teachers alone cannot offer children a full education for life; no single service can be comprehensive and sufficient. School may be helpful to the majority of pupils but can it not also be of value to the disruptive minority?

Teenage in the late 20th century may be thought of as the age of disillusionment. Every schoolchild ought to be able to get some satisfaction from joining the adult world. In the earlier part of this century, except for the war years and a few years in the 1930s, this has been a reasonable expectation. But now? The outlook may be annihilation in a 'European desert' (Lord Mountbatten), bringing to an end a life in which he can find no work, or employment that is only temporary and precarious, or that offends his dignity. Many young people are troubled by the prospect of possible nuclear annihilation (Humphrey and Lifton, 1984; Barton, 1985).

All the disruptive child can say is: to the teacher 'I am unable to take what the ordinary classroom offers'; to the doctor or psychologist 'I am unable to make relationships'; to the police 'Nobody cares how much I am hurt, so why should I not hurt someone else?' Youth leaders expect him to be clubbable when he cannot make one good friendship. Nevertheless prospects for employment and the quality of life may improve and education should be based on the expectation that they will. Indeed as future adult citizens children have it in their hands to see that they will.

The need. We shall consider relevant agencies that may help with problems arising from disruptive behaviour as it affects schools.

Throughout the discussions of the DBIS group we were impressed by the fact that the 'established case' appeared to be at a stage when most methods currently in use for dealing with it in ordinary schools were demanding of scarce resources and largely ineffectual. 'It was too late.' While we have to cope with the present generation of difficult children, and there will always be some children in trouble, it is plain that prevention is in all ways better than cure. Much of the damage may have been done by the time the child is two or three years old. We strongly support the comments of the *Select Committee on Violence in the Family* (1977) on the prevention of harm to children (1). What can we do to spot the problem in its early stages? The family, extended or narrow, is the first and for many years the main group of adults on whom the child is dependent. Influences may begin before the child's birth and be difficult and sometimes impossible to eradicate no matter how skilled the care.

Intervention. Topping (1983) in an extensive review of others' work found that the results of most attempts at intervention had not been rigorously assessed. He reasonably points out that many disruptive children 'grow out of it'. However, such are the palpable needs of children, families, teachers and others for help with children's behaviour problems that we must use empirical methods to provide it until more scientific evaluation becomes possible.

In the following chapters we consider ways in which disruptive behaviour can be diminished. It is often hard to draw a distinction between prevention and treatment since the 'treatment' of a young child will in many cases prevent the appearance of similar or worse problems at a later age, and in the offspring that the child may have when he or she becomes an adult. Since most children are part of a family, intervention is usually in the family as a whole. Different agencies specialise in different types of intervention: medical, where the problem is largely due to illness or handicap; social, when the problem has its causes in the environment; educational, when it is a problem manifesting itself in learning difficulties or disturbing behaviour at school. Needless to say the causes of behaviour problems often overlap, as do the skills of those assigned by training and qualifications to help with them. Professional overlaps and sharing of loads are assets in problem solving if there are good relationships and well-developed communication systems between disciplines.

In this study we are mainly concerned with problems in secondary schools. Services provided by the education department and special skills provided by educational workers (teachers, psychologists, counsellors and welfare workers) are available to be called upon for recognising and remedying school problems, and often the combined services of several specialists are needed. We believe that many secondary school problems can be forestalled by intervention in earlier school years, if not before.

In the UK, services have grown up piecemeal, sometimes in response to a specific need, sometimes because of the whims of someone in authority, and sometimes to satisfy a pressure group. Some people serving a particular function are given different names in different parts of the country. Labels tend to be changed from time to time to give the job a better 'image', for example the 'attendance officer' (AO) (the old 'truancy man') has become the 'education welfare officer' (EWO). With the change of label comes some change in the nature of the work: the EWO is more of a social worker than the AO was, but as he is paid by the Education Department he cannot be given the title of social worker. There is, too, the danger that change of name may be an excuse to avoid facing the need to change attitudes, or to provide resources (finance and staff), to bring about the desired results. We use names generally familiar and hope that this will not cause readers confusion or misunderstanding.

Notes

1. *First Report.* Vol I. Para 54.

   Our recommendations begin . . . with prevention. In their memorandum the Royal College of Psychiatrists said of prevention that it was a general biological truth that organisms . . . undergoing rapid growth were particularly vulnerable. Prevention . . . was basically 'a matter of cultural, economic and political aspects of child rearing practices' . . . Yet the Government in their reply to the Report of the Select Committee on Violence in Marriage (1976, Cmnd 6690, para 21) said 'when resources are limited preventive work is liable to receive less attention than statutory duties or crisis intervention.'

Chapter 5 — Remedies for family problems

The family

Salimbene described Frederick II's experiment of the thirteenth century as follows:

> ... he bade foster mothers and nurses to suckle the children, to bathe and wash them, but in no way to speak to them, for he wanted to learn whether they would speak the Hebrew language, which was the oldest, or Greek, or Latin, or Arabic, or perhaps the language of their parents ... But he laboured in vain because the children all died. For they could not live without the petting and joyful faces and loving words of their mothers.

— Quoted by Professor Sinclair Rogers in his evidence to the *Select Committee on Violence in the Family* (1977) (1).

John Wesley on how to bring up children, quoted in the *Observer* (21/12/1980):

> Break their wills betimes; begin this great work before they can run alone, before they can speak plain or perhaps speak at all. Let him have nothing he cries for, absolutely nothing, great or small. Make him do as he is bid, if you whip him ten times running to effect it. Break his will now and his soul will live and he will probably bless you to all eternity.

In this chapter we examine the needs of parents, especially mothers, when bearing and caring for children, and indicate ways in which help and advice may be offered. We emphasise the direct connection between a good or bad start in life and the child's later behaviour. We have referred to 'good enough' families and these constitute the great majority. The sensible mother has a good understanding of her young baby's needs and this can be enlarged in discussion with the health visitor or other mothers.

Teachers believe that a high proportion of disruptive children come from a disadvantaged environment. There are still a great number of disadvantaged families (Floud *et al*, 1956; Douglas, 1964; Field, 1977; DHSS, 1980b) in which the bread-winners are among the least skilled and the lowest paid. Such families are likely to be badly housed in a socially disadvantaged neighbourhood, with a higher incidence of illness and a higher mortality rate at all ages than the population as a whole. These are people among whom unemployment and delinquency are particularly high, and to whom the inverse care law applies — the greater the need, the less the provision.

Immigrants from Asia, Africa and the West Indies who find themselves in the lowest socio-economic categories and who, rightly or wrongly, feel persecuted and discriminated against, bring additional problems. They have difficulties in communication, and often fail to understand our complex social laws. The children tend to mature earlier, and some of the parents are less 'child-centred' than is expected by teachers and others. Because of their cultural traditions both children and parents may regard it as futile to keep in school and treat as 'children', large, mature teenagers, keen to take their place in the adult world. While racism and inter-racial hostility create their own difficulties, there is a tendency for those who believe themselves to be down-trodden minorities to have similar attitudes towards the more privileged. Thus both West Indian mothers of large families, and single parent white women, tend to regard social workers as enemies rather than helpers.

It seems absurd that we have a department of state concerned with the education of persons of all ages, but none specifically with the care of children. Ministries concerned with social services and the education of children should work more closely together.

The first baby. In spite of all the advances in obstetric care, mothers in 'western' societies are often less prepared for motherhood than their forebears or than women in less 'developed' countries. Nevertheless the majority, happily married, influenced by their natural maternal instincts, with deep memories of their own childhood and beguiled by the 'attachment behaviour' of their baby (Bowlby, 1951), quickly learn to be good enough mothers and make use of help and guidance from doctors, midwives, health visitors, relatives and friends. But some may have feelings of guilt about increasing the population, or about the kind of world into which they are bringing their babies. The multifarious and complex social pressures that may be brought to bear on parents over having children, and the effects of these upon the child are discussed by Kitzinger (1978). Parental inability to make use of the help available is one of the many factors accounting for teenage behaviour disorders. First-time mothers (and fathers) may be inept at dealing with babies. A health visitor, at a first-time mother's instigation, helped to set up home groups of mothers with young children who, by discussing their mutual problems, were able to help themselves (Hiskins, 1982). Those who have reason for unhappiness, among whom the mother left without a partner is perhaps the leading case, often fail to behave maternally because they do not feel maternal.

The single parent. Some unmarried mothers have their own parents to turn to, but many have become detached from their families. The single mother is beset by social and economic difficulties as we have mentioned. Until she can get her child into a creche or nursery, she cannot go to work and is dependent on social security payments. Housing departments are slow to provide anything more than 'homeless families' accommodation, usually dismal and discouraging. A single parent tends to have an undue share of illness and so does her child (DHSS, 1974). When mother is ill the child goes into care; when the child is ill, he goes into hospital, and is sometimes kept there for 'social reasons'. We have seen cases where the child has spent barely half his first five years with his mother. Social workers are rightly concerned about these cases, but far too often their only remedy is to take the child into care.

Some social workers seem to take children into care too readily, and to be inconsistent in their decisions. The same worker who refuses to respond to a mother's plea for removal of a child even though placing him on the 'at risk' register may insist on removing from his home a child greatly wanted by a mother whose main need is help in mastering the skills of bringing up a difficult child. Social workers seem seldom to know or enquire about the mother's *need* to have a child, and do not help her to mobilise her positive feelings to assist the child to develop satisfactorily. They do not see the need to help to 'mend the home' suggested by Bowlby (1951) as the best form of 'treatment'. If the mother cannot get this kind of help, then the outlook for the child is bleak. Life in a children's home seldom promotes good personality development; many foster placements break down; returning a damaged child to a damaged mother is courting disaster. Many single mothers and their children fail to find ways out of this impasse. The baby of the single girl under 16 years of age is especially at risk, and the emotional and social needs of such mothers are poorly catered for (Page J, 1979). There are organisations to help the single parent family (The National Council for One Parent Families; Gingerbread), but they cannot always give enough help.

The parents

Whether the child has one or two parents rearing may not be 'good enough'. Different kinds of deprivation and children's varying responses to them were set out by Bowlby (1951), though modification of some of his ideas has become necessary (Rutter, 1981; Tizard, 1986). Studies of parent/infant attachment are giving us greater understanding of the needs of both parties for the development of stable emotional relationships as the child grows. Much suffering could be avoided if mothers were given help and support when they first show their sense of helplessness. The problems of parents may show themselves before the birth of the child, at around the time of birth, or later when the first or earlier child is a toddler and the mother becomes pregnant again. If parents are inexperienced all 'problems' are likely to be more pressing, and to require more and earlier help in child bearing life.

The antenatal period: help for the expectant mother

Excellent services are available for the care of the pregnant woman but they are not fully used, especially by women who are most in need — those in the Registrar General's social classes 4 and 5; and even those women who get admirable physical care are often denied the opportunity to discuss their anxieties with a professional person — to give one common example, their fears of giving birth to a mentally or physically handicapped child. They may find doctors unsympathetic: 'In the main, antenatal consultations are managed so that there is no place for mention of social/emotional factors. The relevance of a woman's other roles is considered only where employment or marital status (ie — working, being unmarried) are perceived as in conflict with the goal of the production of a live, healthy, full-term infant. In other cases the intrusion of "personal" considerations into medical decision-making transgresses the prevailing norm of reproduction as a medical process' (Oakley, 1980). A survey, quoted by Thomson (1981) indicated that a third of all recently qualified general (medical) practitioners (GPs) felt that they should not have to deal with patients' family problems, which were regarded as irrelevant to medical practice.

The mother and the baby are both at greater risk when the pregnant woman does not attend the antenatal clinic until late in the pregnancy, or attends irregularly. Staged payment of maternity benefit contingent upon attendance at an antenatal clinic as in France, though it may help, does not appear to be an entirely satisfactory answer (Chalmers, Oakley and MacFarlane, 1980). Women with young children facing the cost and difficulty of travelling to the antenatal clinic may be irregular attenders. Antenatal clinics that are accessible, and run in a welcoming fashion by staff with perceptive attitudes would encourage higher attendance. Use of GPs and community midwives can greatly improve uptake of antenatal care and reduce perinatal mortality. The maternity grant of £25 should be raised to a realistic level. Britain lags behind most of Europe in maternity pay (Equal Opportunities Commission, 1982). All expectant mothers in France receive over £400.

Statutory notification of maternity bookings (as with notification of births) would enable health visitors to be aware of pregnant women on their 'beat', so that they could start to build a relationship with the mother before the birth. The general practitioner can play a key role at this time. The Park Hospital, Oxford, has shown that it is possible for the health visitor to diagnose families 'at risk' of harming their children by working in conjunction with the family doctor and community midwife, and taking a psycho-social history at the antenatal clinic. Further, it has been shown that such families are amenable to group therapy at a health centre (Beswick, 1979).

Currently more women are drinking more alcohol and perhaps as many as 5 per cent of pregnant women drink enough to risk producing babies with the foetal alcohol syndrome, characterised by unusually slow growth, abnormalities of head, face and various organs and mental handicap. (Sclare, 1980; Streissguth, Clarren and Jones, 1985).

The Select Committee on Violence in the Family (1977) (2) recommended the education of parents antenatally not only about childbirth and the perinatal period but what to expect of life with young children and what miseries as well as joys it can bring. There are many good books about the care of mothers before, during and after birth. A useful one has been produced by the Scottish Health Education Unit (Docherty, 1980) and is available from some National Health Service (NHS) Health Education Units to GPs and pregnant women. However, to forewarn the prospective mother is not necessarily to forearm her. Indeed unless it is done with care her anxieties may increase.

The birth and perinatal experience

In most primitive societies women are not left alone once labour has begun. In our own maternity units they often have been. Kennell (1980) quotes the work of anthropologists who found that in all but one of 38 cultures studied a woman stayed with the mother during labour and assisted at the birth. There is evidence (Sosa, Kennell, Klaus, Robertson and Urrutia, 1980) that this may reduce the length of labour and the number of complications; the behaviour of the mother to her newborn infant becomes more positive. In western societies there is a growing custom of having some well-disposed person, if possible the husband, present throughout labour. Brazelton (quoted by Klaus and Kennell, 1976b) makes an important point: 'The feeling of autonomy, of being in some control over a rather frightening crisis in your life, of *having a choice* about what happens may be critical as a force for development in both men's and women's, fathers' and mothers' lives at life crisis'. It should be the aim of the whole obstetrical service to make the delivery not merely as little unpleasant as possible, but a rewarding experience for mother, father and infant, even if the rewards for the infant take time to mature. A good start in life sets up a chain of good experiences and is to be regarded as the beginning of prevention of excessive adolescent rebelliousness.

The fact that UK figures for perinatal mortality and handicap have been higher than in many other countries should be the stimulus to make us examine standards of antenatal and perinatal care of the mother in addition to concentrating on the infant after birth. A shorter labour should result in easier delivery and less likelihood of death or handicap for the baby. There are no labour ward specialists, though there are now a few neonatologists (paediatricians). The overall perinatal mortality for England and Wales as a whole is falling (Office of Population Censuses and Surveys (OPCS), 1983) and is now similar to that in the rest of Europe. However, the rates of perinatal and infant mortality in the north of England, and for legitimate births in social class 5, are about double those respectively for the south and for social class 1 (DHSS, 1980b; Office of Population Censuses and Surveys, 1982). Short shrift was given (DHSS, 1980a) to the (House of Commons) Social Services Committee Report (1980) on perinatal and neonatal mortality. Most of the Committee's recommendations concerned material and technical facilities of the service. The report hardly touched on the impersonal quality of the service or the social causes (eg, undernutrition and drug abuse) of maternal and infant morbidity.

We see the reduction of handicap as good not only in itself but as a factor in preventing later antisocial behaviour. The causes of perinatal mortality and handicap are not all fully understood, and there is argument about how to reduce them. Estimates that the reduction of brain damage in the new-born could be reduced by as much as 40 per cent (Loring and Holland, 1978) have been disputed. Some bodies are concerned with social factors such as poverty, the quality of hospital care for mothers and babies (DHSS, 1980b; Chalmers et al, 1980), and encouragement of attachment (3) (4) (5). Doctors urge the provision of more hospital equipment, supported by the Maternity Alliance (6). Whatever progress there has been in the development of the maternity and neonatal services, and there is much to praise, there are yet deficiencies in the care given by hospitals and professionals that have been eloquently documented (Kitzinger, 1978; Clayton, 1979; Oakley, 1979; Greig, 1981; Bidder, 1981; Boyd and Sellers, 1982; Ellis, 1986). Information collected by such organisations as the Association for Improvements in the Maternity Services make it clear that still many mothers are dissatisfied with the care they receive during the birth of their babies, and particularly with the attitudes of medical and nursing attendants. One of the greatest impediments to progress, and one that receives too little attention, is the natural defensiveness of professionals in the face of apparent criticism. The development of self-learning in supportive circumstances will accelerate solutions for this serious problem. Resources are also required.

After only 3 years of existence the Children's Committee (a joint committee of the Central Health Services and Personal Social Services Councils set up by the Government in 1978) was disbanded. In its short life it made useful contributions, including a paper on perinatal mortality (DHSS, 1979). Its demise must strengthen arguments for the introduction of a Minister for Children, for in succession the Court Report (DHSS, 1976b), the Black Report (DHSS, 1980b) and the Short Report (Social Services Committee, 1980) have been consigned to oblivion.

Encouragement of attachment between infant and mother. Nearly thirty-five years ago Bowlby (1951) wrote: '. . . let the reader reflect . . . on the astonishing practice which has been followed in maternity wards — of separating mothers and babies immediately after birth — and ask himself whether this is the way to promote a close mother-child relationship. It is to be hoped that this aberration of western society will never be copied by so-called less-developed countries.' The growth of medicine since the turn of the century has resulted in a tremendous development of services in obstetrics and for the neonate. But in the welter of justifiable anxieties about cross infection, complications of pregnancy and other relevant physical matters, we have come only lately to understand the psychological and emotional needs of babies, parents and the developing family, and to appreciate the severe psychological and social consequences of not satisfying them. Although in the majority of families need and love are reciprocal, in a minority learning to love is not natural and spontaneous. Child psychiatrists, influenced by the work of Bowlby, now pay great attention to the development of 'attachment' between parents, principally the mother, and their very young baby.

The work of child psychiatrists, combined with that of ethologists and anthropologists, has alerted us to the value of 'primitive' behaviour of animals and humans, and of the interactions of the young with person(s) in the parental role (Klaus and Kennell, 1976b). There is evidence that immediate breast-feeding and skin contact between newborn infant and mother leads to breastfeeding for longer, the mother showing more affection for the baby, with fewer infections and more rapid weight gain in the infant (Klaus, Jerrauld, Kreger, McAlpine, Steffa and Kennell, 1972; Klaus and Kennell, 1976b; Sosa, Kennell, Klaus and Urrutia, 1976; de Chateau, Holmberg, Jakobson and Winberg, 1977; de Chateau, 1979). Traditional hospital routines have restricted the time babies could spend with their mothers (Gunther, 1976; Lozoff, Brittenham, Trause, Kennell and Klaus, 1977) and may have led to maternal indifference to the baby (Robson and Kumar, 1980).

Low birthweight babies need special care. Babies weighing less than 2500g (5.5 lbs) are born more often to mothers in social classes 4 and 5 than to those in higher socio-economic groups. Single, widowed or divorced women also have more than the average number of small babies. Separation of mother and infant at birth for any reason is thought to be one cause of failure to thrive. But the dangers of separating mothers from their babies in special care baby units, because for example, of prematurity and low birth weight (Leifer, Leiderman, Barnett and Williams, 1972), are becoming recognised (Klaus and Kennell, 1976b; Brimblecombe, Richards and Robertson, 1978; Lancet, 1979) and are being overcome (Tafari and Sterky, 1974; Richards, 1978; Davies, Herbert, Haxby and McNeish, 1979; Derbyshire, Davies and Bacco, 1982). Even limited contact with the baby is better than none. Klaus and Kennell (1976a) believe that immediate spontaneous mother-infant contact is more likely with births at home, and that fathers can behave like mothers with their neonates. Support then, for the mother, especially by the husband, before, during and after the birth of her child, and immediate and pro-longed contact between mother and child in the earliest postnatal period, are among the most important means of enriching the quality of maternal care, and so of increasing the mother's ability to identify herself with the child and to tolerate the vicissitudes of baby care. The cared-for mother tends to have the cared-for baby: the cared-for baby becomes the secure school child who is unlikely to become the disruptive teenager. Although we have begun to learn about the need for attachment and how to promote it, more work needs to be done on the factors influencing it, and on the long-term effects when it is not sufficiently developed (Ross, 1980).

It is one thing for psychiatrists and ethologists to propose good practices; what of those who are to perform them? In recognising the nature and value of maternal support systems and infant/parent bonding not only do parents have to be alerted to them but maternity services are having to change their attitudes and practices. It is not many years since husbands were the only relatives tolerated as visitors in a maternity ward, for about half an hour a day. Babies spent many hours in a cot often at the foot of the bed, or even in another room. Now visitors are more welcome, including other members of the family, even siblings. Mothers now stay only a few days in hospital. Some hospitals are assessing parent/infant relationships and talking to parents about the importance of bonding (Ounsted, Roberts, Gordon and Milligan, 1982). The cost of such discussions, and of a couple of photographs of the baby when in a special care baby unit (one for the father) (Sills and Handley, 1978) (7) are a small price to pay if these measures help to avoid emotional deprivation in the child.

Even if the pregnancy progresses to a normal delivery, some strain is imposed on the marital relationship. In the happy home where both parents are equally delighted at the prospect of starting a family, when the husband supports the wife throughout labour, is present at the birth and from then onwards shares with his wife the care of the baby and some of the household chores, a new but probably deeper and more durable relationship between the partners is likely to come into being. But, alas, those are the happy few. Between the good enough mother and her baby there tends to be at the start a biologically determined, inevitable relationship which excludes even her husband. Many husbands have little warmth of feeling for the infinitely demanding baby, see it only as a rival, and resent their wives' absorption in the child. Attention should be paid to ways of helping parents to cope with the strain of such vicissitudes as wakefulness at night, crying or illness (Valman, 1980). Parental incapacity under these circumstances may lead to emotional and physical harm to the child.

We also have to find ways to help maternal bonding in those mothers who find it difficult because of their own deprived childhood. Whether for long-term follow-up, or immediate attempt at 'treatment', the lack of capacity for attachment must first be diagnosed. This would entail a history, taken antenatally, of the mother's experience while she was being reared, and the father's too. Doctors and midwives need training to observe deficiencies in maternal bonding. It is sad to hear of one maternity department in a district general hospital that has given up collecting data on maternal behaviour because no use was made of it. A hospital like this, with full paediatric and psychiatric services, should be ideal for mounting a long-term study in conjunction with the community health service. We know that the behaviour deplored by teachers in the secondary school is often related to neonatal problems but we need more detail, more precision. It is not much use insisting that babies must be loved, to parents who themselves suffered rejection when young. So there is the delicate question of how such a parent, mother especially, can be 'trained' to love her baby. Not much can yet be done for some mothers who have themselves been severely deprived. Support systems of various kinds should be devised for more 'treatable' cases, starting with recognition of the problem as early as possible in the pregnancy, and the establishment of helpful relationships with relevant services.

Postnatal and later periods

For a few weeks or months a healthy infant may be 'no trouble', though it is astonishing what may go wrong. The most caring parents, if inexperienced, may not notice that their crying baby is cold because insufficiently clad, or too hot. Then comes teething with the child fractious. Many children have coughs, colds, pharyngitis, measles, chicken pox or ear infections, and are restless, grizzly and sleepless. Mother's milk may be insufficient; parents may not notice that the child is hungry. The most loving parents find a screaming, protesting child hard to tolerate. If parents are unloving, they may be driven to injure their child. It is not so many years ago that 4-hourly feeding of babies was de rigueur. It was of a piece with the notion that babies might be left to cry as a form of 'discipline', in the belief that they were 'taking advantage' of their parents. There was never any evidence to support such views and mercifully they are now less fashionable (8). A significant statistical correlation has been found (Jones, Ferreira, Brown and Macdonald, 1979) between aggressive behaviour in older children and absent or delayed response by the mother to the infant's crying. It was disturbing, therefore, to hear in that popular BBC programme *The Archers*, support for the outmoded doctrine that by not responding to his demands, parents can train a baby a few days old to be undemanding (9).

Many women go out to work to provide for a better standard of living in the home at a time when so many men are either out of work, or earning a low wage. But paid work is often boring and tiring, and most workers have little control over it, and play no part in decision making. One study observed the deleterious effects on the health and attitudes of women in such work, and related them adversely to their home lives (Shimmin, McNally and Liff, 1981). If, as is all too common, the husband is not very helpful in the house, the wife having two jobs, may become even more tired and depressed. Her resentment at her husband's behaviour weakens her feelings for him and their relationship deteriorates. A tired despondent mother will have less patience over her children's constant demands, with predictable effects upon their behaviour.

The child at risk of non-accidental injury: predictive factors. We have indicated in Part I, Chapter 3 that child abuse is probably commoner than was thought, and perhaps increasing. Prevention is clearly of supreme importance. To be effective it will depend on both prediction and intervention at an early age. Various authors (Lynch and Roberts, 1977; Gordon, 1977; Brown and Davidson, 1978; de Chateau, Holmberg and Winberg, 1978) describe factors they believe predict the likelihood of abuse occurring, or at least rejection of the infant (Collingwood and Alberman, 1979). There are significantly more post-neonatal deaths in families known to be abusing (Roberts, Lynch and Golding, 1980).

Not all children at risk will be seriously injured and this may be so especially in social classes 1 and 2. However, unchecked family instability is likely to lead to personality and behaviour disorders in older children and adolescents (Pringle, 1973). Other factors such as marital disharmony, unemployment, parental ill-health, unwanted pregnancies, financial indebtedness (Tables 3 and 4) and lack of play facilities (families in high rise flats), could also be discovered during the child's first months or years of life but so far these have not been the subject of scientific enquiry.

Douglas, Kiernan and Wadsworth (1977) found that males who committed sexual and violent crimes were known to have had a considerably greater likelihood than others of experiencing emotional disruption before their fifth birthday caused by divorce or separation of their parents.

The British Medical Association (1977) has advocated a register of 'proved at risk children', that is, of children who have sustained non-accidental injuries. Doubts have been expressed about 'at risk' registers because of the dangers of incorrectly labelling parents.

Intervention by health visitor, general medical practitioner, hospital, clergy or other agents. Accepting the leading part played by the family in the causation of the child's emotional disturbance (although there may be other aggravating factors), the problem must nevertheless be known for it to be 'treated', and for this access to the home is likely to be necessary. Before the child goes to school the problem may be known only to the health visitor, the family doctor or possibly a midwife or social worker, and these would usually be the only people whom the parents would allow into the home. The health visitor is the central figure in this scenario for she should be well-known to the mother and trusted by her, and is likely to visit the home on many occasions (Select Committee on Violence in the Family, 1977) (10) though neither she, GP, midwife nor social worker has any right of entry. The value of the health visitor in observing home factors that might be predictive of later childhood physical illness has been recognised (DHSS, 1976a; Wadsworth and Morriss, 1978). With sufficient health visitors all families could be visited regularly after the birth of a baby, and those known to be in difficulties rearing their children could be visited more frequently (*Select Committee on Violence in the Family*, 1977) (11). France and Scandinavian countries, using different methods, have improved the frequency of examination of children particularly in backward areas (12). A study from the Thomas Coram Research Unit (1975) in London showed that by systematic home visiting health visitors could reach 97 per cent of children. The Short Report (Social Services Committee, 1980) recommended the use of health visitors, preferably with midwifery training, working in the postnatal period in conjunction with community midwives or in their stead.

Nowadays patients in a practice may approach the nurse or health visitor before the doctor. All professionals involved in family care need to be perceptive about clues to a family imbroglio, although these may be difficult to interpret. Doctors and nurses receive little training in picking up cries for help, often heavily disguised, though many learn the art during years of practice. Studies by Dowling (1980) showed that there are ways of improving home care for children; that clinics will be used much more if mothers see them as attractive; that the quality of health visitors' work may be enhanced by changes in its organisation; and that GPs can play an active part in relieving social and environmental factors affecting their patients' health. Doctors who run family planning clinics find that women may mention domestic problems that they have not spoken about to their GPs. What channels of communication are open to such clinic doctors? There is no reason why antenatal and postnatal clinics should not keep a weather eye open for signs of family distress. Incorporating the medical social worker into the routine work of the health care team would help this process. Professional acumen in diagnosing predictive factors is unlikely to be developed in the absence of easy communications between client and service. Communications between doctors and other health workers are often poor. Clients may find that doctors and social workers are not easily approachable, but there are few women who are not glad to confide in a health visitor.

We have been unable to find studies in which health visitors, GPs, social workers, hospital staff or clergy have cooperated in studying or helping families in the perinatal period or at any other time. However, a project in Oldham (13), examining the problems of the pre- and perinatal periods, is run jointly by a health visitor, a social worker and a psychologist with the interest of a GP and a vicar. The project's central aim is prevention.

It has been concerned to find the most effective ways to intervene as early as possible to prevent the problems of parents becoming entrenched, and less amenable to resolution.

A large number of people are still married in church, and like to have their babies baptised and to this extent parents have contact with clergy. Clergy may be aware of signs of emotional immaturity in parents. Many of these act on their knowledge of family problems but there are at least as many who do not. Relatives, especially grandparents, and the good neighbour may be acceptable to the family, and be in a position to observe family stresses and deficiencies. Some will be able to give advice and practical support, but often the parent who damages his child is either following a family or neighbourhood pattern, or else lacks family or friends to help. What the woman needs, who is not coping with motherhood and feels in a trap, is *help* not advice. Visitors (and husbands) are best when they roll up their sleeves and get on with the house work. Drugs will often not be necessary, or will be needed only temporarily. The mother's mental and emotional state will be improved by a change from the constricting household scene, such as sharing responsibility for running a pre-school playgroup (Keeley, 1981), or through part-time occupation that the use of a playgroup makes possible. A short period, even only a few days away from home and family, can be a tonic for an over-burdened mother.

Apart from infections, physical diseases, as opposed to disabilities, are now uncommon in young children. Many of the symptoms with which children present at hospital do not have a physical cause, and are due to emotional disorders. Hospital specialists usually pursue the matter with the GP and may hesitate to cooperate with the school and social services. In such cases it has been our experience that direct personal communication with the school, made with the knowledge and consent of the older child, parents and GP, has resulted in amelioration of school attitudes, helpful responses, and pleasure by the school at being taken into professional partnership. The child has benefited and parental anxieties have been reduced.

A study of the effect of intervention to prevent child abuse when predicted disappointingly failed to show much effect (Lealman *et al*, 1983). However, the intervention was somewhat limited. More resources are obviously needed but by itself an improvident expansion of services might hinder rather than help to provide what is most needed, namely a change of attitude to the care of children, in both services and society (*Select Committee on Violence in the Family*, 1977) (14).

Family violence

Help for parents. 'Though the law no longer allows husbands to beat wives the double standards which domestic violence provoked in the nineteenth century still exist today. Everybody is concerned about violent crime in the streets, but only a minority by violence in the family. Yet of the two, violence in the home is potentially far more harmful. Its effects on children can be devastating. All this was recognised by the Select Committee on Violence in Marriage which reported in 1975 and by the MPs who drafted the 1976 Domestic Violence Act' (*Guardian*, 1977). Overwrought parents may need help if their child is to escape suffering and if later troubles are to be avoided. There is the crying baby advisory/ relief service provided by one Health Authority (Hunt, 1980) and similar services elsewhere. An association — Parents Anonymous — with a phone-in number has been formed. There are the National Society for the Prevention of Cruelty to Children (NSPCC) 'Lifeline Units' in different parts of the country. The National Children's Centre may be able to help. There is CRY-SIS that offers comfort and advice to parents distraught over sleepless or crying infants. Some local social services are now providing a form of emergency service for parents in difficulties over their young children, and are coordinating and making available information about relevant voluntary agencies (*Select Committee on Violence in the Family*, 1977) (15). Doctors can help by interesting themselves in their patients' domestic and social problems. Solutions to family difficulties will usually call for the continued efforts of a number of people and agencies. Playgroups, mothers' clubs, nursery schools and creches can relieve family isolation.

Punishment of the batterers, for which public and media clamour can do little good. If, more sensibly, they go to some establishment where care and psychotherapy are available, they will be recognised for the pathetic inadequate creatures they so often are. But what happens when they return to the harsh conditions of their disadvantaged environment when support will still be greatly needed? Most child batterers have themselves been so badly damaged by ill-treatment when young that it is difficult to change them; and children must be protected. When, in spite of all the help and care available, the child is still at risk, then the only safe course is to remove him to a substitute home. The decision whether or not to leave a child with his parent(s) is most taxing to all concerned with making it. If social workers recognised and responded to mothers' needs, more children might remain in their own homes. Early intervention is impeded by the shortage of skilled staff and because it is just those families where help is most needed who resist or reject it. Moreover the emotionally battered child may go unnoticed. The tradition in this country is to respect the rights of parents and only in the extreme case to resort to compulsion; much depends on the skill of the worker. Those obliged by law to compel, such as probation officers, police liaison officers, and the NSPCC have a good record of achievement. At best, nothing approaching 100 per cent success is to be expected and the money required makes it unlikely that a large scale effort will be made in the next few years to train sufficient skilled manpower.

Two agencies — The British Association for the Study and Prevention of Child Abuse and Neglect, and Kidscape, have been formed to increase understanding of child abuse and to help treat and prevent it. Kidscape deals especially with teachers' problems in this field.

Refuges. Physicians and psychiatrists who care for patients with self-poisoning will elicit in a significant proportion a story of marital violence. The growth of women's aid projects as refuges for victims of family violence, pioneered by Erin Pizzey in Chiswick, London, has been spectacular and indicates a pressing need that officialdom has been slow to support. So far refuges have served only women and often their children, but Erin Pizzey has recognised that husbands may also need help in these unhappy predicaments. Many refuges are overcrowded, most are seriously under-funded. Information is available about help for battered women, refuges and women's aid from the National Women's Aid Federation.

We suggest that something along the lines of Querido's proposals (1946), for supervising psychopathic families should be given a trial. The treatment of tuberculosis by caring for whole families in the Papworth Village Settlement 40-50 years ago is a possibly appropriate analogy. There the breadwinner lived with his family, was medically treated, and worked hours allowed by his medical condition in the Settlement's factories, for normal wages. Ounsted's unit in Oxford attempts something similar for mothers and children (Lynch, Steinberg and Ounsted, 1975; Lynch and Ounsted, 1976).

Help for the child. In the complex task of predicting child abuse; of helping the parents; of persuading adults to accept, or at least to cope with childhood behaviour they find intolerable; of stimulating professional people to be alert and responsive, it is a spur to remember that all these efforts are directed primarily to alleviating the *child's* predicament: the child who is at risk and, as we know from working with children, often most unhappy. The bystander tends to see the treatment of child abuse in unrealistically simple terms: separate the child from the parents, who should be punished; chase up the social workers ('it should not have happened'). The matter is much more complex and many cases pose to social workers, who mostly have the responsibility for dealing with them, conundrums that would test the wisdom of Solomon.

Whatever is done after the event, about either the child or the family, the child suffers; and so again prevention is likely to be much more effective than treatment. It must be remembered that child batterers are usually people who were themselves rejected in childhood. Social workers need special training, encouragement and *help* from other professionals in dealing with probable batterers. The child is certainly not helped if relationships break down between parents and social worker, as is likely to happen when attempts are made to separate the child from the parents, especially if there are legal proceedings. Then the social worker will be seen as someone working against the parents. Long delays ensuing from court proceedings and finding the best substitute home for the child, serve only to alienate parents further from social workers. Such quandaries concerning the care of dependent creatures, can best be avoided by the relevant professionals tackling these problems at or before the birth of the child.

Local Review Committees (16), constituted broadly of many disciplines, are powerfully equipped to enlarge their field of interest and activity to cover also the child who is *emotionally* 'battered'. Much research is still needed in order to help these children and this might best be organised through university hospitals and district general hospitals in conjunction with the Review Committees. A manual describing procedures for dealing with suspected cases of child abuse was prepared by some of the old Area Review Committees.

Childwatch is an organisation that aims, among other things, to have more social workers specially trained to deal with child abuse. Incest Crisis Line offers supportive counselling to people of all ages who have been sexually abused in childhood, and works also with the abusers.

Fostering and adoption

> It was a blow when I learnt at the age of six or seven
> that I was paid for ... I cried all night and it was my
> first great sorrow.
> — Romain Gary, *La vie devant soi* (1975)

The best help for the child is to rear good parents, to help those who fail to be better ones, and to minimise the ill effects of removing the child from his own home when this must be done. For these purposes we cannot do better than refer the reader once more to Bowlby (1951) whose chapters on substitute families are a model of clarity and good sense. In view of the cost of residential care, the difficulty of finding a sufficient number of the right people for the work, and the inevitable institutional nature of even the best residential homes, it is believed to be worth trying to place disturbed children in foster homes whenever possible. Not only are carefully selected foster homes seen as better ways of caring for children than institutions, but they are also much cheaper even if foster parents are paid realistically as they should be. Nevertheless the number of children in care (up to 25 per cent) with a history of failed foster placements (Benians, 1980) emphasises the need to review fostering policies. Some social services departments have adopted the practice of 'contract fostering' for older children. The foster parents commit themselves for a limited period though some continue after it expires. Social services support the foster parents through counselling and discussion groups.

Beyond this there are now schemes and agencies to promote fostering and adoption of handicapped children, such as Parents for Children, and Adoption Resource Exchange. Children who are in some ways the most difficult to place are those who have lived for years in an institution, or have been moved from institution to institution, or foster home to foster home. These children, often teenagers, usually have great difficulty in making relationships and may be delinquent. The majority of foster placements for children previously in care break down, the failure rate being as high as 60 per cent for older children (Watts, 1984). Nevertheless Kent County Council has run a family placement scheme for such children (Hazel, 1981) and there are other projects elsewhere (National Association for Care and Resettlement of Offenders (NACRO, 1980). Shaw and Hipgrave (1983) describe the problems of specialist fostering. They report some success by careful selection and training of foster parents, and through subsequent social work support for them and the children. 'For most of the foster parents, the major source of the improvement in their position was the foster parent group itself, initially established as a preparation and training medium but continuing . . . as a support group and a forum for reviewing and revising the project as it proceeded.' Specialist fostering promises advantages to the child, the community and the borough finances. However, the results need further evaluation for they are mostly reported by interested parties.

Fostered children may be helped if they know about their natural parents. There is no good reason for termination of parental contact and secrecy about children's origins as happens in England but not in Scotland (Benians, 1982).

Day care parents. This is an arrangement for 'fostering' children under 5 years of age during the day for five days a week by substitute parents. The children sleep at home and are at home over the weekend. Such 'foster' parents have a brief six-session training, and when they are caring for a child continue to meet in a group once a fortnight and have close contact with a social worker. This is a better system than mere child-minding partly because more money is usually available for fostering. The parents pay a proportion based on an assessment of their resources. Some parents take time to accept this arrangement and some cannot do so, preferring the child(ren) to be taken into full-time care or nothing. This scheme may operate with the help of a worker from the Family Welfare Association.

The pre-school stage

At this time the health visitor may note the reactions of the child within the family, for example his behaviour towards brothers, sisters and parents. If the child attends a playgroup his behaviour in this may be substantially different from that at home. Any behaviour disorders should be discussed sympathetically with the parents, and if necessary with GP, paediatrician, and psychiatrist. Immediately prior to starting school any outstanding behaviour problems should, with the knowledge and acquiescence of the parents and their GP, be reported in writing by the health visitor to a senior medical officer responsible for the supervision of the health of school children. This report should be available to the school doctor.

Services for the under fives. These are provided by three different kinds of agency — the NHS, local authorities and voluntary bodies. In a joint circular the DHSS and DES (1978a) considered that resources for the under fives were far from adequate and they urged local authorities, through coordination of all available services, to make maximum use of existing resources in education, social services and health fields provided by statutory authorities, together with those from voluntary bodies. It is valuable to combine administrative expertise with local energies though authorities may be chary of coordinating bodies that include their own officers and people from voluntary organisations. The London Borough of Ealing is succeeding in this with its innovation Unified Community Action (see Part II, Chapter 8 (iv)). Another good example of this kind of joint effort is the Gloucestershire Association for Family Life (Seacome, 1982).

Pre-school playgroups and nursery schools/classes. Allowance must be made for illness, accident, death or other untoward vicissitudes that any member of a family may suffer. It must be acknowledged that some parents are so ill, physically or mentally; so damaged, or so inadequate; that no measures available to us at present will transform them into 'good enough' parents. So their child(ren) will be at risk of developing behaviour problems in adolescence. But, as can be observed, any good school for maladjusted children and, as Rutter and colleagues (1979) have shown, many ordinary schools can go far towards mitigating the effects of adverse conditions in the outside world. This is particularly true of nursery and primary schools in which few children show an unalterable pattern of difficult behaviour, and to which most parents are obliged to bring their children and so have an opportunity to talk with a teacher. There are few parents who will not be glad to use one of the teachers as a 'counsellor' and gain a better understanding of children's feelings and emotional needs. At such times the teacher might learn something of value for her care of the child.

Primary schools can take the initiative in setting up playgroups with the help of parents and voluntary workers. They may cater for non-English speaking mothers with both school age and pre-school children. The Warnock Report recommended increased provision of playgroups, 'opportunity groups' and nursery education (DES, 1978b). The opportunity group is a special form of playgroup catering for children both with and without disabilities. It enables the mothers to meet each other. Such groups range from informal clubs to structured sessions devised and supervised by psychologists and therapists. The Warnock Committee discovered from the evidence of opportunity groups that the best support and understanding for parents of handicapped children came from other parents of handicapped children. The value of mother and toddler clubs, child minders and pre-school playgroups is well recognised.

Parents may prefer playgroups to nursery classes because of their relatively friendly informal atmosphere, and because they tend to take more interest in parents' problems. Some of the limitations of nursery schools were studied by Tizard and Hughes (1984). In nursery school the child is asked questions and does not ask them himself. This often stops the child's conversation. Keeley (1981) showed how valuable for the development, indeed the health, of some mothers was the active sharing of involvement and *responsibility* in the running of pre-school playgroups. This is much less likely to occur with professionally run nursery classes because most teachers feel threatened by parents being active. A higher form of professionalism is for professionals to be less obtrusive and encourage parents to be active in 'learning by doing', as Keeley says. Naturally not all mothers have the inclination or the time for such involvement, and they may have other interests or employment.

Poulton and James (1975) believe that support for families offered only on the provider's terms, will not fully realise the potential for intellectual growth and emotional development in the child. They point out that there are more opportunities for collaboration between education and social services at nursery and infant level than later since, when children are young, there are more contacts with parents. The best family service might be from a centre combining educational facilities for children aged 3-8 years with home visiting and medical/social services. Teachers might well play a coordinating role, and parents should be encouraged to play a full part in their children's education. The centre's operation would be 'catalytic rather than ameliorative, contributory and not compensatory', and open to people of all ages, particularly older children. Poulton and James think that such centres might easily grow from component parts already operating independently within the community.

Measures for dealing with family isolation. The Select Committee on Violence in the Family (1977) (17) were impressed by the frequent mention in evidence to them of social isolation as a factor contributing to non-accidental child injury. In many families, not only those living in high-rise flats, children and mothers are isolated. This may be associated, in West Indian and social class 4 and 5 families, with failure of the parents to play with the children, read to them, or even talk much with them, so that their development may be seriously retarded. Teachers have had 5-year old children whose speech was severely limited because people had not talked to them, though this is infrequent now. There are a number of educational home visiting (EHV) schemes and 15 of them were reviewed in 1973-4 by Poulton and James (1975). An EHV scheme ('Home Link') using parents in their own neighbourhood was set up in Liverpool (Where, 1977). The National Children's Bureau (1977) will supply information about EHV schemes, and see also Pugh (1977) and Aplin and Pugh (1983).

Another method, developed for reaching isolated families and helping them to inter-relate with the community, was launched in an educational priority area in the West Riding (Smith, 1975). The 'Scope' project for parents and children in Southampton uses methods of helping families to help themselves: 'Groups of parents and children meet regularly in their neighbourhood once a week. While the children play in a creche, the mothers examine the way in which they bring up their children and learn from the results. They share their experiences with each other and provide support within the group for members who may need it' (Scope Family Centre Annual Report, 1979-1980).

The ILEA have appointed nursery liaison teachers to help forge home/ school links and to initiate cooperation with other agencies concerned with the under-fives (DES, 1980). There are some day hospitals for emotionally disturbed children run by child psychiatric units in general hospitals. These, while treating the children, also offer various kinds of support for the parents. Some people with special knowledge of emotional development are running nursery groups to help both children and parents. All these schemes reduce isolation though very young mothers may be difficult to reach. If the child also goes to nursery school the effects are even more striking. The bond between mother and child is strengthened — the skilled educationist unobtrusively helps parents to feel more responsible for their children's education (Jayne, 1976).

We know of one mixed comprehensive school that compiled, with the active help of many children in the school, a detailed brochure of all kinds of facilities, voluntary and statutory, provided in the locality for young children. Many self-help groups flourish around the country. Information is available about them from a number of sources: there is a National Council for Voluntary Organisations Directory, a Disability Rights Handbook from the Disability Alliance, The Patients' Association, The King's Fund Directory of organisations for patients and disabled people, *Help! I need somebody* (1980), the Mutual Aid Centre, and Local Councils' voluntary services officers.

Child and family development

There is still much to learn about how to overcome the effects of rejection in childhood. While the many schemes for improving the lot of very young children and their parents are impressive, less is done for older children. Children aged 7-12 are those in the 'latency period'; a high proportion of those attending child guidance services are in this age group and need more care than they get. But it is perhaps the teenage group who need a more caring attitude towards their real and intense internal torments. Without it, not only the adolescent but society may suffer, and sometimes young people are driven to killing themselves. What is lacking is the will to use the knowledge and resources that are possessed by professional people — teachers, social workers, psychologists and doctors. Some local bodies publish information about health and social matters, and about agencies that might help with them.

Educating children in human development and personal relationships for marriage, parenthood and life. Many people have inadequate resources for dealing with conflict in marriage. About one in three marriages now ends in divorce at an annual cost to the country, it has been estimated, of about £1000m (Dominian, 1981). The cost in family misery cannot be computed. If more marriages remained happy, so that the number of single parent families was reduced, there would be fewer children in care. Many people get married with unreasonable expectations of their new state, of sexual relations and of parenthood. The strains imposed by a demanding baby or toddler should not be glossed over. Education about the things that make for good marriages and happy children is especially needed for children who have themselves been rejected by their parents: it might help to break the 'spiral of deprivation'.

When husbands are not supportive and helpful in the home the relationship between the spouses may be strained. Fathers may find difficulty in accepting new roles at home when they have been out to work. However, many fathers are now working short time, or not at all, and should have more time to support their wives in home tasks, and with the children. After all, wives with children work all day. It is easy for spouses to take each other for granted after some years of marriage. The couple has the task of ensuring that husbands do not feel rejected when children begin to arrive. The key lies in parents sharing the care of the family and of being caring for each other. Demonstrations of affection never come amiss.

Teachers are not trained in health education and Tizard and Hughes (1984) pertinently ask if they know how to train children to be good parents. Nevertheless each school should have some teachers who are able to teach children all they need to know about the anatomy and physiology of human reproduction. This should be supplemented by health visitors and health education officers reaching all children of appropriate age with health education programmes. They would deal particularly with emotional development and cover physical and psychological aspects of sex, pregnancy, contraception, abortion and VD; all in the context of human relationships. Boys need to be introduced to the different expectations that girls have about sexual activity. For this is where relationships between men and women are frequently put under strain. When a head of a boys' grammar school was asked if he would like his pupils to have talks on sex education in the context of personal relationships he declined saying that the boys knew it all and could teach the staff a thing or two. Male chauvinism is a long time dying but unlike Charles II is not apologetic.

Boys and girls in their last two years at school should discuss the prospects of marriage and parenthood, and the responsibilities and rewards that go with them. They should be impressed with the need of the baby to be loved. In our experience young people welcome health education that includes classroom discussions of personal relationships. Why not involve parents and children in health education? In one instance older children took on some of it with successful results. It is encouraging to hear about courses in child development and social adaptation for older secondary school pupils — parents to be.

It is heartening that London University set up a chair in child development. Practical methods ('Active tutorial work') have been introduced by Button (1971, 1974), Baldwin and Wells (1979), and Button (1981, 1982) for developing children's self- and social-awareness, and their relationships and attitudes. The Schools Council has a Health Education Project (18) with material developed for various age ranges from 5 years upward. Some health authorities produce detailed and well illustrated books on pregnancy and parenthood, and the care of young children (Docherty, 1980). Several other bodies are taking initiatives in this field that should help schools (National Council for One Parent Families, 1979; Pugh, 1980; Seacome, 1982; Coyne, 1986). Let us hope that universities will collaborate in producing enlightened curricula. Aston University, Birmingham, has reported a detailed study of 'Preparation for Parenthood' topics now available within the secondary school curriculum of some schools in England (Grafton, Smith, Vegoda, Whitfield, Bamford and Comber, 1983).

Whatever schools strive to do, and whatever people achieve in the way of changing their own attitudes, and this is seldom attained without inner struggle, resources must be safeguarded. Economies in social and health services that reduce resources for the care of children are a recipe for social failure, perhaps now appearing as increasing vandalism, crime and rioting.

Notes

1. *First Report.* Vol. III, p 495.

2. *First Report.* Vol. I, para 66.

3. Association for Improvements in the Maternity Services (AIMS).

4. The National Perinatal Epidemiology Unit (NPEU).

5. The National Childbirth Trust.

6. The Maternity Alliance is supported by the Spastics Society, the Child Poverty Action Group and the National Council for One Parent Families.

7. Estimated cost per baby of two photographs was 58p; total annual cost in one unit was about £50.

8. *The First Report from the Select Committee on Violence in the Family.* Vol. I Report. Para 40:

   > There seemed to be a widespread popular view that it was wrong to respond and pick up crying babies, and that babies could be spoilt by too much attention. Such views were countered both by parents who gave us evidence, and by some modern research. For instance, Mrs. A ... told us that her baby's crying episodes only became less when she followed her NSPCC social worker's advice to respond when her baby cried rather than to ignore it ... Mary Ainsworth's research (showed) that babies are more communicative and contented and easier to control if their crying is regarded as a signal to respond to immediately rather than to be ignored.

9. *The Archers.* BBC Radio 4: mid-Feb 1983. This programme was repeated twice.

10. *First Report.* Vol. I, Recommendation No. 38.

11. *First Report.* Vol. I, Para 133:

    The Minister of State reminded us that the DHSS's consultative document *Priorities for the Health and Social Services* (1976a) had envisaged a 6 per cent increase per annum in the number of health visitors ... We recommend that this target should be achieved.

12. *Ibid.* Vol. II, Evidence from the Royal College of Psychiatrists, p 166, para 48.

13. Family Start: project report 1. (Project coordinator: Joy Courtney, 46 Poynter Walk, Sholver, Oldham OL1 4PA), 1979. Also: A summary of the project development so far, May 1981.

14. *First Report.* Vol. III, Evidence from M Richards of the Medical Psychology Unit, University of Cambridge, p 498.

15. *First Report.* Vol. I, para 155.

16. Area Review Committees were set up after the 1974 reorganisation of the NHS, to deal with non-accidental injury to children. Their constitution varied with local circumstances but the aim was to make them representative of all the disciplines concerned with non-accidental injury — social services, housing, education, police, probation, medicine, nursing and such bodies as the NSPCC. They were set up jointly by local government and local health authorities. They were to be policy making bodies, their purpose to monitor and strengthen measures to prevent, diagnose and manage cases of non-accidental injury. After the 1982 reorganisation of the NHS the committees became mostly based on Boroughs, usually with broadly similar constitutions and purposes.

17. *First Report.* Vol. I, para 73.

18. Schools Council Publications: Thomas Nelson and Sons, Lincoln Way, Windmill Road, Sunbury-on-Thames, Middlesex TW16 7HP.

Inspection material for teachers is available from Cambridge University Press, PO Box 92, London NW1 2DB.

Chapter 6—What can be done in the school for teachers' problems? Help within the school: self-help

If society is paralysed today, it is not for lack of
means but for lack of purpose.

— Lewis Mumford (1940)

Learning is a social process. All the evidence is
that persons learn with and from each other when
each has an interest in a common problem: 'The
mother cannot teach her baby to talk unless the
baby first teaches its mother to speak' (Martin
Lewis); "Unless patient and doctor become a
problem to each other, no cure is found" (Carl
Gustav Jung) . . .

— RW Revans (1982b)

We consider the resources available to schools for dealing with the
difficult behaviour of children. What may be regarded as treatment in a
young child may have value as prevention of trouble at a later stage.
Although our main interest is with problems in secondary schools, we
nevertheless give attention to what goes on at earlier ages, for the young
child becomes the adolescent. Before compulsory school age the
behaviour of a child causing concern to someone in contact with him is
largely a family problem. Once a child goes to playgroup, nursery class,
nursery school or primary school, teachers or others are likely to notice
unusual behaviour and may become friends and counsellors of the
mothers. A perceptive and welcoming headteacher is likely to learn
more about the mother's troubles than any other professional person
except a health visitor. Young children are easier to deal with than
adolescents, if only because it is possible to pick them up, remove them
from the scene of crisis and provide physical comfort. Most schools have
rules, and recognised sanctions for those who break them, and with
these competent teachers can control the average pupil, teach him and
find the teaching rewarding. Their 'failure' is with children whose
behaviour is outside normal limits in degree and frequency, and who are
unresponsive to the discipline of the school.

Those who study human behaviour, including teachers, formulate their
definitions and explanations of behaviour problems, and their treatment,
differently. They may espouse either a psychodynamic or a behavioural
model to explain the child's difficulties. Many teachers employ a mixture
of approaches to children's problems.

The child and the teacher

A school teacher does not have an easy life. To be single-handed with a group of thirty children with different backgrounds, different cultures and different levels of ability, and to be given the task of keeping them all occupied, interested and achieving, puts the teacher under considerable strain which on the whole increases as the age of the class goes up: there is the not too taxing unruly self-centredness of the young child, and the much more unruly rebellious ganging up of teenagers. Most school children are at school for purposes decreed by someone other than themselves; the teacher's job is to prevail on the pupils to accept these purposes; to like doing so if possible, but to do what is required of them whether they like it or not.

The under fives. Some young children are emotionally undeveloped and their ability to learn and their social functioning are below what would be expected for their age. While there must be sorting and referral to appropriate agencies by caring professionals, could treatment in the pre-school period avoid some of these difficulties? Holmes (1980, 1982) concluded that some children needed a period of consistent individual help before they could learn in a group, and the earlier it was provided the better. She showed that over a twelve-month period a daily ration of a half to one hour of individual attention for deprived children could significantly alter their behaviour and social development. The good effects of giving institutionalized infants an extra hour's attention each day has been noted by Rutter (1981). Young children do very little 'learning in groups'. There is a great difference between learning in isolation and learning with support at all stages of learning.

Holmes compares the difficulties (not inconsiderable) of arranging this special attention and its moderate cost, with the problems these children cause later to schools and society, and the enormous cost of dealing with them, for example £10 000 per child per annum in a community home with education on the premises (DHSS, 1978b).

Primary schools. The teacher's lot is not so difficult in the primary school. There the pupils' span of attention is short and the school may include such things as imaginative play, dancing, drama, art and other creative work; the basic subjects are made interesting and the time given to them is largely determined by the child. Primary schools provide a happy experience for children. The teacher may have a wide range of ability in her class, children with undetected handicaps, children whose behaviour is puzzling, or disruptive. For instance a child whom no one else can control may spend all his time in the head's office; another may not speak, but may look deceptively bright and intelligent, only to be diagnosed after a time as 'autistic', or as mentally sub-normal; another, equally puzzling, may after lengthy investigations, be found to be the victim of ill-treatment at home. When these problems are not sorted out in the child's early school days they are likely to continue and to get worse.

Diagnostic classes for first school children are of great value. They are literally diagnostic, revealing for example that a child's true level of intelligence is higher or lower than was estimated when he was first seen. They are remedial in changing attitudes of children and parents. They are a means of establishing cooperation of professionals with one another and with parents, so as to give young children with special needs special help. The persons concerned in a diagnostic class are the staff (usually the head and at least one other member of the 'donor' school), one or more representatives of the child guidance service and the parent(s). Of course the parents have the last word since a move to the diagnostic class usually means a move to another school; they seldom object. There must also be consultation with the receiving school though this is more of a formality. In particular cases, many other professionals may be brought in to the discussion — the 'community paediatrician' (school doctor), health visitor, social worker, GP, play group leader and perhaps others. Medical treatment of a relatively mild handicap such as myopia, or slightly impaired hearing, may solve the problems of a child who seems slow to learn. It may be found that the child has, in addition to all that is provided in the diagnostic class, special educational needs and a decision can be made about which is the most suitable service or person to supply them.

Such decisions may not be made until the child has spent some time in his new class, but since in an average sized borough, there are not many more than fifty children in diagnostic classes, it is possible for professionals to pay several visits each term and at some time, at least well before the age of eight, those concerned must collectively decide what type of school and, perhaps, what particular school is the right one for the child to go on to, and what help should be given to the family as a whole. Some children will be best placed at a school for those with moderate learning difficulties; a few at a day school for the maladjusted, for the autistic, or for some other handicap. It may be, too, that a few will be better away from home, at least for a time. These are difficult decisions, but easier to make when a multidisciplinary team has observed and discussed them over time.

Secondary school. Children aged 8-12 are taught in middle schools in boroughs with tripartite schooling and all go at 11 or 12 to secondary schools. At this time education becomes more formal with pressure to get good academic results.

Some children are born troubled, some acquire troubles, and some have troubles thrust upon them. Whether they bring their troubles with them or whether they gather them during secondary education, the problems of teenagers may be hard to solve. This is partly due to the normal turmoils of adolescence, but the children's difficulties tend to be aggravated by many features of the secondary school, particularly, perhaps, by the relatively impersonal nature of the relationship between teacher and pupil. Size, split sites, and difficulties of communication with colleagues are among the factors which contribute to disruptiveness. However, a large school with a large staff has, or should have, certain advantages: experience, expertise and wisdom among its own staff and remedial departments. The school can draw on a number of specialised agencies within itself or provided by the local education authority (LEA). The school should be in a position to obtain help for younger teachers, and be able to match the curriculum to the child so that it includes some subjects to give him satisfaction. A withdrawal unit (Part II, Chapter 7) could help to remove or reduce some of the strains which burden the pupil; a school counsellor would be able to form a positive relationship with him and help him gain or regain his self-esteem.

It has long been evident, though not always appreciated by teachers, that the transition to secondary school is a major event in the child's life. Among other adaptations, he has to change from being a 'senior' person in his primary school, to becoming 'small fry' in the secondary school. His security systems have to be rebuilt. Fortunately most children are adaptable, and enlightened schools and LEAs make efforts to lessen the strains of the transition. Discussion before transfer about pupils' behaviour problems, preferably through the pastoral system (school counsellor etc), is a system some secondary schools use to treat the children understandingly. Clubs whose members are in the main the younger secondary school pupils, but which encourage final year primary school pupils to join them, form a valuable link between the stages of 'middle' education and remove some of the rumoured terrors of starting again as a 'new boy'. Increasingly schools for all age groups make parents feel welcome, present the staff as people ready to be helpful in many ways to the whole family and show the parents that their help is wanted and appreciated.

In this chapter we are concerned with measures to help prevent or redrce disruptive behaviour and with ways for dealing with the 'established case' in the secondary school. An appropriately trained teacher can deal with the milder forms — the common 'stroppiness' of mettlesome young persons; severe cases will require the help of a special environment and specially trained staff, as for example in a school for maladjusted children. Much has been written, mainly in the USA, on the management of behaviour problems in the classroom. We do not mention in detail the various theories and practices, some rather narrowly based, that have been developed there. Many American authors do not attach much weight to emotional or environmental factors in the causation of difficult behaviour. Different writers offer useful advice on how to deal with it in the ordinary school (Wills, 1945, 1960; Dinkmeyer and Dreikurs, 1963; Shaw, 1965; Dreikurs, 1968; Dreikurs and Grey, 1968; Bower, 1969; Dreikurs and Cassel, 1972; O'Leary and O'Leary, 1972; Gordon and Burch, 1974; Rutter, 1975; Caspari, 1976; Jones-Davies and Cave, 1976; Macmillan and Kolvin, 1977; Laslett, 1977b and c; Gilham, 1978; Redl, 1980a; Wilson and Evans, 1980; Wolfgang and Glickman, 1980; Upton and Gobell, 1980; Gilham, 1981; Galloway, Ball, Blomfield and Seyd, 1982; Hargreaves, 1982; Laslett, 1982b; Barker, 1983; Wheldall and Merrett, 1985). Some, such as Robertson (1981) are preoccupied with the status and authority of the teacher as a means of control. We commend especially books by Glasser (1975), Marland (1976) and Laslett and Smith (1984). Many teachers in the UK seem to be unaware of much of this literature. Teachers should get the best of both worlds by appropriate use of others' experience and their own supportive facilities. No one is better qualified to give advice about child psychology than the school psychological service (Part II, Chapter 8 (i)).

Prevention or reduction of conflict between adults and children

Appropriate curriculum. It is difficult to arouse the interest of a child in a subject he does not wish to learn, and he may react in a number of ways. The teacher's task is to take the lead in arranging the curriculum (DES, 1978a). Governing bodies, parents and pupils also have a proper interest in the curriculum and should be able to offer advice (DES, 1977).

Work experience in the last year at school should help children to decide what they want to do after school. There should be some form of assessment of the child's response by a team that includes the employers, along the lines perhaps of schemes that seem to work in France with local industry, commerce and services (Dobinson, 1975). Courses and qualifications closely linked with industry and commerce, such as those provided by the City and Guilds, and by the Royal Society of Arts (1), are likely to help children to find employment after school. The Grubb Institute (1981) has done useful work examining the transition from school to work, and is exploring practical ways of facilitating it (Bazalgette, 1978; Reed, 1980; Reed, Bazalgette and Armstrong, 1982).

The hours that people work, even in full-time jobs, will get fewer, and so schools must also be geared to helping people to find enjoyable, and preferably creative, leisure activities. Schools have for too long been based unthinkingly on our industrial system and should redress the balance by regarding the pupil more as *product* than *worker* (Handy, 1984). The position is made difficult by the great contraction of industrial work. Wirth (1981), discussing Dewey's immense contributions to the philosophy of education, criticises educationists for their puny efforts at modifying western industrial ethics and practices, which have such harmful effects. Dewey saw the need to relate learning to work if people and institutions were to develop. Wirth echoes Dewey's desire to make 'democracy' not only a form of political organisation but a 'name for a life of free and enriching communion' in which a 'social return is demanded from all and opportunity for development of distinctive capacities is provided for all.'

Responsibilities of school staff. Discernible leadership is required with staff realising the importance of their attitudes towards:

a. children

b. others working in the team (Silberman, 1969)

c. themselves

and the effects these have on the children

The caring, predictable and reliable environment: cooperation between teachers and parents. What of the needs of the 60-80 per cent of 'average' children who are neither at the top of academic achievement, nor at the bottom? In life, as in architecture, order with variation is to be desired. At home a basic pattern of more or less fixed getting up times, meal times, bed times and so on gives a sense of security but changes in detail are appreciated, and big 'surprises', if they are pleasant, are remembered with delight many years after the event. In the same way a good school is basically 'reliable and predictable', but there are the occasional variations in the form of treats, outings, or school journeys that do not undermine security but dispel monotony and boredom. The child is shown that he is cared for not only by what adults say and do but by the school environment

110

they provide (Blishen, 1969). An ordered series of events (routine), and of surroundings that continue independently of hostile or seductive feelings gives support to the child. Many secondary schools are 'good enough' in these respects but others fail to meet requirements.

Material surroundings. Although secondary school children have a form-base they seldom work in it. Sixth forms usually have a common room where pupils can relax and talk to their friends during break times. If the ideal of an individual desk in a specific room cannot be achieved suitable time-tabling might reduce the frequent changing of form rooms, and it might be possible to find space for sitting rooms — 'defensible space' (Newman, 1972) — that groups of pupils could call their own. All children need a place where they can keep their belongings reasonably safe and not have to bring them back and forth daily. The provision of amenities is evidence of a caring attitude towards the children and engenders a feeling of belonging in the pupils. Under these conditions vandalism is probably less likely (Stone and Taylor, 1977). A few secondary schools, such as Countesthorpe in Leicestershire (Watts, 1977) are aware of children's needs for this kind of stable, secure background, particularly when they first arrive, but we know of none which has yet fully overcome the peripatetic nature of the secondary school day.

Pupil participation. Children should be involved in as much decision making as can be contrived. Meetings and discussions are legitimate opportunities for expressions of discontent, hostility, jealousy, concern and unhappiness. The value, and sometimes harm, of peer opinion and group pressures need to be remembered; and, if they are openly discussed, good ideas can be made use of. Often pupils themselves want more firmness, not less, in classroom handling. Dreikurs and Cassel (1972) have described the advantages of a weekly class discussion period, genuinely open to pupils to raise any matter they wish. It promotes understanding between children and teacher, and between children and children; and it has other merits. In this country such methods seem to be confined largely to private progressive schools, or special schools for maladjusted children. Not a great number of secondary schools have school councils, but some now have pupil governors. Davies (1976) describes the thoughts, perceptions and drives of sixth-formers in a comprehensive secondary school. He recounts how, after stiff opposition, sixth-formers secured representation at staff meetings.

Reward systems and behaviour modification. The realisation that adults relied largely on punishments, rather than rewards to influence children's behaviour in an acceptable direction was responsible for the development of 'behaviour modification'. Though forms of this are almost universally used in bringing up children, mostly by adults who have never heard the term, most English educationists and psychologists who are concerned with causes as well as symptoms think it too mechanistic to be used alone. American psychologists, led by Skinner (1953, 1969) adopted the view that rewards could be at least as effective as punishments, and developed two forms of 'operant conditioning'. If the child does what is acceptable to the teacher, the teacher rewards him — not on the spot except perhaps by a word of praise — but by as it were putting some points in his bank account to accumulate until he has enough to buy some coveted object (a toy or sweets, for instance) from the class 'shop'. Alternatively points may be exchanged for being allowed to use some special school facility. If the behaviour is unacceptable, points are deducted. At the end of the week if the points balance is 'in the black' the child exchanges them for what he wants; if 'in the red' he has to go empty handed away. A repetition of behaviour that is approved of (or refraining from that which is disapproved of) will be reinforced with additional points; that which is disapproved of will, it is hoped, be extinguished by the deduction of points and the resulting lack of reward at the end of the week. In some cases behaviour that is disapproved of can lead to what is known as 'time out' or withdrawal of the pupil from the class.

Behaviour modification is really no more than a system of manipulating the learning environment. It certainly encourages teachers to be polite to children. A smile, 'the soft answer', as a reinforcing event may work wonders in a difficult situation, or indeed at any time. Reinforcement procedures, though long used, remain rather simple and primitive, their effectiveness not rigorously evaluated. Not many people are trained in their use. One study described how disruptive *pupils* were able to modify the behaviour of their *teachers* (Gray, Graubard, and Rosenberg, 1975). Some people promote behaviour modification methods with almost missionary zeal (Wheldall, 1981). Without suggesting their uncritical adoption, we feel these methods offer a positive way of dealing with the aggressions of childhood, and even the uncertain behaviour of some adults, but they are only one tool among many for this purpose.

Relationships

Between teachers and children. Not everyone can get on with everyone else, but some children have difficulty in socialising because of private problems (home life etc). Sometimes a child may have to be moved, for a school cannot tolerate all children, nor some children a particular school. If teacher and child cannot develop a good relationship the child will not learn and underachievement will add to his difficulties. Teachers are human and they may sometimes be thankful that 'awful Johnny' is absent from the class, rather than enquire where he is and what he is up to. Nevertheless, a disaffected child needs teachers with caring attitudes. Responsiveness to the client has to be developed. Respect for, and confidence in, their teachers is the basis on which children build their own self-respect.

To forge relationships teachers need time to talk with the children, singly or in small groups, not only about subjects taught, or episodes in the classroom, but about all manner of topics. The skill of listening to the child, the teacher giving him *his attention* and listening at another level for what he isn't saying, is one that can be learnt. Some schools run a 'third session' or an 'extended day', a suggestion in the Newsom Report (Ministry of Education, 1963). It is relatively informal and provides an opportunity for staff to get to know the children better. Clegg (1980) quotes with approval the views of probationer teachers on the value of class discussion and the virtues of justified praise to encourage learning in the child and good relations between child and teacher.

Between teachers and teachers. Relationships between teachers and children are influenced by the way in which teachers behave towards each other. If teachers work within a rigid hierarchy in which they have little say in running the school, it will colour their behaviour and attitudes to the pupils. In turn pupils have less respect for teachers who have little authority over the organisation of the school. Teacher participation has been debated at a number of teachers' conferences for ten years or more, and many schools are now run less on the head's fiat. However, changes in the fount of schools' authority are not all plain sailing. They require cooperation from the staff. Sometimes a head who is too innovative for the current school culture may, like Rob Mackenzie, lose his job (2). The account by Holmes (1977) of Teddy O'Neill illustrates the dangers faced by innovators, and the power of antagonistic local opinion. Staff-room relationships, and attitudes of senior teachers to juniors, are sometimes frankly unhelpful to the inexperienced teacher. It must be difficult to run a comprehensive secondary school smoothly and efficiently without attention to staff relationships, participation and sharing of responsibility.

Between teachers and parents. It is not too much to say that schools have, in the past, seen parents as a nuisance, to be kept at bay. Schools are modifying this attitude especially in the case of younger children and are welcoming contacts with parents and relying on their help in various ways. The problems presented by the disruptive child are largely expressions of disadvantage which is not confined to the child. Diffident parents may be depressingly aware of their own incompetence, illiteracy or inadequacy. It helps the school to take account of parental feelings, failings and difficulties. The timing of meetings is important and schools could help by organising playgroups or creches while parents are at school. Should the teacher try to make contact by visiting the home, as is done with some success in the USA? Whatever methods are used the development of relationships with parents depends mainly on the initiative of the teacher. Some teachers feel parents do not want them to visit. Children, it is said, do not always welcome teachers in their home (3). However frustrating it may be, help may have to be deferred until child or parents request it. Liaison teachers offer some prospect of resolving this dilemma as Clegg (1980) found.

How much power should schools or the community exercise over parents? The disruptive child is the parents', and parents are independent. However, other parents have rights too and may reasonably expect the school to control disruptive behaviour to ensure undisturbed schooling for their children. Possibly most parents would consent to psychiatric help for behaviour problems if the threat of exclusion from school were used. It is generally agreed that this would not be justifiable for 6 or 7 year olds. For many parents it is a horrifying thought that a child of seven or less should need to see a psychiatrist, and they may demur. Moreover psychiatrists do not want a patient got to them by intimidation unless his behaviour is quite extreme. Nevertheless when the child is older, and his problem entrenched, it may be more difficult and costly to help him. We shall argue that reference to other professional agencies will usually be more readily accepted if the parents and the child recognise staff from those agencies as part of the school scene.

If parents of young children can accept advice, there should be fewer refractory problems at a later stage. A form of binding relationship may be promoted by making use of the LEA's legal powers to induce parents to encourage their (usually older) truanting children to attend some special form of schooling such as a one-to-one relationship in a teacher's home. Though normally relationships will be formed on a basis of confidence and trust, this may be insufficient to secure cooperation from the 'reluctant parent' whose child is most at risk. Erica Cobbett (1975), a headteacher, described studies she made visiting parents' homes to try to discover why they did not visit the school. She makes suggestions for drawing parents into school activities, and above all advises teachers to let it be seen that parents are not expected to do all the adjusting.

114

Between teachers and other caring services. Whatever is attempted in the pre-school period, some children will not be ready for school when they reach it. When teachers find that a child has learning difficulties, or that his behaviour interferes with other children, they may need assistance to elucidate the causes of the child's problems and how to remedy them. Such help may come from teachers with special experience of various kinds, for example — remedial teaching, pastoral work, counselling; or from other agencies such as the child guidance service, social services or the education office. Later we deal in detail with these relationships.

The concept of reciprocity between teachers and the person with whom they are interacting is basic to the professional relationship. Teachers' work may be facilitated and lightened by accepting the input that children, parents, other teachers and staff from other agencies can provide.

Awareness of services available, and communications with them

Teachers are coming to see themselves as more than just pedagogues. If the prime purpose of a school is to be a place of learning — and why should it not be, like a college of further education, a place of education, learning and research? — then is it not also under an obligation to be a place with few impediments to this purpose, where teachers understand how it is that some children have difficulty in learning? Other professionals devote time to research in learning and teaching, but this will never be sufficient to relieve teachers themselves of the task of understanding children's learning problems and applying what they find out to their own job.

Schools tend to be parochial in outlook, even to the point of obsession with their problems. Traditional attitudes about their 'completeness' could be softened by schools becoming more welcoming to other professionals such as psychiatrists, teachers from special schools, social workers, nurses, and doctors. More open pathways would encourage the trend, for example, for maladjusted children to move part-time to ordinary schools when their behaviour is improving. The evident reluctance of schools to seek help with a difficult pupil until they can no longer cope with him suggests that *amour propre* has made it difficult to accept 'failure' and ask for specialist help. The school may feel insecure, indeed vulnerable, at a time when authorities, society, parents and children are changing their expectations of teachers. Nevertheless if schools and their children are to receive the help they need, some internal changes of attitude seem essential.

Local education authorities should examine their communication systems to see if they are not actually hindering the flow of information. One LEA asked its secondary schools to submit a return of the names of their disruptive pupils, but some schools, lacking confidence in what the authority would do with the information, made a nil return. Some LEAs require that schools refer children to special services through the education office. This leads to delays, and some referrals may not get through because they are lost or re-routed. This frustrates the referring parties, who blame the agencies from whom they hope for help as being unresponsive. Such requirements are often ignored because they are unworkable. Communications and relationships between different agencies concerned with disturbed adolescents were critically examined by the NHS Health Advisory Service (HAS) (1986). Their report quotes many instances of lack of interprofessional collaboration. Some teachers, working in multidisciplinary teams, were instructed by their LEAs not to join in multidisciplinary meetings during school hours. 'On many visits (HAS) teams were instrumental in introducing senior officers to each other for the first time.' Research to aid improvement in poor services for young people might begin, the report suggested, by asking the young people themselves for their opinions.

Some parents ask schools for help with their children. This can often only be provided in concert with members of other agencies, who for this purpose would need to be brought together with the child's teacher or teachers. But there are still gulfs of uncertainty and distrust to be bridged. Finding time is always difficult but meeting other services to discuss children's needs should be regarded as an essential part of a teacher's work, with timetables arranged to permit regular meetings, and surely it is for teachers to take the initiative in promoting coordination of this sort. If adequate numbers of health visitors and school nurses were attached to primary schools, continuity of care would be possible before and after starting school. Teachers would recognise them as co-professionals in home-school liaison. Social workers attached to primary schools could try to ameliorate environmental causes of learning difficulties. All this would be in line with the proposals of the Court report (DHSS, 1976b) to make health care and education into a truly child-centred service.

Parents vary in their belief in the existence of emotional problems. A teacher may not understand what a psychologist writes in his reports. He may not comprehend the roles of members of the child guidance team, and may not particularly welcome them to the school. On the other hand child guidance staff may believe that they cannot find time to visit a school or engage in discussions with its staff. If services are to be of assistance, there must not only be knowledge of their existence and function, the serving and the serviced must interact. It is lack of communication between the agencies involved with disruptive pupils that effectively renders the problem insoluble.

Professional relationships and the general theme of communications are examined in more detail in Part IV.

Discipline

> The commonest technique of control in modern life is punishment ... the suspicion has ... arisen that punishment does not in fact do what it is supposed to do.
>
> — BF Skinner (1953)

One disruptive pupil can interfere with the work of a whole class; a disruptive class can disturb those in adjacent rooms and disturbance may spread. Something has to be done. What it is depends on the nature of the trouble, the teacher's beliefs and perception of the child, the general ethos of the school and of the society to which the school belongs. How can agreement be reached on any aspect of school culture and policies when there are 60, 80, or more teachers on the staff and a large number of parents and others with an interest in the school? All the varied pressures on schools, not least the pupils' academic aspirations, are relevant to discussions of these questions, discussions that would be best initiated by teachers themselves.

There are simple ways of maintaining good relationships with children. Do not humiliate them; avoid punitive attitudes; show concern and empathy; try to discover why a child is upset; and develop mutual respect between teacher and pupil. A teacher's firm disapproval of behaviour is more effective if the teacher obviously cares for the child. Unfortunately many children come from homes where anger is common and ineffectual. A child needs rewarding for trying as much as for attaining. What a child absorbs is influenced by his feelings. Children have to adapt to teachers, and they talk to psychiatrists about their experiences with them. Children work harder to conform to teachers' ways than teachers may realise. A child of nearly 8 pressed her teacher rather hard about the reasons for underlining headings. The teacher finally said that the child must just accept that she, the teacher, was a rather old-fashioned person who wanted things done that way. The child replied 'But I don't like to think of you as that kind of person'. Teachers should not be too concerned if a child fails to conform absolutely to school culture. While there is now

117

more appreciation of the emotional problems of children, their causes, and the behaviour they may give rise to, there remains a large group of adults who continue to believe in the efficacy of more, and more severe, punishment for the control of non-approved behaviour.

If discipline is defined as the maintenance of order in a group, the group must have some rules. We believe that in schools they should be as few as possible, and that parents and children should regard them as reasonable. A mother, sent for by a housemaster, was relieved when she found that the complaint was only that her son had been seen at some distance from the school without his cap. A twelve-year old girl from another school, while agreeing that some rules were necessary, said 'but at our school there are more rules than there are children'. Too many and too trivial rules make for contempt for all rules, even those essential for life and safety. There must be some methods of enforcing such rules as there are. In the majority of schools these are punitive in some degree. For minor transgressions of the 'normal' child, mild punishments may act as 'reminders' which give the teacher the satisfaction that justice has been done and that the incident can be forgotten. What is to be deplored is reserving the worst punishments (expulsion, long-term suspension, corporal punishment) for the 'worst' offences, since these are so often committed by those who are already suffering from painful social or emotional difficulties.

Teachers, and indeed most children, derive support from a system of unequivocal limits to behaviour and clear understanding among staff of the use of punishment. Hamblin (1978) suggests that teachers should ask themselves after a disciplinary encounter, 'Have I strengthened this pupil's belief in himself as a responsible person or as a good for nothing?' Teachers should regard their disciplinary task as 'to build up an ideal for their pupils, sending them rewarding messages which enhance their sense of responsibility, rather than attempting to control by inhibitionist checks'. As Redl (1980b) says, 'punishment' must have a clear-cut goal to help the child. Adults who punish should understand the complex thought processes they engender in the child, involving his most sensitive and vital psychological organs. During punishment children need support, and help with assuaging guilt.

The governors of a special school for maladjusted children were told about violence inflicted on teachers by pupils, a frequent occurrence. The head described how this was met by 'talking the child down', without counter-violence and emphasized how such aggression could be contained without rejecting the child. When the outburst was over, and the child's anxiety had lessened to a tolerable level, the teacher might, by counselling techniques, help the child to learn a little about himself from the whole experience. The governors wanted the Education Committee to know about what happened to the teachers. Admirable as that would be, it proved difficult for them to understand that the Authority should also arrange for the expertise of these teachers in dealing with aggressive children, to be made available to teachers in other schools, to social workers and even to the police. Teachers should support each other in maintaining discipline and staff need opportunities to discuss unresolved conflict with children in quiet circumstances, on a one-to-one basis. There is a view that disruptive behaviour tends to make schools less liberal, perhaps an expression of their inability to cope with it.

We emphasize the uselessness of teacher violence for controlling the behaviour of disruptive pupils. It makes such children more disturbed and aggressive and so the teachers are not helping themselves. What sort of relationship do teachers believe will be developed with any child they attack physically? Some teachers cling to the use of physical force to instil discipline and learning in children, in the face of a mass of evidence that it does no good, that there are much better ways of achieving these ends, that it is inconsistent to beat children when it is illegal to beat adults, and when most other 'advanced' countries (including Russia) have ceased to do so (4). The ILEA has abolished corporal punishment and the National Union of Teachers (NUT) has resolved to do away with it. Trends in local authority rulings and in teachers' attitudes indicate that corporal punishment is on the way out but constructive alternatives must be available (Highfield and Pinsent, 1952). As for the suggestion that 'children prefer it' this is no argument. It is in the main for adults to decide what is good for children and one of the purposes of a good school for maladjusted children is to help them to see the harm that corporal punishment does.

The Advisory Centre for Education set up the Home and School Council in 1967 to help teachers and parents to come together. Michael Young (1967), director of the Institute of Community Studies and first chairman of the Home and School Council, has commented: 'The thing that many teachers fear they might lose is authority ... almost all other countries ... do not need corporal punishment because they have the parents, whereas in Britain, which does have it, teachers probably have to face more severe problems in maintaining control than almost anywhere else. In other countries much of the discipline is work for parents, not teachers ... so the latter must communicate with the former ...' The responsibilities of being in loco parentis should be shared cum parente. Parents could then be allies.

Suspension. If a child is suspended, it means that the school has given notice of its unwillingness to accept him, perhaps for a day, for a week, or indefinitely. All but the shortest suspensions have to be notified to the education authority. The head may tell the parents that the child needs a short rest from the turmoil of school or, more frankly, that neither teachers nor pupils can stand his behaviour and that they hope he will come back, after a day or two at home, in a more tractable frame of mind (an example of the school working *cum parente*).

The process should be used for constructive purposes and not punitively. It offers an opportunity for a systematic effort by all concerned to seek solutions to the behaviour problems that have led to a young person being debarred from attendance at school. Parents should be brought into consultation at the first sign of difficulties. If they are reassured by the concern of teachers for their child's future, their support will be helpful to action that the school may wish to take. The helping agencies (education welfare service, child guidance service, school counsellor, withdrawal unit) should be involved at once if it seems appropriate. This can be done before any question of suspension arises. Parents are usually cooperative if included in discussions that emphasize their child's needs. This happens even more readily in schools where parents are invited to discuss the good as well as the 'bad' doings of their children.

However, not all parents cooperate with teachers or are much interested in their children's progress. It is then that teachers need a clearcut procedure to be laid down by the education authority, for it helps neither them, nor parents, nor pupil if actions are uncoordinated or infirm. Some authorities have simply noted suspensions and taken no further action, the children being left to their own devices, perhaps to roam the streets or engage in crime. If expulsion seems inevitable, either another school should be found willing to take the child or home tuition should be considered. There must be many LEAs with good practices in this difficult area of school administration.

The attitudes and policies of schools and teachers

We have discussed briefly (Part I, Chapter 3) how the way schools are run may aggravate children's behaviour. Daines (1981) thought schools needed 'treating' as much as disruptive children. Lawrence *et al* (1984), going further, see the school environment and teachers' demands as the main causes of disruptive behaviour, a theme pursued by Galloway (1985a). If, as is all too often the case, children are simply expected to adapt to the school, the difficulties of those with special educational needs will be exacerbated. Responsibility for special educational policy should not be put on to specialists ('experts'). The ideal is for a well staffed special education department to help mainstream teachers to adapt their curricula and teaching methods to their pupils' needs (Galloway, 1985b). If rules could be not only *agreed* with some pupil participation, and *known*, and *not too inflexible* (for example pupil time-keeping) children might be more cooperative. Cunningham (1978) quotes Tyrrell Burgess: 'If democracy is not merely to be oligarchy tempered by electoral defeat, people need to know how to run democratic institutions.' He goes on: 'Yet if schools are operated in an authoritarian manner no amount of "civics" or "political education" in the curriculum will get students to develop the skills and motivation to run democratic organisations.'

Teachers vary in their reactions to different children. Six teachers in one school were asked to compile a list of ten pupils each thought of as the 'nastiest and most difficult children in the school.' When the lists were compared it was found that 29 different pupils had been mentioned (Patricia Goldacre, personal communication). Laslett (1977b) believes it would help teachers to cope with difficult children if they defined their attitudes to all children, distinguishing between those who do and those who do not fit in with the average teacher's expectations. The teacher should write down the names of the children in an 'attachment group', with their IQs, attainments, social class, etc, and the particular items of behaviour found acceptable. He should do the same for an 'exclusion group' with behaviour especially disliked. He should ask himself: does this latter group of children puzzle him? Do they make him anxious, angry or frightened? Is a child not merely disruptive but also handicapped in any degree? Has enquiry been made about it? Is his behaviour due to lack of ability? Can he read? Is he numerate? Is he otherwise disadvantaged?

What of the learning relationship between child and teacher? The concept of the teacher teaching, the process resulting in the acquisition by the pupil of remembered facts and knowledge, a one-way form of communication, is too simple. Indeed, feedback to teachers from responsive pupils is a form of communication that the child needs and that the teacher appreciates as a reward (Revans, 1965). Two-way communication in the classroom is a device at all ages for securing interest and attention. As someone has remarked education is a mingling of mature and immature minds. An important element in all professions is that of service and it should be at the heart of the relationship of teachers with child and parents.

Although, as we have noted, there are not in absolute numbers many severely disruptive or really troublesome children of secondary school age, and while there are those who genuinely enjoy what the comprehensive school has to offer, for many children time at secondary school is time endured. Maybe without protest, but not without underlying resentment, smouldering and ready to be stirred into flames. A disruptive 'hero' or an anti-authority gang may be more influential than teachers or parents. In some secondary schools it is hardly too much to say that there is a state of 'cold war' between teachers and pupils. Skill and tact are needed by the staff, however trouble-free the school may appear.

Teachers who are aware of what pupils think of them, their methods and the way the school is run, have a ready stimulus to examine and modify their policies. Unfortunately teachers seldom have the benefit of this kind of feedback. Such exercises in communication demand a sense of personal security. The possessive attitude of teachers to the curriculum is an example of professional isolationism. But then people like to teach what they know about. This is being slowly modified by parental and political pressures, pupils' ambitions, and schools' growing awareness of community and industrial needs.

To change schools from 'education factories', concerned mainly with the instillation of 'programmed knowledge', to 'learning communities', will need teachers, pupils and parents to work out together the kind of school and teaching the children need. None of this will be possible unless the energies and initiatives of younger teachers also are harnessed. Yet in most schools most decisions are taken at the top. A questionnaire to elicit information on participation by staff in school management, was circulated to members of the NUT Young Teacher Section in one Borough in 1971. In most of the schools junior teachers played little or no part in making decisions on school policies. Few heads wished even to hear teachers' suggestions, and meetings were few. We need a less authoritarian role for the head and senior teachers, and more pupil and parent participation in the determination of the curriculum. When schools are run on open lines with all the teachers deciding school policies, the staff may experience a great boost in morale (5).

Teachers' professional problems must surely be solved mainly by their own efforts. Professionals should expect support if they discuss with colleagues problems they meet in their work (Laslett and Smith, 1984). School as a learning forum offers teachers a chance to learn from events in their work, and the effects they have upon the children. Older teachers can pass on wisdom and practical hints to the inexperienced who may have been taught little enough about class management and child psychology during training. But if old hands make cynical remarks about the school or the children, or indulge in one-upmanship in the staff room, they will hinder communication and undermine self-confidence in colleagues. One meeting a term of all teachers in a school is worthless, yet this may be all that they have and then mainly to receive information from above. There are even heads who fear sectional meetings, such is the vulnerability of authoritarian systems.

Learning of any kind does not necessarily mean a large outlay of time or money. However, extra remuneration may have to be paid for time taken by meetings outside school hours if there is no time for them in the 'normal' school day. There is much to be said for paying professional people a good salary to cover a day of variable length. People may reasonably feel that school holidays could provide time for teachers to do *their* 'home-work' — postgraduate education, and the examination of school policies, client needs, the effects of teachers' attitudes and methods, school management, and other elements of school life.

Cooperative learning — an action learning project

Examination of educational and organisational matters jointly with teachers from other schools, administrators, and members of other professions and the community would transform schools into learning communities, and this should help them with their problems. One of us (NFC) arranged an action learning project to examine the problem of disruptive behaviour in secondary schools, with the cooperation of an LEA and borough department of social services. A description of action learning is given by Revans and others (Revans, 1982a, 1983a; Pedler, 1983) and a definition in Appendix 2. A 'set' of six fellows — two teachers, a social worker, an educational psychologist, an assistant education officer (administrator) and a parent (school governor, PTA member and engineer) met over a period of time to examine how disruptive behaviour affected them and the educational arenas with which they were concerned. The insight and perceptions that were gained helped the group to make many constructive suggestions. Learning and development in the fellows' own organisations, always slower and more difficult than individual learning, was promoted and monitored by the set. The exercise demonstrated that people with essentially similar problems can help themselves by learning with and from each other in a supportive milieu, by sharing experiences and questioning afresh old ideas and attitudes (see Part II, Chapter 8 (i)).

Notes

1. The open sixth: many hands make more relevant work. *Times Educational Supplement*, 27/1/1978.

2. Rob Mackenzie, at Somerhill Academy, Aberdeen, tried to abolish corporal punishment, and to create a 'family atmosphere' with encouragement for the ordinary child. The school staff opposed his methods and induced the Education Committee to terminate his headship. — *Guardian* 6/4/1974; and Wilby P. — Dissident teachers bring down a progressive head — *Observer* 7/4/1974.

3. Auriol Stevens described in the *Observer* of 11/3/1979 the re-opening of Hornsey Girls' School after the caretakers' strike was over. The pupils had had to do most of their studies at home and in their teachers' homes. The school staff were quoted as saying: 'There has been an enormous gain in friendship and appreciation. Children have been into our homes and realise we're ordinary.'

4. Information from the Society of Teachers Opposed to Physical Punishment (STOPP).

5. Most free schools are run in this way. See also Stewart H. — Carry on Croxteth. *New Statesman* 29/10/1982. Croxteth is a community school in Liverpool fighting closure, and now run on open lines. All the teachers decide teaching policy, such as discipline and the syllabus, at a weekly meeting. One teacher is quoted: 'It's a complete dream after the rigid administration structures I've worked under.'

Chapter 7 — Services in the school or closely associated with it, for children with special needs

Children with Special Needs

The Warnock Committee. The Warnock Committee on *Special educational needs* (DES, 1978b) recommended the 'integration' of some children with special needs into classes in ordinary schools. It is generally accepted that if a child has special needs those who teach him must have appropriate training.

Under the 1981 Education Act (the Government's response to Warnock) the comprehensive secondary school is to provide for the 'whole range of ability', though seldom for those of very low intelligence or those whose special needs include elaborate equipment, for example the visually handicapped, or those with hearing difficulties; those who need special physical care and protection such as haemophiliacs, or for whom medical and nursing care have first priority. The less severe the problem the easier it is to provide for special needs in the ordinary school. Some schools make provision for the partially sighted, the partially hearing, and for those with mild difficulties of locomotion, but in a borough of 50 000-60 000 children of school age the numbers of such special cases would be very small, and few if any ordinary schools could make the appropriate provision. Two types of special need for which several or all schools will have to provide are disruptive children, including some mildly maladjusted, and 'slow learners' or 'backward' children. Warnock did not envisage doing without special schools for maladjusted children or social adjustment units (withdrawal units).

We agree with Warnock that it is vital for parents to be fully involved in the education of children with special needs. The child's needs may be complemented by the teacher's needs which may even be the cause of the child's special needs (Galloway, 1985a).

Remedial Teaching

Many children are unable to make use of what the school has to offer and there are others who fail to achieve the standard of work expected of them. Although there can be few who go through their school days without the need for a little extra tuition on some subject or other, from somebody, even a fellow pupil, here we are dealing with something deeper, where the child has fallen behind his peers and his potential. His capacity to learn is impaired partly because of this. Children requiring remedial teaching may be difficult to teach, and may demand a disproportionate amount of attention. Some behavioural problems are associated with learning difficulties, and remedial teaching may be all that is needed to overcome them.

Remedial teachers can list a number of reasons for under achievement (Mortimore, 1982), but there has been insufficient research into its causes and many puzzling cases remain. Methods of dealing with it are described by Gulliford (1971). The Warnock Committee concluded that one child in five might need some tuition in addition to standard class teaching for some part of his school life. Unfortunately the Committee did not say for how long this extra help was likely to be required and some people have the impression that one child in five has special needs whereas probably the majority need only a short period of extra help to make good some relatively mild falling behind.

Reading is an essential skill with which most children are expected to have made a sound beginning during their primary schooling. Tests for 'reading readiness' may not be suitable for all children, but attempts to teach children before they are ready may confuse them and leave them unable to read until quite an advanced age. Very minor disabilities of sight, hearing or speech may set them back and even locomotor disorders, not at first sight related to the acquisition of reading skills, may be a serious obstacle. There are children who are slow developers in all departments concerned with language, having 'low verbal ability'. This backwardness may be due to 'constitutional' deficiencies, or result from growing up in a non-verbal environment, a home or district in which books are hardly ever read or, now that most families have at least one TV, even a newspaper.

It is said that the popular press caters for a public whose reading is not above the nine year age level and we learn from psychologists that if a person does not reach the average vocabulary of an eleven year old before his school-days are over, reading skill will soon decline. In Great Britain where 148 different languages have been identified among our school children quite a number of children will be half way through primary school, or even reach secondary school, without hearing much spoken English. Though children learn a second language more quickly than adults, our irrational pronunciation and spelling present difficulties. English children, who through illness or living abroad or moving from one district, and therefore one school, to another may not get an adequate command of their native language because they have had an insufficient or confusing 'exposure to education'. Others find it hard to learn to read because of social or emotional disadvantage. It is no easy task to find the solution of these difficult problems when almost every individual pupil presents a different one. All but a small number learn to read in the end, but it is a skill easily lost: many children said to be reading satisfactorily when they move from primary school are found to be poor readers when, six or seven weeks later, they enter secondary school. Is this a reflection on how children are taught to read? A comprehensive secondary school may find that 20 per cent of pupils transferred from primary schools require remedial teaching, with about 100 pupils spending some time in remedial work during a year. The large number of non-reading intelligent adults now being discovered shows how easily the basic and essential skill of reading is lost.

A highly skilled and caring remedial teacher may achieve a near miracle in an hour a week of individual tuition. Some remedial classes in schools do well with small groups, but teachers of larger ones, even if the children attend nearly full-time may achieve very little. Remedial education may be provided in a school either in a class or department, the latter more commonly in a secondary school because of its wide age range. A remedial department may have several classes, pupils progressing from one to another doing very little in the mainstream though it should be the remedial teacher's aim to get as many children as possible back with their normal age group. There are also centres which a backward or non-reading pupil can attend for several sessions a week. Unfortunately in some secondary schools remedial teaching is provided only in the first two years, after which children are assumed to be ready for the mainstream when, by other standards, they are not. Remedial subjects taught are reading (mainly), writing and less often arithmetic. The most difficult children are those who have lost motivation. In these there is usually a crippling sense of failure and worthlessness, leading to learning blocks and poor self-image (Rist, 1970). Such children may respond to a one-to-one (therapy in disguise) approach or may need some form of psychotherapy before any response to teaching can be hoped for. Daines (1981) considered that remedial teaching might be the most important therapy in many cases of disruptive behaviour.

Remedial teachers need special training and should have full support from their colleagues in carrying out their difficult task. To achieve any result the child's self-esteem and confidence must be restored. If the bottom stream of the fourth year are repeating basic maths seven times a week (it does happen) all will be utterly bored. Here would be a case for using applied maths through practical subjects such as wood- or metalwork, or by setting up a small computer science unit.

Within the school the remedial teacher may feel his role is under-valued, and be relatively isolated in his work. Most remedial teachers have taught at some time in cloakrooms, corridors, staffrooms and odd corners.

Unless a remedial teacher has a recognised and accepted role, he or she may be called upon at a moment's notice to take the place of an absent teacher. This should be avoided because it disrupts the work and also the teacher/pupil relationship, so important for success. Remedial teachers need recognition not only within the school but also as an integral part of all the agencies in or outside it dealing with the problem, including the home. They know the children better than most and can make a useful contribution to discussions about them. Unfortunately many ordinary teachers are unaware of what goes on in a remedial unit, and may, for various reasons, be reluctant to take back a child from it. Galloway (1985a) comments on 'the extraordinary lack of liaison between many remedial teachers and their mainstream colleagues'. Classroom teachers have a tendency to say the child is 'not bad enough yet' for special help. It is a mistake to defer it, for remedial teaching is often successful over a short period of time, if the child has not fallen too far behind.

There are excellent materials and books on remedial teaching, and many projects dealing with it. Resource and teacher centres hold training courses. Interesting new departures are being developed by Inter-Action (Caldwell, 1972). The possibilities of all this have yet to be fully appreciated and applied in the school service.

Pastoral Work and the School Counsellor

We have emphasized that good relationships are requisite for learning; inappropriate teaching methods and learning tasks may prevent the growth of bonds between teacher and pupil. The pastoral system should try to eliminate inconsistent discipline, detect pupils 'at risk' and prevent escalation of minor difficulties. 'Pastoral care should be undertaken by teachers who are prepared to examine continuously their own actions' (Hamblin, 1978). It may be helpful to replace punishment by restitution and reparation. Education authorities adopt various measures to promote pastoral care (Evans, 1981). A system of tutors and housemasters enables the large secondary school to monitor the child's activities and the degree to which he achieves or fails. Sometimes year heads who deal with the pastoral care of the children of the year of which they are in charge, move up year by year with the children. Some schools have both systems.

It is the practice in many schools nowadays for pastoral work to be put into the hands of designated senior staff who mostly have no special training for it, and this limits the classroom teacher's contact with other agencies and the parents. While it is true that an inexperienced teacher may have difficulties in dealing with such people, if he never does so how will he learn? At what point does a teacher become able to tackle this important work? Seniority seems to bring the burden. Ideally all teachers should be aware of, and interested in, their pupils' social and emotional problems, and it has been argued that classroom teachers should do much of the practical work (DES, 1978a). The attributes of the recently qualified — youth, idealism, energy, 'withitness' and the natural sympathy and identification of the young with teenagers are assets the school should use, with help and guidance. Classroom teachers find it frustrating not to know which of their pupils are under the care of child guidance or social services. Of course pastoral work takes time from teaching, but if class teachers did more of it, senior staff would have more time for teaching. Not all teachers are inclined to undertake pastoral care and some will not do it. Marland (1976) emphasized that teachers had to combine good classroom management with being seen to care for children.

Pastoral work is likely to be effective only if the teacher can distance himself sufficiently from the establishment for a child to feel confident to be open with him about his troubles. However, in avoiding an establishment position, he may create problems for his colleagues. For this and other reasons some schools have found it helpful to concentrate pastoral care in the hands of one or two experienced teachers with special training — school counsellors. The proportion of schools with counsellors varies in different parts of the country. Some counsellors are much better fitted than others to carry out their *pastoral role of facilitating good relationships between staff, children, parents and services.* Conflict between the professional and social perspectives of teachers is in proportion to their ability to communicate with supportive agencies, and to work with them to assist the physical, intellectual, emotional and social growth of pupils, parents and colleagues (Bartlett, 1974).

Some teachers regard the counsellor as a 'cop out' for the child, an attitude derived perhaps from the authoritarian nature of schools. The only way to nurse a child with hostile behaviour back to a state of mind that will make it possible for him to learn is for the school to demonstrate a continuing caring attitude to him. The best counsellors are those who not only offer the child the most appropriate care but who are able to communicate with the rest of the staff so that their colleagues can learn about a child's special difficulties, rather than merely losing the child to the counsellor, and thus making the counsellor a 'cop out' for the *teacher.*

The counsellor should be available to make relationships and gain the confidence of the disgruntled teenager-with-a-problem and with his parents. He has time to give attention to the attention-needing child. Counsellors work in different ways, though most do some class teaching which helps them to form relationships with the rest of the teaching staff whose confidence they must retain. It also helps to overcome the resistance of heads and staff who feel threatened if people who know something about how the mind works, refuse to pass on information given to them in confidence. The child psychiatrist can tell the parents what sort of help the counsellor can give, and the counsellor can give them a more realistic view of the psychiatrist. Counsellors cannot operate successfully on their own and it is up to all teachers in a school to see that they are not isolated.

Even when trained for pastoral work, teachers may, like most people, find it easier to understand some problems than others. Conversely, some 'clients' are better than others at eliciting sympathy and at 'opening the eyes' of a counsellor to the sufferings underlying intolerable behaviour. If a problem is to be solved it must be understood and this may need the help of other caring professions.

Withdrawal or social adjustment units

Academic success is enough for the majority of bright children from good homes and that may cover some 40-50 per cent of children — those who achieve 'O' and 'A' levels (depending on the school). What of the rest? Teachers admit that in comprehensive secondary schools the system in effect labels 50-60 per cent of children as 'failures'. It is a fact that most children cope with life well enough, or to put it better, they cope with the system. Nevertheless in many cases we are failing, as shown by the figures for delinquency, crime, depression, breakdown and inadequate young adults at all ranges of ability, who are unable to bring up their own children happily or preserve their marriages. It is significant that the majority of suspensions are in the 13- to 15-year age group, and this suggests that early problems have not received sufficient attention.

Most teachers would be pleased to get rid of one or even several children from their teaching group but, nevertheless, feel that the school has a commitment to the children it has accepted. There are various ways in which with goodwill the staff can rearrange the child's programme so as to reduce the burden he imposes on those who find him particularly hard to tolerate. Whatever they do, there is still the small group of 'disruptives' whom all or nearly all the staff find intolerable. Neither 'loving care' nor 'discipline' in all its forms, including corporal punishment 'make any difference'. The child whose behaviour is unacceptable should be regarded as a child with special needs.

Withdrawal of difficult pupils, temporarily or permanently, has gone on for over 100 years. For a long time the practice was to pillory the trouble-maker by placing him in some prominent position, maybe outside the head's door. A less punitive approach began about 20 years ago, when 'sanctuary' or 'adjustment' units were started, based on the expression of a caring attitude to the child; they provide a more satisfactory means of withdrawal. 'Tutorial classes' serving the same purpose for younger children had been set up by what was then the London County Council in the 1940s (Hill, 1971). Since the majority of children at that time were educated in elementary schools, most of them left at the age of 13 and were then of course no further trouble to the schools.

The Brislington Project (Jones, 1971) was school-based to maintain the child's integration in the school's mainstream while supplementing mainstream activities with something of a frankly pastoral nature. The headmaster sited his adjustment unit at the end of one wing of his buildings, with small cosy rooms, saying that these might be for children with special needs but they had the same need as every other pupil for an agreeable environment and a setting that presented the school in an attractive light. It has been suggested that the truly disruptive child who may have decided he has had enough of formal schooling and has no intention of cooperating (but can even this be certain?), probably needs to be handled in some kind of facility somewhat separated from the main building but not necessarily off the ordinary school campus. A unit that was simply containing final year pupils should provide them with training skills and work experience. It seems to be generally agreed that it should at least be the *aim* for a child in a withdrawal unit to continue with normal schooling in those departments where he can manage it. However, this may be unrealistic for many 15-16 year olds (Wilson and Evans, 1980) although there is no reason why the aim should not be retained. Some children need the continuous, though not necessarily full-time, support of the unit to be able to cope with the vicissitudes of their lives and get some benefit from their school.

There has been a rapid growth of withdrawal (behavioural) units in the last 15 years. The total number in England in 1977 was 239 (DES, 1978d). 72 per cent of those served only pupils of secondary school age; 9 per cent served primary age groups only; 19 per cent served primary and secondary age groups together. 22 per cent served one school only; 78

per cent two or more schools and about a quarter served 20 or more schools. About half the children in behavioural (withdrawal) units for 14-16 year olds had been suspended from their schools. Since the 1978 DES report the number of units has probably more than doubled. Holman and Libretto (1979) and Wilson and Evans (1979) described different kinds of withdrawal units. Rodway (1981) and Tattum (1982) give accounts of the setting up and running of on- and off-site withdrawal units. Depending on the way they function they may or may not be appropriate for disruptive/truanting children. The variety of methods used to deal with children's behaviour problems, ranging for example from the Brislington Project (Jones, 1971) to the more structured arrangements of some LEAs, probably reflects uncertainty about their causes, the differing attitudes of adults to childhood and teenage behaviour and the lack of appropriate training and experience of teachers.

Evans (1981) and Daines (1981) mention criticisms of withdrawal units. The curriculum tends to be limited and teachers may be inadequate for the task. Sometimes the unit is seen, even unconsciously, as a punishment for the child. It may not be regarded by the rest of the school with much respect. While it may help the *child* to spend time in a unit, the unit's presence should not lessen the onus on teachers to examine the reasons for a child's behaviour, so as to avoid the 'fault' being always located in the child rather than the school (Rabinowitz, 1981b). Information and views about adjustment units for day pupils is given by Jones, McKeown, Noel, Kerridge and Dr Plat-Taylor (1981). Mortimore, Davies, Varlaam, West, Devine and Mazza (1983) survey their own and others' data about the working and value of support centres for disruptive pupils, and include comments by pupils. Lawrence *et al* (1984) discuss the arguments for and against withdrawal units.

In this country the child is entitled to a free education. This alone does not guarantee the right to equal opportunity to develop abilities, individual judgement, a sense of social and moral responsibility, and to become a useful member of society. If we do not do all we can to help the child realise these aims, we are failing with our 'captives' in the educational 'service'. The withdrawal unit can not only be appropriate for the needs of certain children, it may be essential for keeping them where they have a right to be: in an ordinary school.

On-Site Units. Experience has shown that spending some part of the school week in a small group where the expectations are different from those in the ordinary classroom results in some change in the child that carries over into the ordinary classroom where conformity and conventional standards of behaviour are required. However, a unit that is really nothing more than a 'sin-bin' may merely give the child one more

134

experience of rejection. If the school and the unit have a therapeutic out-look, the child can get special care from the unit while still having access to the numerous resources of a big school. Ideally the withdrawal unit is a place where there is at least one, and preferably more, caring adults able to allow hostility and aggression to be shown and assimilated; a place where a disruptive child can feel certain of making one worth-while relationship, and grow to make more. The unit may occasionally take children full-time, but usually takes them for several sessions per week. Since it belongs to the parent school the social and educational objectives are likely to be closer to those of the rest of the school. If all goes well the child, after beginning with a variable number of sessions in the unit gradually moves back for an increasing number of periods into the mainstream of the school.

What is important is that the child gets discussed at a series of case conferences in which the senior staff and those closely concerned with him are made aware of his personal problems, his background, and any other circumstances accounting for his difficult behaviour. The staff will also be introduced to the need to examine the role of the family as a factor in the causation of the child's difficulties, and of the necessity of working with it to complement what the school is doing. If the unit is truly a sanctuary or haven where strains and pressures are reduced, where the adults have a genuine sympathy with the over-burdened child, where they look for and emphasize his assets and good points, he will lose the sense of being rejected and go back to other teachers a 'changed child', though it may be that there is change also in them. Teachers will change if they are compassionate, and if they are able to learn from the unit staff the secret of bringing out the best in the child.

Off-Site Units. Some LEAs prefer an establishment for disruptive pupils to be at a distance from the school. It may serve only one school, but more often serves several or, as in the London Borough of Hounslow, two nearby secondary schools. The London Borough of Brent has an off-site unit serving several schools which it calls an 'Educational Workshop', for 15 children. There is great variety among these units but their ultimate goal is said not to differ from that of any other withdrawal unit — to get the children back to normal school. In fact off-site units are usually less effective at returning children to their own school. They take a larger number than most on-site units but the staff-pupil ratio is at least as high, if not higher. The whole unit is small and groups are small which reassures the pupils.

On-site and off-site units compared. The child is usually only part-time in an on-site unit and he meets his peers in the playground, in his tutor group, and in the ordinary lessons he is able to attend. In this way the needs of the younger teenager are particularly considered. A well-organised unit is as much part of the school as any other group. Other staff, particularly seniors, continue to feel responsible for the children in the unit, and work with the unit staff to plan and make such changes in curriculum and teaching as seem necessary for the child's welfare. Re-integration of the child into larger groups is facilitated through frequent informal discussion (DES, 1978d). It is possible to share knowledge about the pupils, and school records can be consulted. The unit in the school should have a therapeutic effect upon all the staff. It can make them think about their attitudes to all the children in the school and the children's problems (Holman and Libretto, 1979). Other children may better understand deprivation if the disturbed child remains among them. A referral to an on-site unit can be arranged quickly and informally between the staff concerned who know and are likely to trust each other. A unit in a school may sometimes be able to take a child waiting to go to a special school for the maladjusted; and is also useful for children returning from such schools, as a half-way house. Its presence is likely to make a school willing to take a child already labelled 'difficult'.

A feeling of rejection, which plays such a large part in the genesis of the disruptive child's condition, tends to be confirmed if he is placed outside his school's curtilage. Difficult children have problems with relationships, and transfer out of their school means they will have to start all over again. Nevertheless in an off-site unit the children know all the teachers, there is almost always more informality than in a big school and, even if the unit has conventional views of acceptable behaviour and inclines more to the punitive than to the therapeutic approach, the small size and the greater preponderance of practical and creative activities makes it less threatening to the children. If one teacher is absent there is not the same crisis as when the staff consists of one or at most two teachers, as in an on-site unit.

Off-site units often cater for certain children, usually older (15-16 year olds), who cannot be easily handled by school-based units and are an alternative when a special school seems called for. They can work well for truants. It may not be possible to provide tuition in specific subjects that the child is good at, but the head and staff are free to develop the unit according to their own beliefs and theories and can make experiments that might not be approved by a school housing an on-site unit. Many have several teaching groups and to that extent are nearer in concept to an ordinary school. Indeed it may be hard to distinguish them from a day school for maladjusted children, particularly if the majority of their pupils attend full-time. There is a danger of the off-site unit being used as a dump to get rid of children whom a school no longer wants to be troubled with.

Admission to off-site units is more complicated for it involves the education bureacracy, and separate staff. Local authorities say that off-site units are easier to administer than those that are part of a big school, and are more economical of skilled staff. There is usually a head with whom the education office can have direct contact. If it should prove impossible to find the right kind of staff for withdrawal units in sufficient numbers, this would be an argument for off-site units where the few specialised staff could be concentrated. However, this is really an argument of despair. Return to ordinary schooling may be more difficult if not impossible from off-site units (DES, 1978d). Grunsell (1978) found that an ordinary school that had been thankful to get rid of its disturbing children, felt no further commitment to them, and did little to welcome them back. Truants may refuse to go back to an ordinary school once they have become integrated in an off-site unit. Sometimes parents are fearful of their child's return to the ordinary school because of previous failures there (DES, 1978d).

There are advantages in both kinds of unit, some favouring the child and some the administration. There is convenience for the LEA in setting up and running an off-site unit; and for the school staff who no longer 'own' the behavioural problem. These may be described in managerial terms as structural elements. The advantages of the on-site unit may be summarized as integrated care of the child (less rejection); learning by school staff, parents and children about individual and group problems; learning by staff about themselves and the effects of their methods on children — all because the school continues to 'own' the problem. These are functional elements. There are some disadvantages in both kinds of unit. Structure exists to serve function and we believe that on-site units are more dynamic, and socially useful, at least for most children aged 14 and under. However, off-site units have the advantage of relative independence and are probably best for 14+ children and for persistent truants.

Organisation and running of a withdrawal unit. Why are most secondary schools without withdrawal units? A few have such advanced pastoral systems that they feel no need of a unit. Some have tried them and given them up when their pastoral work improved. To form a successful therapeutic unit within a school needs commitment in terms of time and support at the highest level. It will only work well if it has staff with the qualities required to teach disruptive children, to show their colleagues how to handle disturbing behaviour and to get appropriate help by working closely with parents and professionals from other agencies. It is not easy to find such staff. The units need supervision. To satisfy these requirements means regular meetings and case conferences to discuss particular difficulties and the children's progress. Some specialised training for the staff makes a great difference. Courses available help teachers to understand why behaviour difficulties arise, and provide them with techniques for helping the child to find other means of 'crying for help'.

It must be admitted that withdrawal units are not all organised in this way. Case conferences may be few and far between. Teachers may say they have neither time nor inclination to learn about the *home* which is considered to be a problem for other agencies such as the social services, or the pastoral department of the school. Schools' systems of self-examination are seldom sufficiently developed to see if they are themselves a cause of the problem (Galloway, 1985a). Working in a withdrawal unit is stressful for teachers who, among other attributes, must practise a high level of awareness and concentration to cope with the children's demands and changing moods. Teachers in an ordinary school are sometimes critical of the staff working in such units (Jones NJ, 1977), mistakenly believing that they have an easier time. It is difficult for teachers in units to set up good lines of communication if the rest of the staff regard them in this way. Even more than the presence of the unit, it is the atmosphere and attitude of the school that is helpful to child and family (Galway, 1979). Only the teachers can take the initiative in removing barriers to communication within the school and between it and other agencies.

If the LEA is unsympathetic and gives little or no money towards setting up a withdrawal unit, the teachers for it will be chosen by the school's senior staff who may know little about the qualities needed to make the unit effective. There may be questions of status, gradings and pay. Some schools fence off their unit from the rest of the school so that the children are segregated and cannot mix with their friends. Some units are set up without any reference to the CG service.

The presence of a withdrawal unit does not deter parents from sending their children to the school. Both Highfield School at Letchworth (Holman and Libretto, 1979) and Brislington School in Bristol (Jones, 1971) were much sought after by parents. A survey of parents (Evans, 1981) found no opposition to withdrawal units. In fact schools get a bad name when parents find their children's progress is impeded by uncontrolled classroom disruption. Anxious parents have been known to make direct approaches to teachers in charge of units. Heads should resist the temptation to make them into compensatory units to cover all educational problems, and children should not be refused admission to them merely because they have no learning problems. Teachers express fears that children in withdrawal units may be labelled by staff and peers as being different or odd. In practice when a child is 'diagnosed' as difficult to the point where action has to be taken, it implies that staff have come to terms with the problem and this may be a relief to the child as much as to the staff.

The organisation of the withdrawal unit, and the arrangements for transferring pupils into it, should be well thought out, properly resourced and business-like (Jones NJ, 1973; Wilson and Evans, 1979). Numerous facets of children's behaviour and their problems have to be considered. Many people are usually involved in admission procedures including: teachers, heads of department, house staff, senior teachers, educational psychologist, parents, school counsellor and psychiatrist. Jones (1974) has described the selection procedure for the Brislington School special adjustment unit in its early days. The children themselves were brought into the process. Those who were not settling down in their first term at the large comprehensive secondary school were brought together for a time-tabled discussion period each week with the head and an educational psychologist. Children were free to raise any topic for discussion and very soon personal problems began to emerge. From these sessions certain children began to progress in school. One or two children clearly needed help from the child guidance service and were referred. Some could not use these group therapy sessions and were considered for the special adjustment unit. In all cases where children moved on to the unit it was found that they had considerable personal problems which only emerged clearly during their stay there.

A withdrawal unit should be separate from a unit for remedial teaching though working closely with it. However, we note that of 108 withdrawal units visited by HMI (DES, 1978d) the staffs of 16 per cent claimed to concentrate mainly on remedial work, 54 per cent on the emotional and social needs of their pupils, and the remaining 30 per cent equally on both. The concentration on remedial English and mathematics was thought to reflect the belief that disruptive behaviour could lead to under-achievement and vice versa.

Schools that have withdrawal units find that when properly staffed they work well. 20 or 30 children may pass through a unit in a year and there are usually no more than 6 to 8 in it at a time. As children's behaviour becomes more normal, the initial outlay is recouped from the results: children, staff, parents and the authority benefit. Both on-site and off-site units cost money to set up. Though the on-site unit costs relatively little it may, at least in part, have to come from the school's allocation. The cost of withdrawal units is discussed by Topping (1983) and Mortimore *et al* (1983).

We suggest that while units are therapeutic for the child they could also help schools to change the system. This would be truly and efficiently preventive (Rabinowitz, 1981b). Teachers seldom know what other schools are doing so periodic joint seminars with schools running similar socio/educational projects would be useful for learning and supportive purposes (DES, 1978d). There is need for experiment and variation.

Chapter 8 — Services and resources available to the school

i   Resources for teachers and children

We talk about maladjusted children but not about
maladjusted adults. Adults are neurotic, psychotic,
silly or criminal but not maladjusted. Yet when we
look around at other people, or at ourselves, we see
far more foolishness and self-defeating behaviour
than we ever see among children.
— Michael Roe (1978).

So far, we have concentrated on the ways in which teachers might help
their pupils, themselves, and one another, by forming a caring, less
hierarchical society in which *each is valued*, where senior teachers help
their junior colleagues to create an atmosphere in which children's
self-esteem can be nurtured, and parents are welcomed and respected.
Teachers do their work *in* society and really they do it *for* society.
However, some teachers feel that to be obliged to have recourse to
agencies outside the school is a stigma on themselves and on the child.
There are many resources from which teachers can get help, set up by
LEAs as part of their educational service, by other statutory departments,
and by parents and voluntary organisations. Innovations elsewhere can
act as a stimulus to local initiatives. Every LEA will have 'advisers' and/or
'inspectors'. Most boroughs will have a child guidance service with
some staff (though probably not enough) with special training and
qualifications. This provides individual help, either with educational
difficulties or with social or psychological problems and can provide
individual, group or family therapy. It can recommend fostering or that
the child be placed in a children's home, at a special day school or at a
school away from home. In most boroughs there will be centres for
children with various kinds of learning difficulties; arrangements either
in the borough or in neighbouring boroughs, to provide special education
for children with handicaps; or small units whose aim is rehabilitation
which may be attached to the child guidance clinic, or to a single or a
small group of schools.

Voluntary bodies such as the Spastics Society, may set up treatment
centres, schools and special play facilities. In the same way holidays for
those with handicaps may be provided by statutory or voluntary agencies
to give the child an experience he would never otherwise have and, also
important, give the parents a few days relief from the unceasing care of a
child with a disability.

A service like education is bound to be costly. In times of economic
stringency expenditure on education is cut. Schools go short of staff and
equipment; in-service training is curtailed; initiative is frustrated; and
school work constrained. HMIs and chief education officers have found

143

that expenditure policies causing staff cuts, and shortage of books and equipment, are depressing morale and efficiency in ordinary schools (DES, 1981, 1982a, 1984d, 1985, 1986; Bedfordshire County Council, 1982). However, in many places implementation of the 1981 Education Act is leading to increased provision for children with special needs in ordinary schools.

The business of rearing and educating children must be seen in a wide context. In 1913 *The Times* wrote 'children . . . are the children of the nation (which) owes them all the care that a mother owes to her own children . . . the nation's children are the nation's opportunity' (1). Halsey (1981) echoed this when he said 'The reproduction of generations is everybody's business.' If we are to develop our children's capacities fully, and to generate a society interested in unselfish values, we should be looking at rather different ways of running many parts of the education service. Halsey makes a powerful argument for systems of self-management in schools and local education, that would provide exciting new ways of educating young people, and would have the added advantage of offering teachers and children democratic participation at many levels.

Support from the employer and other agencies

Teachers have their own problems. Quite a number break down: the fortunate ones have friends or colleagues whom they can use as counsellors and through whose good offices their work load or teaching problems may be lightened, but disruptive children may be too much for them. There is need for a teachers' counselling service. Advisers and inspectors have a counselling role but there are not enough of them. The child guidance service may be helpful in this field (Tizard, 1973), but could be more so. Both teachers and pupils may be helped by the same teacher/counsellor. What is most needed is for teachers to help each other. Unfortunately teaching traditions tend to point away from mutual support which, as the practice of medicine and the law shows, enhances rather than hinders development of the individual worker. The supportive methods of action learning could help teachers here (Appendix 2). Complaints by teachers of lack of support from other agencies have been mentioned. If 'defensible space' (Newman, 1972) is necessary for pupils it is just as much so for teachers, if they are to do their work properly. Falling rolls *could* mean lower pupil/teacher ratios with consequent easing of teacher loads.

Individuals and services with special roles

Education welfare officers

These are at present part of the education service and, as things are, they are probably best located there. However, they are widening the scope of their work to include school and family problems. In some boroughs they receive training in social work and have been attached to social service departments for the purpose of developing better in-service training. Although their interests tend to be in social work, and they are valuable for liaison between schools and other agencies, perhaps because of their descent from the old 'truant officer' they often tend to be the Cinderella of the education service, poorly trained and paid, and not encouraged to make use of their interests and aptitudes. Many EWOs are housewives, or retired professional people or policemen.

Advisers and inspectors

At local authority level these terms are virtually synonymous, some LEAs preferring one, some the other. Whatever they are called their work is similar and they have monitoring, advisory and counselling roles. Though they will have been teachers for many years their experience may not be as wide as could be desired. Nevertheless their main function is to raise standards of work using methods of analysis, coordination, encouragement, education and persuasion. Ideally they should act as compendia of 'good practices'. They may be helpful about the needs and problems of disruptive pupils.

The school doctor

Every school has a doctor attached to it, employed by the local health authority. The doctor visits schools for routine physical examinations and may be called in at any time. There is no reason why teachers should not discuss behaviour problems with the school doctor and some schools make much use of him though there are many in which no teacher communicates with him (FitzHerbert, 1982). Perhaps teachers believe that the doctors are only interested in the physical health of the children, a belief that could be fostered by the doctor's attitude or apparent lack of time. It was originally envisaged that the school doctor should play a primary role in the selection of children who needed special educational treatment (Ministry of Education, 1946).

At routine medical examinations a parent, usually the mother, comes with the child but this tends to happen less often at secondary school age. In the ILEA the head sits in at medical examinations, but other authorities believe that this interferes with confidentiality. Arrangements do not seem to conduce to a parent spontaneously offering information about her child's behaviour or psychological difficulties. School doctors could probably be used to greater effect to help teachers and children with their relationships, and they should take the initiative to improve communications.

Physical and mental health. Some families are singled out early in their careers as likely to provide a disastrous environment for their children who

a) may be inadequately cared for — smelly, ill-kempt and poorly clothed; as a result they are unpopular with peers and staff, and this helps to make them unhappy at school,

b) may often be late coming to school or absent,

c) may fail to attend routine medical inspections and follow-up appointments at clinic, hospital etc; as a result defects in vision, hearing and teeth go uncorrected, contributing to learning difficulties and poor self-image, and exacerbating behaviour disorders.

Drug taking. We have noted (Part I, Chapter 1) that currently many young persons are taking addictive drugs, greatly increased amounts of which (especially heroin and cocaine) are coming into the country. Children are ignorant of their fate if they become addicted to hard drugs. Anyone who has tried to treat drug addicts knows how difficult and unrewarding it is. The NHS will not be able to provide more *treatment* of drug addiction without extra finance. *Prevention* is so very much better in this case but it entails social and political decisions rather than medical ones. However, the school doctor should be well placed to help teachers with children at risk.

The health visitor and school nurse

Most schools have health visitors and school nurses attached to them. Although health visitors are expected to visit schools weekly, they may be too busy to do this. It seems that some secondary schools may not even know who their health visitors are or what their role is (FitzHerbert, 1982). The health visitor's statutory authority in a school is very limited, so that her ability to influence events in the school and persuade teachers to consult her over behavioural problems will depend on the relationships she builds up with the staff. These will be tenuous if her visits are infrequent. She may already know of problems within the families of some of the children. Health visitors would make a greater contribution to schools if there were more of them and if they knew more about adolescent psychology. They could then play a useful role in health education of both pupils and staff. Most schools have regular visits from their school nurse and teachers may have relatively close contact with her.

Careers services

These are part of boroughs' education services. Schools have careers departments in the charge of trained teachers and there are usually several careers offices in a borough. The service usually has strong links with the probation and social services as well as with schools and other agencies concerned with children's welfare and education. There are many publications about careers for school leavers.

In spite of claims by local authorities it is generally acknowledged that the needs of industry are commonly not met by schools though some, through the careers services, are cooperating with local colleges of further education (FE) so that pupils make use of both school and FE facilities. The plan (DES, 1984c) to switch funds from local authorities to the Manpower Services Commission (MSC) for the training of young persons for industrial tasks seems to have been designed to force the issue and has met predictable opposition from local educationists. Unfortunately the MSC's track record with its youth training scheme is little better. When careers departments arrange progressive work experience for pupils many will be able to continue the work after leaving school.

A difficulty for schools is that industry and services are not clear what they want. 'Although the rhetoric of our public life stresses the importance of creativity, originality and a critical approach, these qualities are not in truth valued by most employers who are, not surprisingly, more interested in the conformist virtues' (St John-Brooks, 1985). Outward looking attitudes in schools would start to create the dialogue without which employers will not fully comprehend their own real needs, nor schools learn how to meet them. But most industrial managers have not received the training that would facilitate this process and have tended to move away from nineteenth century entrepreneurial behaviour. The amount and quality of training available for young people in Britain is much less than in other industrialised countries (St. John-Brooks, 1985).

Treatment of the established case

In order to suit the wishes of schools and parents, and the needs of the child, it is necessary to arrange a wide safety net in the form of alternatives for dealing with the variety of problem children in schools. The first step is to refer the child either to the child guidance service or to the psychiatric adviser to special schools and units. These may then recommend one of a number of different courses.

When the home is not providing proper care for the child:

- Boarding school — maintained or non-maintained
- Foster home.

When the home is thought to be satisfactory or likely to become so with help (all ages):

- Day school for maladjusted children
- Facilities on the ordinary school campus or available to the school:

School counsellors

Social adjustment (withdrawal) units — working together

Remedial departments.

- Facilities for 5-8 year olds:

Infant diagnostic class.

- Facilities for 8-12 year olds:

Opportunity class — in ordinary schools

Assessment centre — (Part II, Chapter 8 (iii)).

It takes a long time for disturbed children to establish confident relationships with adults. When a severe breakdown has occurred in a family it may be necessary for a child to go away for some years and return home only for holidays, or in rare cases not at all.

Schools' special facilities have been described and summarized by Topping (1983), and should now include special educational provision as outlined in the Warnock Report (DES, 1978b). School facilities should be complemented by systematic efforts by social workers and counsellors to reduce home stresses. This should be one of the most constructive tasks of social work departments.

Some LEAs have set up multi-disciplinary education support teams to help children, teachers and schools with their problems over disruptive behaviour. An account of one in Tower Hamlets (ILEA) is given by Ellis (1985). A similar unit was set up in a borough elsewhere some years ago but failed partly because its work was not integrated with that of the child guidance clinic.

The senior tutorial centre

These centres are quite separate from withdrawal units. Originally set up to help high school children to catch up if they got behind in basic subjects, they have often been pressed into taking 'difficult' children though they resist taking more than a certain number of the most disturbing. This is a facility for secondary school children with school phobias and learning difficulties, for psychologically withdrawn children, truants, and for those suspended. It does not deal with those who are slow learners because of low intelligence or perceptual difficulties. The pupils attend the centre for 2 or more half day sessions per week, otherwise remaining in the mainstream of their school. Entry tends to be through the child guidance or school psychological services, to avoid being swamped with direct referrals from schools, though teachers' views about children are taken into account. Attendance should cease when the child has made enough progress. This intention is usually carried out with younger children, but those who are nearing the end of their school career may come to spend more and more time in the centre and less or none in their school.

The centre acts as a resource for remedial education in schools and is able to give advice and assistance in this field to teachers, a side of its work that could well be expanded. It needs to be part of a coordinated team if it is to work to the best advantage of pupils and schools, with direct communication between its staff and other teachers. The centre works with the home tutor service. Coordination of the various educational agencies requires more than one local authority adviser/inspector for special education, but this condition is not often met.

The home tutor service

Many authorities arrange home tuition for those children who, for a variety of reasons cannot attend school. Children may be kept at home for months or even years because of physical or mental ill-health. An increasing number of pupils have been excluded from school for unacceptable behaviour, usually over the age of 15 years. Some of these pupils may be subject to care or supervision orders. Home tutors may be married women with teaching experience. Pupils go to a tutor's home if she is unable to leave it. Some home tutors take small groups, some prefer to have one pupil at a time. The relationship is therapeutic and even difficult cases may be helped in a matter of months. Home tutors visit children who for some reason are not attending school. They liaise with other agencies, notably the child guidance service. Home tuition is especially useful for children with feelings of inadequacy, and those who feel rejected (Jay, 1973).

Alternative education

It has to be recognised that whatever pressures are put on some children, they will not attend ordinary schools. Even the practice of the Leeds magistrates (2) failed to get much more than half the truanting pupils back to school. So the free school came into being, often a way-out place run by one or more enthusiasts for 'freedom'; tolerating language, behaviour and dress that would offend most teachers. They are permissive about punctuality and may give only small attention to academic skills. Nevertheless, they often have a high attendance rate. Such a unit might be housed in any available premises — a hut, short-life house, or a basement belonging to a well-wisher; barely adequate in standards of sanitation and hygiene, and short of resources.

Some authorities have tolerated, welcomed or even assisted 'free schools' set up by pioneering innovators. A few have set up their own alternative schools. An example is the London Borough of Hounslow, whose first was so successful that two more were set up. A social worker and an educational psychologist are employed full-time for the three units. It has been a feature of these schools that from the first it was accepted that the children should not go back to ordinary schools. There is some support for the concept of state assistance for alternative schools (Advisory Centre for Education, 1979).

The child guidance service

From small beginnings in 1927 a service acting on La Fontaine's 'plus fait douceur que violence' has grown into a nationwide service regarded as essential by education authorities. Its functions are many and various but they are concentrated on the aim of promoting the health and welfare of children and young persons up to school leaving age whose problems are primarily educational and psychological but may indeed also be physical.

Child guidance services are set up by different authorities in different ways, but the majority are now the responsibility of the local education authority, having a basic team of one or more child psychiatrists (employed by the local health authority), educational psychologists, and social workers (who may be employed by the social services or the education department). These until recently had a specialised training that was of inestimable value in helping them to understand and solve family difficulties (they were called psychiatric social workers). In most clinics the staff is expanded by increasing the number of these core workers and by the addition of remedial teachers and psychotherapists. The director of the CG clinic has in the past often been a child psychiatrist, but is now more likely to be a principal educational psychologist. The organisation of the service and the manner of integration of the educational psychologists into it vary (Chazan, Moore, Williams and Wright, 1974; Child Guidance Special Interest Group, 1975; Sampson, 1980). In some services they are relatively autonomous as part of a school psychological service, referring cases to the psychiatrists and social workers. Sometimes the psychiatrist is relatively detached from the CG team but is available on request. Not all authorities have a CG service; in some it consists of a solitary educational psychologist. For simplicity, in our usage the term child guidance service subsumes the school psychological service.

The CGC, as a multi-disciplinary team, provides valuable training for juniors aspiring to work in child guidance or in allied professions. Clinics see children referred directly by parents, teachers, doctors, social workers, health visitors and any other person who may be concerned about problems affecting the child and his family, which may be anything from mild to severe, from medical to social or educational. Occasionally an older child himself seeks help. It is obligatory for statutory agencies to obtain the parents' consent for referral, and it is customary to notify the family doctor of it. No channel of referral should be blocked. We know of two children referred by a taxi driver in whose cab they had taken refuge, and of one referred by a bishop.

The clinic offers the child and his family diagnosis, advice and treatment, which may be psychotherapy of some sort, remedial teaching or, in a small number of cases, full-time treatment, either in hospital or in a school or hostel catering for maladjusted children. Parental consent is required to treat the child. The child guidance service is being asked to take on additional functions such as advising and helping special schools or units (day or boarding) and (occasionally) ordinary schools, either in a routine way or when they have a problem; and to do more work with families.

Assessment. The CGC will accept referrals of children up to the age of leaving school which may be at 18 or 19 years. The assessment by the child guidance team, more often than not in cooperation with members of other professions, has an important part to play in the management of the disruptive child. Psychological examination may reveal an unsuspectedly low or high level of intelligence, difficulty with basic attainments, or family problems. Help from a remedial teacher may be what the child requires. The term remedial teaching allays parents' anxieties but there is only a fine dividing line between the child guidance clinics' remedial teachers and psychotherapists. Most cases are discussed by the clinic team as a whole. The investigation into the home background of disruptive children almost always reveals a home fraught with difficulties in relationships, some or all of which may respond to he'p from the child guidance service. The process of assessment as it concerns social workers is considered in Part II, Chapter 8 (iii).

Treatment. Provided the family understands that there is a problem and seeks help with it, it may be possible to formulate a worthwhile treatment programme for the child, or for the parents who in some clinics are seen with the child as a group, for 'family therapy'. Multiple problems in the home may preclude a satisfactory contract for treatment. However, a worthwhile, if small, percentage of families are seen regularly and with this help the children may survive even the most disadvantaged family backgrounds.

Support. Many teachers feel that the child guidance service fails them when they look to it for support. In their view it is understaffed, its contacts with schools are infrequent, there may be long delays before a child can be seen, and if it is decided that he should be seen regularly, his appointments may be infrequent. But there are complaints either way. If the child goes daily he 'might as well not come to school at all'; if he goes once a week he always misses the same lesson; if he goes once in six weeks 'what good can that do'? The therapist could reply, but the complaint is seldom made directly to him. The clinic's reports, verbal or written, may appear to the school to be unhelpful. If the child guidance team makes an assessment, teachers would like its findings to be available to them and other members of the school. Most of the work of a CGC is time-consuming and, however good and numerous its staff, it is not surprising that those calling upon it complain that the service they receive is sometimes too little and too late.

Ideally the clinic's report would be followed or replaced by a discussion between teacher(s) and one or more members of the child guidance staff. As things are there is not always time for this. Child guidance workers feel that schools expect too much — the clinic either performs a miracle or it is useless; not only that: teachers expect the clinic to do all the explaining. Many seem to forget that there is the telephone; that if the clinic has not answered a question it may not have been asked. The school does not always feel an obligation to help the CGC. In particular, teachers may not recognise the obligation the clinic is under to respect information given it in confidence.

In theory the child guidance team is in a position to help teachers develop the type of relationship they need to have with a disruptive child and to make other arrangements to give him help and support: for example should he be in a particular group, be given a one-to-one relationship for some part of the day, or be allowed to give up one or more subjects, and so on? Are there features in the school that reinforce rather than extinguish the behaviour complained of? The child guidance staff cannot cover all this ground. Orientation is also a factor: the CGC is essentially child-centred, the school more likely school-centred.

The role of the child psychiatrist. Schools and educational services in general would get more help from the child psychiatrist if all concerned appreciated better his professional role, what he can offer and what is beyond his powers; and if they could bring themselves to think of him as an ordinary human being struggling with a number of conflicting demands, most of which are time-consuming. He is so often seen as a demi-god-demi-devil. To many, if he is shown not to have magical powers, he is a charlatan; to others he is a threat likely, in some unspecified way, to do incalculable damage to those so unfortunate as to fall into his hands. It is only fair to say that these attitudes are changing and it is again largely a matter of communications. Once teacher and psychiatrist get together, they often find that they have a lot of common ground and can exchange ideas to their mutual benefit. A practical problem is that every person or body who calls upon psychiatrists would like their full-time attention. Most psychiatrists hold that their first duty is to the individual patient and their second is to help the CG team deploy its resources in the best possible way. Such time as is left has to be shared between the numerous demands for their services and this does not leave enough to satisfy any one of those wanting their help. Child psychiatrists are in short supply. Some child guidance teams have less than the equivalent of one half-time psychiatrist.

Some teachers need help in managing delicate relationships between child, psychiatrist and other people. An intelligent adolescent orphan at a girls' secondary school had such difficulty with her relationships and her work that her 'O' levels were in jeopardy. Her chief school friend was the daughter of a doctor ('K'). He suggested to the head that she should see a child psychiatrist, initially using the device of arranging some psychological tests. The head called the girl to her room and introduced the business by announcing brusquely 'Dr K thinks you should see a psychiatrist'. She did see one but not surprisingly nothing came of it.

Whatever happened to child psychiatry? 'Yes doctor, I'll do anything you say, so long as I don't have to go near any of those psychiatrists' was the concluding remark of a charming and probably appreciative mother to whom one of us (PGH) had been talking about her son's problems. It is not often put quite so bluntly, since most parents know, as this one did not, to which branch of the medical profession the psychiatrist belongs. But it is not hard to know what they think. Psychiatrists are, by tradition, doctors who deal with the mentally deranged — with patients suffering from a definite clear-cut illness and usually one with bizarre, alarming and threatening manifestations. Many doctors, including some psychiatrists (Curran, 1952; Lewis, 1963) believe that doctors, whatever their specialty, should deal only with recognisable and circumscribed 'diseases' and deplore the tendency of modern psychiatrists to presume to an expertise in human relationships and the ordinary business of life. But most psychiatrists, especially child psychiatrists, are unwilling to narrow their sphere in this way, and the majority of organically oriented physicians and surgeons now accept the existence of psychological and social factors even in patients whose condition may be due primarily to the most clearly demonstrable organic pathology.

These doctors welcome the cooperation of psychiatrists but even when it is accepted that behaviour as well as disease is their affair, the view still tends to persist that it is behaviour of the most extreme and intolerable sort with which they should be concerned. How often when discussing a child, a teacher will say 'I could give you twenty worse than he is'. To this there are two answers — 'Why don't you?' or, more to the point 'I don't want twenty worse, I'd rather have twenty less bad'. No one would say this to a surgeon or a cardiologist. For them the hopeful case is the early one, but there is this regrettable tendency either to reject the help of the psychiatrist altogether or to regard him as the last resort. Then, when he fails, the whole race may be written off as useless. Nevertheless if the psychiatrist is to be engaged early in the case he must be available.

Far too many children have had no help when they move to the secondary school. There, the quiet, the psychologically withdrawn or the neurotic tend to be overlooked because attention is focussed on the disruptive. Serious and persistent disruptive behaviour of teenagers can in its way be as severe a problem as cancer. Cancer will kill the patient seen too late; disruptive behaviour if not treated in time may ruin much of the person's life — say another 50 years; and inflict suffering on other people. If a disruptive young person marries, his/her spouse, their children, and probably the grandchildren will suffer and possibly their children, as well as many outside the family. What he and those affected by him will cost the state in purely financial terms is incalculable and innocent people who cross his path may lose anything from property to limb or life. Surely it is worth an effort to forestall this! Most education authorities will do *something* but they tend to take the short rather than the long view, to resent money spent on their 'bad' or unrewarding pupils, to believe too much in the efficacy of punishment and to shrink from investigating to what extent child 'sinners' are and have been sinned against. It is, of course, wrong to make sweeping statements against the whole educational world. Many primary schools recognize these children as 'wounded' and see it as folly to try to cure one wound by inflicting another. There are many splendid schools for maladjusted children. But most schools complain of such things as poor material conditions, lack of resources, too few staff, too little outside support. We know of only one ordinary secondary school (though there may be many more) where the head insists on equally good conditions for *every* child in his school and has persuaded the LEA to give him an advisory team of psychiatrist, psychologist and psychiatric social worker to investigate the reasons for any difficult behaviour of his pupils and to cooperate with the school in finding ways of reducing it.

It may seem to the psychiatrist (and by psychiatrist we mean the team of which he is a member, often, but by no means always, the leader) that educationsists do not appreciate his valuable role in the delicate and difficult matter of making the decision whether a child should be sent to a boarding school and if so where. This has hitherto implied 'deeming' the child 'maladjusted'. The DES has argued (Education Act, 1976) that since the child will be taught by teachers, then 'educationists' (educational psychologists?) and teachers are better people than psychiatrists to make the decision. But the deaf, the blind, the spastic and most other children with handicaps will be put into the care of teachers, though this is never given as a reason for removing the task of diagnosis and recommendation for placement from the hands of otologists, opthamologists, neurologists, etc. The only explanation we can think of for the DES taking this exceptional view of maladjusted children is that they see them as suffering from a handicap that requires quite different handling from that of physical handicap. The educational psychologist should certainly have a major part in the decision making process about children with learning difficulties, but even here there are factors other than the child's ability or behaviour, to be taken into consideration. If the handicap is a rare one, mere geography — the remoteness of the child's home from any suitable day school — may be the determining factor. If the child is regarded as maladjusted, it is the total environment that has to be assessed. Yet it is precisely this that most educationists have regarded as beyond their purview. If he is taken into care he may go to a good home but a bad or relatively uncaring school. If he is a conforming sort of child he may be discharged from care and returned to the family which imposed the stresses that he was unable to bear, with possibly some new ones added. A good psychiatric team and a good school for maladjusted children, working together, are aware of these subtleties and may realise that a child still needs some degree of protection and some further help in building up his inner strength, however well he may be responding to the environment the school is providing. They will also recognise the help needed by the parents and other members of the family, and do their utmost to see that it is provided (Holman, 1967).

In such ways the psychiatrist and the psychiatric team have certain skills relevant to the diagnosis and treatment of children in difficulties. It may not be easy to get their view accepted by parents and teachers but, in general, the simpler views are derived from an imperfect understanding of children's needs and of what is required for good personality development. Some parents retain a Victorian attitude to ways of teaching and have no idea of modern methods, so they do not accept the need for psychological help.

Psychiatric units. Another source of help for a difficult child and his parents is a day unit in a local psychiatric hospital. Unfortunately, while there are a certain number of inpatient adolescent units, it is not easy to find day centres, especially those that a child may attend part-time while remaining on the books of his own school. The great value of these units is in the high ratio of staff to 'patients' — teachers, psychotherapists, doctors, occupational therapists as well as nurses, social workers and volunteers. Varied forms of therapy are practised in them (Perinpanayagam, 1978).

For the greatest benefit to be derived from psychiatric work with children and families, close liaison is needed not only with schools but also between psychiatric units and social workers. It is difficult to achieve good results if social workers cannot attend case conferences regularly, and if they are insufficiently experienced to make use of all the information available about families. Some special experience is needed to resolve such difficulties. After all psychiatric social workers were not only highly trained and experienced, but they had specialised in the field of psychiatric work.

Future relations between schools and child guidance services

Though many complain that the child guidance service is inadequate teachers are often ignorant or ambivalent about it; others expect too much of it, and are not always prepared to work *with* it. Though child guidance services must necessarily expend much of their effort on the home, no one should belittle the part the school can play in treating these problems, even though the child spends only about 30 hours a week in it, and only in term time. The school is important to a distraught child, not only as a haven from a horrid home, but as providing a chance to learn how to cope with life's problems and opportunities. On this score alone schools deserve all the help they can get from social and child guidance services, but they will get it only if they ask for it. Nevertheless some CG staff do not regard help for schools as a high priority.

It has to be remembered that psychiatrists are *doctors*, trained in general medicine and general and child psychiatry. Hearing virtually nothing about school problems during their training it may be difficult for them to accept the role of entering schools to help *teachers* (not *children*) to cope with behaviour problems. While a social worker or a member of the child guidance team, as 'experts', may be needed to solve a school problem, they are unlikely to be able to do it alone. Their advice and help, though necessary, will seldom be sufficient. Teachers and parents, all perhaps 'experts' in the sense that they have some special relevant knowledge and experience, must also be committed to the problem. Good solutions are most likely to emerge when everyone concerned gets together to examine the matter, so that each may learn with and from the other. The total of learning is greater than the sum of the individual inputs. A day may come when all this is taken for granted, but at present the psychologist and the psychiatrist are not in the school *by right* but by invitation, and the school is free to dispense with their services.

Groups of individuals, as 'institutions', need to learn about themselves — their attitudes and the way they perform — if they are to modify their behaviour. For they may be oppressive, or insufficiently accountable to their clients (those they serve), as well as to their members. In another social institution, a hospital, it was found (Coghill, 1976), when examining the need to 'counsel' nurses, that the largest category of nurses possibly needing help were those in conflict with the hospital. When the problem arose because of the *hospital's* actions it would have been absurd to 'counsel' the *nurses* merely to induce them to conform: this would not influence the cause of the trouble (the institution would learn nothing) and might leave a grievance unredressed. The group of nurses discussing this matter saw that it might at times be the institution that needed 'counselling' and further that the nurse, even the student nurse, in the thick of the experience, might be the appropriate person to do it.

What we badly need is more understanding of what helps people to get on well together, what makes them suspicious and hostile, and what renders them more, or less, willing to accept the need for change in working practices (Abercrombie, 1960; Coghill, 1981) (3). Sutton (1978) emphasizes the potential of the educational psychologist for monitoring and evaluating many of the problems of schools. Public debates about schools' difficulties are conducted without benefit of scientific field-work and analysis, and the issues remain unresolved. The defect, Sutton suggests, lies not in professional incompetence but in the linking of educational psychologists' work to the status of local government officers rather than of scientists, or even help-agents. Monitoring and evaluation of the outcome of professional work would be most effective if it were done jointly between interacting agencies. Initiatives must come from LEAs and professionals.

When limited resources are over-stretched it must be asked whether they could be used to better advantage if used differently. Tizard (1973) observed that 'The average teacher doesn't get much help from any of the special services: contact with the school doctor is often fleeting or nonexistent, remedial teachers often take children out of the class rather than help teachers in the class, educational advisers may visit only infrequently, and the psychiatrist and social worker not at all.' He commented that it was less effective to treat children in a clinic away from their usual environment; and systematic studies of how day-to-day school life affects children were overdue. Tizard thought that the child guidance service was expensive and ineffective. It dealt with very few children and was insensitive to the needs of the community and schools. 'The child guidance service should be centred much more closely on the school.' Others have come to similar conclusions (Cave, 1973; Cline, 1980; Gilham, 1981). Current doubts about the effectiveness of psychotherapy (Prioleau, Murdoch and Brody, 1983; Wilkinson, 1984) have added fuel to the debate on its value in the treatment of children. Rutter (1975) and Kolvin, Nicol, Macmillan, Wolstenholme and Leitch (1981) thought that individual treatment was sometimes useful and it has a place in some cases. It is nonetheless true that children and parents feel that they get sympathy and understanding from the CG service in welcome contrast to what they get from others.

Kolvin and his colleagues (1981) describe an action research project designed to find ways of identifying maladjusted children in ordinary schools, and to evaluate the effectiveness of different kinds of treatment given within the school, using a team of social workers, psychologists and psychiatrists. The social workers did most of the field work. The emphasis was on helping teachers to help their pupils. The team discussed with teachers ways in which the school environment might be altered to help individual children. Evaluation of the project was rigorous. The study showed that professionals other than teachers could do useful work in schools with teachers and children, and could help teachers to use new methods. Greater engagement of child guidance staff to help teachers and for preventive work has been advocated (Hargreaves, 1978; Dessent, 1978; Carter, 1978).

For CG staff to help teachers to develop new relationships with their difficult children would mean close contact with teachers, working on individual cases. If an educational psychologist were able, even for only an hour every week to work alongside teachers, in the school, on the children with behaviour problems, this would give an opportunity for them to examine together the school environment, including school policies and teaching methods so as to assess their part in the child's problems. Such methods of work would give CG staff an opportunity to help teachers to understand and practise some of the new methods of pupil and class management (see Part II, Chapter 6). Forming a 'team'

159

that 'works' is more than merely bringing together different kinds of people. To function optimally means its members learning new ways to work. Some professional people are not used to working with other professions in a close-knit fashion. Teachers have long seen their role as 'on their own in the classroom.' Most social workers have only seldom entered schools. Child guidance staff, who do visit schools relatively frequently, have tended not to do so in the role of a member of a 'school caring team'. We examine team working in more detail in Part IV, Chapter 12.

When child guidance staff work within schools as part of the school team the 'stigma' of referring a child to them is lessened. Furthermore it is easier to secure parental cooperation for psychological or psychiatric intervention if the appropriate specialist is seen as part of the school environment. Communication between child guidance team and school is freer and becomes more rewarding for both. The process of referral is simplified, speeded and made more acceptable to parents who, with teachers and specialists, can work as a team for the welfare of the child (Evans, 1981).

We see teachers, social workers and child guidance staff (usually psychologist or doctor), together with the EWO, and the school counsellor and health visitor if the school has them, as the professional people who should be involved in the treatment of disruptive behaviour. They constitute the basic 'team' within the school, however informally or infrequently they meet, that enables the people concerned to work together — 'alongside' — on individual cases, and offers the possibility of monitoring the performance of the agencies they represent. Not all members of this team would necessarily have to be present at every discussion. We know of secondary schools that have proved the value of regular visits from one of the members of a CG team, to help keep the disruptive child in his own school.

New methods of operation may need more child guidance staff. It should be noted that the recommendations on staffing and training made by the Underwood Committee (Ministry of Education, 1955) 30 years ago, and of the Summerfield working party (DES, 1968) have yet to be fully implemented. If the CG service fulfils its function of helping to manage children whom teachers find difficult, and helps teachers to gain a greater insight into the consequences of their own behaviour, crises might be avoided and teachers have less need of help.

160

The members of the action learning project previously referred to (Part II, Chapter 6) summarized the advantages of the presence of other agencies working in a team in schools:

> There is no doubt that teachers *need* help and support with their disruptive children, and they would be best placed to receive them from the presence in the school of staff from relevant agencies, all working together as a team. Such teams would help to overcome delays in referral of pupils to social services and child guidance that may be due to:
>
> - local school reasons
> - pressure of work and priorities on social workers and CG staff
> - parental blocks about psychiatrists and child guidance staff.
>
> Earlier referral of cases would mean earlier diagnosis; and treatment at a stage when it was easier: these are important elements in prevention.
>
> As members of a team, teachers would be helped to deal with disruptive behaviour themselves, probably a more effective way of tackling the problem than tutorial centres, and cheaper. The disruptive child might then be dealt with in the ordinary school where he belongs.
>
> Teams would be valuable for pastoral care in general and for integrating the work of different professional staff.
>
> Such supportive methods would encourage staff to examine and change the school environment and policies, and would help people to accept changes in practices. Further, working with staff from other agencies would help teachers to:
>
> - modify their attitudes to those agencies
> - learn how to make use of the expertise and facilities they offer
> - learn about and appreciate their work and limitations
> - get help from them more easily
> - give them help over joint problems
> - prevent incorrect uses of information, and labelling.
>
> Closer contact with child guidance staff would offer the opportunity to teachers to learn about methods of pupil and classroom management based on psychological knowledge.

We return to this subject in Part II, Chapter 8 (iii) when we discuss the integration of social workers in the school care team.

161

Notes

1. *The Times*, 7/10/1913. Quoted by Reeves (1979).

2. See Introduction, Note 3.

3. Mrs. Abercrombie stimulated medical students to think freshly about facts and ideas met with in their training, with the implication of the need for some degree of change in their attitudes towards previously held concepts. In Chapter 11 of her book — on suffering change — she comments on the students' reactions to the process of changing:

> Even more frightening than seeing the world change around one, may be seeing change in oneself. 'I can't trust myself now, let alone anyone else', one man said after the first discussion. Sometimes a student may express a strong dislike for the idea that he could change. For instance one wrote, '... I would be sorry if I had changed to any great degree in so short a time. It would show, I think, unstability of former reasoning and I don't think that anyone would like to admit having such a radical fault as that.' In the same vein, some student might jeer at another who demonstrably changed his opinions during discussion, as though this was to be reprehended rather than approved. Here we see the great difficulty facing the teacher. Everything we are trying to teach can be learnt only if it is compatible with the student's present attitude, or if his attitude can be so modified as to incorporate it.

ii A non-medical therapeutic community

Therapeutic communities

At its outset psycotherapy was a one-to-one process in which patients were meant to attend, expecting the therapist's undivided attention, for an hour a day on several days a week. The therapeutic community and family therapy were later developments. Both have rather similar aims. The therapeutic community, first set up by Maxwell Jones (1952, 1962, 1968), seeks to give its members 'an opportunity to achieve the optimal role compatible with their mental state, of becoming aware of new ways of dealing with their own and other people's problems.' Family therapy applies this principle to a group who have been living together and interacting, but also aims to help them see that they are all parties to the problem and can, by seeing it from new standpoints, contribute to its solution. A number of mental hospitals either are, or have wards that are, therapeutic communities. Many schools for maladjusted children, both day and boarding, are therapeutic communities for a given age range, and some go a long way toward incorporating parents as well as children. Cross (1981) describes such a community.

Therapeutic communities are usually thought of as residential. The community lives together and brings out and solves its problems through this complete contact. Family therapy is usually considered as a sessional group meeting, but there is no reason why those who would benefit should not have a combination of the two. An organisation for this purpose exists in several countries in Europe (1) and was introduced into England in 1957 by Grace Goodman and Margaret Gainsford who made their house into a place to which families could come, spend part of their time in their own quarters, and part of the time living as a community, setting aside some hours each day for discussing and solving together problems of social interaction. These were families in which relationships had broken down and the children were in physical or emotional danger, so interaction between parents and children was given high priority in their discussions. In the daytime children over the age of five went to school, and the pre-school children to a nursery on the premises in which the mothers spent an hour or so each day looking after their own child or children under the tactful guidance of a skilled worker. All the adult residents participated in household chores, meal planning and cooking. The average stay was about six months though some families, if a parent got a local job, were able to rent a nearby cottage, and remain indefinitely. Needless to say few people are able to leave their homes for as long as six months, and therefore most families were homeless. They were accepted on the understanding that their costs were defrayed by respective local authorities, who would rehouse them when they were judged ready to leave. This is a resource that might be used to help single parent families whose emotional problems are greatly aggravated by the time they spend in accommodation for the homeless, with their young children going in and out of care.

Special schools for maladjusted children

The Education Act of 1944 placed an obligation on LEAs to 'ascertain' and make provision for handicapped pupils. One category of handicap was *maladjustment*. This condition was vaguely and unsatisfactorily described (see Part I, Chapter 1) but the definition put emphasis on two features: (1) that maladjusted pupils needed 'special educational treatment' and (2) that their 'personal, social and educational' rehabilitation was to be expected. Yet the term tended to be interpreted so as to include mentally ill children for whom hospital treatment was indicated rather than any form of purely educational provision, and others who needed to be away from a damaging family or social environment, though thought to be capable of profiting from a normal school. Many children who might have been included under the heading failed to be identified without very searching investigations such as those of Stott (1966) and Rutter (1967).

Not all those deemed maladjusted are transferred to special schools. DES regulations permit the child guidance team to send them to any school 'recognised as efficient' by the DES. Careful selection and matching of child to school have proved remarkably successful when the child is intelligent and his main need is removal from home. Some, who have even been expelled or indefinitely suspended from secondary schools, have gained university places, even awards. Some, now adults, occupy prominent positions in public life, or one of the professions. Teachers seem to think of maladjustment mainly in terms of antisocial, hostile, anti-authority or violent behaviour. Thus it is that many children who conform to standards of discipline imposed by schools, and who therefore go unnoticed in the classroom, will cause trouble later: for example the Kray brothers and Mary Bell were considered to be normal in the schools they attended. In a school for maladjusted children there are concentrated all the behaviour problems that an ordinary school meets in only a scattering of children. Expertise possessed by the staff of such schools could be helpful to ordinary schools (Dessent, 1984). A survey by Dawson (1980) provided information about these schools.

Special education is expensive, but of all the handicaps maladjustment makes the smallest demands on the budget for day or residential treatment, and unlike physical and mental handicap, it is often of relatively short duration.

Administrative considerations and facilities available

Guidance for ascertainment of maladjustment was given after the 1944 Education Act (Ministry of Education, 1946), but the process of deeming a child to be maladjusted has varied in different authorities. Since the 1981 Education Act the decision whether to recommend that a child attend a special school for maladjusted children is based, as before, on a report from the child guidance team, but the parents now have to see it. Often the process is initiated by the school because of the child's behaviour. In some circumstances social services may start the process. There are, however, a number of difficulties. A suitable place for a maladjusted child may not be found for as long as two years. Some delay is inevitable since to be effective schools for the maladjusted must be small and may be full. Most ordinary day schools will keep a child awaiting a vacancy but, if they cannot tolerate him, he may spend most of the waiting period out of school with perhaps minimal home tuition. The child's state may deteriorate and his education suffer; he may easily commit crime if only out of boredom.

There are several reasons besides bureaucracy and shortage of money for there being no places for maladjusted children when they are wanted. Since the staff in these special schools is small, the loss of one person may deprive the school of 15 per cent of its staff. Skilled or suitable staff are hard to come by and it may take time to secure a replacement, so new admissions may have to be postponed. Each school has its own ideas of what sort of child it can cope with at any given time. For this reason a school may take a child who has not long been on the waiting list and refuse one who has been waiting much longer. The child's referral is often delayed because referral is seen by the ordinary school as an admission of failure. Going to a special school may be regarded as a punishment and not as a chance to receive skilled help; it is only when the child's behaviour has persisted and become insupportable that referral to a special school is considered. By this time the child's state will probably have deteriorated. Parents may object to a particular school, or be reluctant to 'put the child away'. Schools may oppose the recommendation of the CGC if they are unaware of home circumstances that are making the child's life unbearable.

The child

The prime characteristic of children in a special school is that they have poor relationships with virtually everyone. When the child's behaviour is such that he sorely tries adults, there is only one basis for cure: that no matter how the child behaves, the adult continues to care for him. And the care must be offered within a secure predictable environment in which it is expected that some sensible rules will be kept. The relationship between adult and maladjusted child is complex (Laslett, 1976).

Some psychiatrists like to negotiate a place at a special school and only to recommend that a child be deemed maladjusted when the school has agreed to accept him, and the child and his parents accept the school. Then the paper work can be quickly completed. The child may thus be spared a long period of labelling and rejection. However, in the mean-time the child's school has to make provision for him, and this they may not be able to do. If the child has to wait many months for a place at a special school his school may have to suspend him. It can be argued that, by the fact of his disturbing behaviour, whether or not suspended, the child is already labelled. To be called maladjusted is no worse and may encourage the ordinary school to be sympathetic and patient with him and avoid exclusion. The subject deserves further thought, particularly regarding ways of expediting admission of children deemed maladjusted. It has been found, for example, that liaison with a school to which a child will be going may help an ordinary school to cope with a child until a place can be found for him. It may also help the parents to accept the school that will take him.

The education committee of a local authority may want to place a child as 'maladjusted' without parental consent, but most special schools are unwilling to accept a child whose parents are hostile. Since they may regard the school as a place to which their child has been 'put away' parents may be reluctant to accept advice on how to establish better relationships with their children, and so treatment may be thwarted. A type of 'established case' with a very different background is the school refuser whose parents, professing to be desperate at having a child at home all day, actually refer the child themselves. A special school may find that it is not given enough information about the children it receives, nor enough help with their social problems.

The maladjusted child tends to have had an accumulation of deprivations and disadvantages beginning in infancy and being added to as life goes on. In nearly every case an unsatisfactory relationship has developed between child and parent(s). As the mother of such a child said: 'My mother hit me often but *never* did or said anything to show me that she felt any affection for me.' (2) The woman who has had no experience of warm maternal feeling seldom feels or shows maternal warmth herself. The same is true of fathers though they usually play a less important part in the life of their infant child.

Treatment

Basically, the special school is attempting to do two things in the treatment of the children:

1. To establish a belief in the mind of the child that he is worthwhile (generating self-respect).

2. To inspire the confidence that will make him feel he can, through his ability to get along with people, acquire the academic skills that are necessary for a return to the normal school system so that, even if his family is unable to give him the support he needs, he may nevertheless be inspired with the necessary confidence to face a hostile environment, for that is what the ordinary school tends to be to a maladjusted child.

The staff must be prepared to be tested to the extremity without retaliation, and to restrain, divert and face violence with tolerance and explanation. All the activities of the school are geared to the success of the child. Many are designed to encourage sociability, sharing and helping. When a maladjusted child is able to help others, this is the beginning of the road to success.

Schools for maladjusted children are run in different ways (Colley, 1984). Some have a group therapy meeting every morning, including all the children and most of the staff, run in a variety of ways. The manner in which the environment, including school and home, affects the children is discussed. The adults and whenever possible the children join in the discussion. Sometimes children introduce topics of their own. They like to hear of the good things they have done. It is a place where there is discussion about behaviour, and where responsibility is put on the children for the social environment so that the school may function without the imposition of unnecessary restrictions.

Some schools find the children's court a valuable aid. It acts as a safety valve. Four (say) children are elected 'justices' each term by the whole school. When there is a conflict the staff, or the justices of the court, encourage the belligerents to make a complaint to the head. They go into the head's room, sit down and describe what has happened. Very often, by the time the complaint is written down, the heat has gone out of the conflict, and when the complaint comes to court, which meets twice a week under the supervision of the clerk of the court (the head-teacher), the complainant may be friends with the person who caused the trouble and the complaint is cancelled. The court procedure shows that there are two sides to each question. The children are taught the necessity to wait, and they learn how it is possible to resolve conflicts verbally and constructively without using violence. The court is highly respected by staff and pupils. Laslett (1982a) has described how such a court was used to stop bullying in a special school.

Another device to enable children to talk about themselves and discuss each other's behaviour is provided by a system of graded badges. At a weekly meeting attended by staff, chaired by a pupil, children say what badges they feel they deserve and other children say if they should have them or not. Acquiring and retaining badges is dependent on progress in behaviour. This is a method for increasing the children's sense of security. They know they are listened to when they speak.

Maladjusted children often have maladjusted parents and, in order to help the child, teachers in special schools must comprehend the parents' social and psychological problems, and how these affect their relationships with their children. For this the teachers and the school's social workers visit homes and arrange sessions for parents at the school.

Staffing

It is hard to staff special schools. They need a high staff to pupil ratio and the teachers have to be people who find it easy to form close, caring relationships with children in a therapeutic atmosphere. Since unsuitable staff tend to leave and those suitable to be seconded on special courses, or leave for promotion, there may often be one or more unfilled posts. Many teachers in these schools feel that they acquire a stigma in the eyes of their ordinary school colleagues which may cause difficulty in returning to the main stream of teaching. This is unfortunate, but informality and concentration on pastoral care are not regarded as assets by many appointing bodies.

Many special schools have their own social workers (preferably with psychiatric training and experience) who have an intimate knowledge of the school, the children and their homes and, of course, work closely with other specialists such as members of the CG team and the school doctor. While an ordinary school may find it difficult to reach a working agreement with social workers, a special school is likely to have an excellent relationship with its own and other social workers. Special schools tend to vary in their relationships with psychiatrists. Some feel they need more psychiatric help than they can get, or of a kind different from that provided. Not all schools wish for psychotherapy for individual children. Most of them welcome regular visits from psychiatrists who are able to work in the way that best meets the school's needs.

Volunteers from older pupils at secondary schools or students from nearby colleges visiting regularly and getting to know the children are valuable, particularly if they are able to take part in outings and the school camp. In no schools are the interest and presence of the governors more welcomed and supportive to staff and children. Such commitment helps the children in their difficult task of learning to relate to adults.

Outcome

If a principal object of all the caring services for children is to help them to grow into emotionally mature adults, then pupils in special schools might normally be expected to return to ordinary schools as soon as they can cope with life there. The ordinary secondary school finds the younger ones easier to handle and integrate, but children who are nearing the school leaving age may be reluctant to move from the special school in which they have settled down. Moreover, partially or wholly readjusted pupils need experience of responsibility, and it also helps the teachers in special schools to retain such pupils for a time. The pupils themselves may have difficulty in facing the prospect of the ordinary school and some break down (Dyke, 1985). Return to ordinary schools should become less of a problem when, under the 1981 Education Act, ordinary schools have better facilities for coping with children's handicaps.

Ordinary schools may find it difficult to take back children whom they have known as disruptive, and some refuse to do so even if the special school has gone a long way towards rehabilitating the child. Many factors have to be taken into account, but adequate communication and consultation between the two schools are among the most important. Part-time trial transfer should often be the first step and is easier if the ordinary school has a withdrawal unit. This is seldom difficult from special day schools but may not be possible from boarding schools. The break between primary and secondary education at 11 or 12 years adds a further difficulty to trial runs in the ordinary system. The issue of confidence seems important on all sides. The child's self-confidence can in most cases be increased by at first moving part-time to the ordinary school. The ordinary school and the parents have to become confident that the child is going to settle down there. The confidence of the ordinary school staff would be fortified by fuller knowledge of the work of special schools.

Some people object to retaining teenagers in a school with much younger children. So sometimes children have to be moved from a special school solely because of reaching a certain age, just when they are developing stable relationships. Children are apt to see such breaks as further evidence of rejection. Nevertheless some schools have no fixed leaving age. In practice the age of transfer tends to be elastic. There have been few studies of the effects of changing schools on these children.

Notes

1. Aide à toute ditresse (ATD). *Children of our time.* A policy for children — a twenty year programme. ATD Fourth World, 1979.

2. Information from Muriel Colley.

iii The social services and their relationship with schools

> The fact is, the 'failures' of the system are also the
> conscience of the system. A society such as ours
> owes a considerable debt to its casualties. But all
> too soon the 'failure' becomes the 'outcast', for that
> is how society seeks to keep itself free of guilt —
> and avoids paying the debt.
>
> — Tom Hart (1977)

The profession of social work is a comparatively new one although through the centuries there have been people who felt a social obligation or a religious duty to help those in difficulty. Their view of 'need' was somewhat narrow, and giving help was often a form of self-aggrandisement rather than the outcome of real compassion. It took many years to identify true needs and we can hardly yet say we have full knowledge of them all and of the best ways of meeting them.

By the time the Curtis Committee (Home Office, 1946) was set up children had come to be an object of public concern. Wartime evacuation had drawn attention to the deplorable physical and mental state of many children from families in inner cities, and had led child psychiatrists to direct attention to their emotional needs. Their work indicated the many ways in which too much could be demanded of children even to the point of cruelty; or in which they could be deprived of the emotional satisfactions without which they were unable to develop a normal personality. If home conditions were harmful, growing up in an institution was usually worse. Some institutions, set up by religious or other charitable foundations, were already making efforts to train their staff and welcomed the new understanding of personality development. They came to see the interaction between the generations and the likelihood of a cycle of deprivation (disadvantage) if those with the necessary knowledge did not intervene to prevent it or, when it had been set up, to attempt to break it.

Implementing recommendations of the Curtis Committee did much to get rid of abuses in child care but still left many services isolated and uncoordinated. Almost before the Children's Departments had had time to establish themselves it was realised that a family might have more than one problem, indeed so many as almost to justify the complaint that there were as many workers knocking on the door as there were hours in the day. Understandably families did not like this but some have thought that Seebohm's recommendations (Home Office, 1968) swung too far in the opposite direction, seemingly proposing: one social worker, one training; one family, one social worker. A child deprived of normal home care, an alcoholic father, a depressive mother, a problem of rent arrears or overcrowding, or several troubles which up till then had been the concern of separate and specialised departments, were to be understood and solved by one single worker, though this is not altogether a fair interpretation of Seebohm's intentions. The Committee was concerned that there should be one door on which people with problems relevant to the personal social services should knock and that they should not have to go to several different offices and see several different people to sort out all the problems within a family. However, they might deal with more than one person in one office. Different authorities have interpreted Seebohm's intentions in different ways, but most have modified their practices in the light of experience and reintroduced a degree of specialization for some social workers. The social workers were themselves the first to point out that if two people, for example spouses, were at daggers drawn they were unlikely to be able to take the same person as confidant. It is certainly improbable that one person, especially if lacking in any specialized training, will be equally good in all spheres. A person with a specific gift for persuading a reluctant patient to accept the help of a mental hospital, may have little understanding of the needs of a baby or how to assess adoptive parents.

One of the roles we tacitly impose on social workers is that of scapegoat. It is comforting to have someone to blame. With hindsight it is easy to see that what the social worker did, he ought not to have done. It may be his own negligence or it may be the fault of the system, but the public's (certainly the media's) criticism and hostility tend to be directed to the individual. In this chapter, we in the same way, do not always distinguish the object of our criticism. This, however, is not to be taken as detracting from our admiration for the members of this profession in which decision-making is their most frequent and difficult activity, and who perform tasks in our society that before the advent of social services as a profession were not performed by anyone. Our object is certainly not to undermine the confidence of social workers whose departments are usually under-staffed for the burdens thrust upon them. Some indeed are so underfunded that many cases requiring urgent social work, even children at risk of non-accidental injury, are unallocated.

Social workers may wryly regard as a tribute the manner in which other people — clients and professionals, lean upon them for support and help. One of our main purposes in this book is to advocate that when two or more professionals are interested in the outcome of a decision, the making of it should not be in the hands of only one of them, and that it is likely to be a better decision for having been taken, if not jointly, at least after thorough joint consideration.

The local authority social services department is the largest agency outside the education and health services that is available to support schools, pupils and parents. However, the Barclay Report (National Institute for Social Work, 1982) has virtually nothing to say about the relevance of social work to schools, though it mentions some of the interactions between social services and other agencies. It speaks of the unrealistic expectations that many people, including teachers, have of social workers. It mentions the general need for preventive social work, in addition to work arising from statutory obligations and in reaction to crises. Since they are not part of the education service, social services are under no obligation to carry out the wishes of any part of it, and schools complain that social workers often make unilateral decisions about children without consulting their teachers. On the other hand, social workers are a great support to families and aim to act in their best interests and those of the child. When they make mistakes it may often be through taking too narrow a view of the problem and failing to understand the part a caring school plays in the life of a disadvantaged child.

A case involving one of us (PGH) illustrates the dangers of poor communications between agencies. Two siblings aged 5 and 4 were committed to care in a nearby residential nursery on the grounds that they were at risk if left with their unsupported mother. Later the children were placed at a residential school for maladjusted children without consultation with either the mother or the day school and it was some time before the mother was told where they were. She was 'seriously psychologically disturbed' to begin with but this was not so when the children were sent to the special school. The effect upon the mother, already in difficulties, may be readily imagined. Under the Health and Social Services and Social Security Adjudications Act 1983 parents are given the right of appeal to a court over problems of access to children in care. Failure of communication, exemplified in the cases of Janice Beckford and Tyra Henry, is the root of much evil in making decisions about children's welfare. Teachers might learn from social workers as much as social workers could learn from teachers — if only they could make time to get together.

Functions of the social services department

The following are its principal functions:

1. Casework service (1).

2. Statutory duties as required by the various Children Acts, Mental Health Acts, etc., for example reception into care, assumption of parental rights, admission to mental hospital (voluntarily or otherwise), court work.

3. Responsibility for specific services, for example meals on wheels, home helps, telephones and holidays for clients.

4. Services for the chronically sick and disabled provided, for example, by occupational therapists; work with the mentally ill and mentally handicapped; teachers for the blind; specialist day centres; and community development to enable people to articulate their needs and to help themselves.

5. The provision of residential accommodation for a large number of different kinds of people.

Thus social services have to take the initiative in dealing with social and legal matters, and people go to them for help. With clients' high and confused expectations that social work will provide a solution to their problems, quick results may be unrealistically demanded. Social workers should less often be the 'last resort'. Most teachers, indeed most people, have little idea of the variety and load of work of social workers. Schools and social workers seldom fully comprehend each other's roles in dealing with difficult children. The work load of social workers is heavy. They are concerned with many problems that may well be more urgent than those of schools, even matters of life and death such as baby battering or dangerously violent behaviour. They receive many reports of suspicion of damage to children that take time to investigate. Social workers have matters of common concern with health visitors and the police juvenile bureau, and they are expected to carry out the instructions of the courts, among other things supervision orders and intermediate treatment. All this has to be done in a working week of nominally 36 hours. Nevertheless, a school has a statutory obligation to keep the child and so may reasonably expect some liaison with the social services, even if only to find out what they can and cannot do. Relationships may be unbalanced by members of other professions too readily attempting to off-load problems on social workers, by not treating them as equals, or by expecting too much of them.

Career structure

Social workers in their first post are either unqualified, or, if qualified, usually fresh from their training course. Promotion comes relatively soon. In the past this tended to take the social worker away from case-work just as he became knowledgeable about his job. He would then largely lose contact with clients. This is a problem that besets nursing, the civil service and the law (judges), though usually only after a long period of practical work with clients. Social service departments soon became aware of criticisms of their structure (2) and sought remedies. The situation changed with the restructuring of salaries in 1979 which provided a form of career development for social workers. Although professional development has followed different paths in different authorities all are now tending to adopt the principle of enabling the experienced and able social worker to improve income and status without necessarily giving up the practice of social work with clients. So now there is a trend for senior management to be social work trained, and middle management to be less removed from the client.

The excessive mobility of staff that characterized most social service departments in their early years has now abated. The organisation of social workers into teams, each with a senior, ensures a greater measure of continuity of concern for individual cases than one may always see in other professions, for example in medicine. It is difficult for a relatively inexperienced worker to know where to draw the line between taking a decision himself and when to consult someone more senior. It is our contention that the person consulted might appropriately be a member of another profession and not necessarily a senior social worker. Failures in communication between social services and other appropriate agencies cannot all be put down to social workers.

Social work

Social workers should take more account of the fact that a problem family often sends a problem child to school. Liaison between social services and primary schools is essential and must surely rest mainly with the social worker. However, social workers seldom find opportunity for liaison with other agencies. As a result community care, an aim of contemporary social policy, although embodied in legislation, is not often found in action and this limits preventive and therapeutic work with the disruptive child.

The social worker's load

Lack of practical knowledge in social workers at the start of their career, when they commonly do much of the casework, must affect the volume of work and the number of clients that the social services department can deal with. Problems with low priority may never be reached. Social workers have to make recommendations about children's safety that may constrain parents' freedom. They have day-to-day care of families who abuse their children and it is they who initiate action to take a child from his family, though a child may be compulsorily removed only after a place of safety order, or an interim care order, have been obtained from a court. Recommendations by social workers have usually to be sanctioned by the director of social services or his assistant director. Such procedures can never be dealt with by a system of foolproof rules, and mistaken decisions will inevitably occur. This kind of work has been considered by social workers to be more important than dealing with school problems, a position reinforced by the public's readiness to blame social workers when children are neglected or harmed by their parents.

The very young profession of social work is practised in a society that is itself confused about values to be placed on human life. The social worker bears the final responsibility in many issues of child injury and human liberty. It may be that social workers have too much power. The Association of Directors of Social Services is pressing for a review of the powers of social workers but is anxious to avoid piecemeal *ad hoc* changes which have been such a feature of parliamentary legislation in the last 15 years. The emergence of bodies such as the Family Rights Group and the Children's Legal Centre has been prompted by a desire to control social workers' powers. It would be counter-productive, however, if such bodies, in their just pursuits, succeeded in emasculating social service departments to the point where they could not protect persons at risk.

Social services departments' structure and organisation: future role of social work

Social workers should be able to relate theory to practice according to the situation they find. Traditionally they have placed disruptive children in the framework of individual and family social pathology. The adequacy of this perspective has been questioned in many sociological studies and social workers are now examining the effect on the individual of social policies and the environment. A social class differential in mental and physical health has been observed for at least 50 years, and remains (Morris, 1979; DHSS, 1980b; Smith, 1985). The strike of social workers in 1979 added impetus to the reappraisal of social work. It may well be that some of the work done by social workers should be done by others, even volunteers. However, experience in hospital medicine and the law has shown that social workers can establish a valuable liaison role between professions and caring agencies that is not readily undertaken by anyone else.

If what is done for hospitals were done for schools, then social workers' first duty would be to the schools to which they were assigned — very much as medical and psychiatric social workers 'belong' to the child guidance clinic or appropriate hospital department — and work in a team with an educational psychologist or a doctor. Generic social workers belong to the social services department and work under a leader who may assign them to some job he may consider urgent while they are in the midst of dealing with a problem the school regards as urgent. The Mental Health Course (training for psychiatric social work) provided a group of workers to whom the welfare of the child was paramount and who were not expected to undertake other types of social work. It was a mistake to abolish it in the belief that a 'generic training' would fit all social workers for this specialised task.

The Children and Young Persons Act 1969

The Association of Directors of Social Services (1985) has expressed dissatisfaction with the working of this Act. It would prefer methods that separated judicial proceedings from welfare considerations, at present combined in the Act which, though based on the thinking of the 1960s, operates within a framework of a magisterial system introduced in the twelfth century. The Act has made preventive work more difficult in that social services now have to prove to magistrates that a child has been harmed before he can be taken into care.

If magistrates make a care order it is assumed that the child should be removed from his home unless they make it plain that they want the social services to exercise supervision (usually with the power to remove the child immediately should the circumstances warrant it). Social services accept that if they are not going to remove the child from home when a care order is made, they should tell the magistrates and give their reasons. If the magistrates believe that a supervision order would be the right answer, but it cannot be implemented, social services should say so in their report to the court.

The 1969 Act has been criticised because resources were not made available to bring it into effective operation, and because it was implemented, so far as it was implemented at all, the wrong way round with approved school orders done away with before replacements for those schools were available. The making of residential care orders has probably not improved the working of the Act since they did not make one single additional bed available in a residential establishment. To empower magistrates to make residential care orders at a time when there was a shortage of suitable accommodation for young offenders, would mean either that the young people placed on these orders would sleep on mattresses on the floor and residential staff would leave in disgust, or alternatively, as the newly committed children were pushed into the establishment at one end, those who had not yet had long enough to benefit from residential care would be pushed out to make way for them. Social workers are concerned that the 1969 Act has not been fully brought into use, and that there is now a 1975 Act concerned mainly with adoption, only fully implemented in 1984. After the Criminal Justice Act 1982, and the Health and Social Services and Social Security Adjudications Act 1983, what is really needed now, as we understand the Association of Directors of Social Services has recommended, is a look at the whole situation of children in care. The legislation should be tidied up and the resources provided to implement the final result. Our legislators could get some good ideas from listening to people who have been in care, now well organised in NAYPIC.

The adversarial method of procedure in the juvenile court does not lend itself to establishing the reality of a family situation, or the principle of the welfare of the child being the primary consideration. It tends to impede cooperative action by the agencies concerned with the young person's behaviour (Association of Directors of Social Services, 1985).

Approaches to the problem and relations with schools

Referrals of disruptive children are often made at a crisis point and only with regard to one facet of the total situation, for example the classroom. Although social workers often seem to be more concerned for the families than for the child or his teachers (Part I, Chapter 2) it appears that some are not sufficiently concerned with mothers. However, society is unclear what it wants from social workers. If the child stays at home and is injured they are wrong. If the child is removed before he is injured, they are also wrong. But some children are removed for other reasons than suspected imminent injury and some social workers seem unaware of the potential of 'good enough' mums or of the value to the child of a 'good enough' school.

Social workers consider children's problems in the context of their families' economic and environmental state. Other elements are: the geographical isolation of families; mobility and educational opportunity; generation and culture gaps between parents and children; loss of communication within the family; and children's higher material and job expectations. All these factors aggravate the effects of inappropriate child rearing and have a significant impact on the way a child functions in society. Some things could be put right by legislation provided it was implemented and funds voted for it. However, many are external to the family and many people survive adverse conditions. It is the lack, inadequacy or failure of relationships within the family that principally affect the nature of the child's personality development, and hence his capacity to withstand adverse extraneous conditions.

Social workers' priorities then are different from those of schools. They tend, understandably enough, to concentrate on child and wife battering for example, rather than on emotionally deprived infants who later become headaches to secondary schools, even though they may also become delinquents, or child or wife abusers. Social workers tend to see schools as not coping as they should with their problems. The main contentions occur with secondary school teachers. Relations with primary schools are somewhat easier because they appear to have fewer incidents arousing anxiety, though there may in fact be more than are disclosed, and we emphasize the value of prevention at junior level.

Teachers may resent a social worker's belief that his understanding of a problem is better than that of the teacher. Perhaps teachers mean that social workers do not find disruptive children difficult enough. The social worker, like the doctor, has only intermittent contact with the child. The teacher, like the nurse and her patient, cannot 'walk away' from him, though the social worker sees the teacher doing just that by exclusion of difficult children from school, sometimes then to be cared for by residential social workers. Different approaches and methods of teachers and social workers may cause misunderstanding. For example under a court supervision order the social worker's task is to 'advise and befriend' and this gives him a relationship with the child different from the teacher's. In the broad view that social workers feel they must take of the child's situation, of the home, and of society, the child might be found to be reasonably happy and not troublesome at home, although disruptive at school.

Attempts to remove a troublesome child may be made without first trying alternative methods, say exclusion or referral to the CG service. In most cases the school would really be asking the social services to do something far more fundamental — to remove the child from his *home* and thereby from the school. Even when the social worker's knowledge of the total family situation suggests such a course, he is always in a dilemma. On the one hand if a court can be convinced that a child has been harmed a care order safeguards him from further injury and the social worker from blame. On the other, going into care is often in itself injurious to the child and provides no real solution to the problem. It is, incidentally, very expensive. If what is needed is help or treatment for the parent(s) it may be possible to provide these, if at all, only after considerable expenditure of the social worker's time and a long waiting period for the client. During this time the state of the child may deteriorate and the social worker's anxiety increase. Schools certainly resent lack of help from social workers; social workers feel embarrassed when explaining how little they can legally do, to a head desperate for an answer to a problem he finds intolerable.

There are other points of contention. Frequent changes of social workers unsettle schools and children. Social workers are irritated by schools that hold on until they can no longer tolerate a child's behaviour. There may then be no easy way of solving the problem. Social workers believe that sometimes a teacher who has wanted to refer a pupil, has been baulked by the head. Schools sometimes hide their difficulties, or one member of staff may not know what another is doing. A head assured social workers that a boy had never been in trouble. In fact he had hardly ever attended an art class because he was put to doing his maths work over again in that period. Another head complained that the social work report about a child was different from the school's and that the social worker did not see the boy, whereas the school had him all the time. The boy's housemaster, however, stated that the social work report was accurate and that the head had written the school report without reference to his staff. Social services and schools work under pressure and neither may be aware of the burdens carried by the other: teachers may grumble that social workers do not respond promptly to their appeals for help; social workers may protest that teachers exaggerate the urgency of their demands. Both parties are affected by insufficient financial resources, which have decreased as demands have increased.

Schools complain that early signs of behaviour disorder may first occur outside school, but that schools are not told of them. The children posing the practical problem of disruption in a high school, the spark that brought the DBIS group into being, were known to social workers who had given the school very little information about them (see Introduction). Social workers say that they are reluctant to 'inform' on a child who is troublesome outside the school. He might give no cause for complaint in school, but become labelled as a troublemaker as a result of what was said about him. Social workers have expressed the view that teachers should try to rise above the inhibiting effects of the authoritarian nature of school organisation. If schools expect care from social services they should be prepared to bat on the same wicket. There is no conflict of *interest* between schools and social workers. They are all concerned with the same child. Earlier referral would allow the matter to be handled at a less emotive level, but teachers and social workers, being each preoccupied with their own priorities find it is not easy to arrange occasions when they can talk together. In hospitals doctors, by working with (medical) social workers, have learned much about social factors in illness which helps them to treat the patient as a whole person. Social workers could help teachers in ordinary schools to gain insight into the relevant social elements of their pupils' problems, as they do for teachers in special schools, and they can usually achieve more in the early case.

Many teachers' difficulties with disruptive children could be eased by having a social worker (as well as an educational psychologist) attached to the school. He or she would help in the early diagnosis and management of behaviour difficulties, and in the separation of minor from major problems, giving more time for serious cases. There are ordinary schools that solve their difficulties through close working arrangements with social workers and other agencies (3). Cheshire experimented with a system in which social work support teams consisting of social worker, teacher/counsellor and EWO were appointed to individual schools. The results were promising but a number of problems of communication remained to be overcome (Derrick, 1977). The London Borough of Haringey appoints social workers to work inside schools and they are able to know the child in the school context (4). The study by Kolvin *et al* (1981) showed that even with a limited amount of contact teachers found social workers helped them to deal better with difficult pupils. Good relationships with social services will promote prompt help for schools.

For all this the social worker would need a firm base in the school life, however little time he worked there, with recognition as a professional colleague and a room for records and interviewing. If teachers viewed the disruptive child more in the context of the community, and social workers spent even a little time in schools, these two perspectives might interact to prevent unrealistic demands upon social workers, and social workers might understand better schools' difficulties. Problems of working in an interdisciplinary team could surely be resolved as they are in hospitals where social workers join integrated ward teams while preserving their professional identity.

We have discussed the need for educational psychologists to work in schools, as part of a team and we believe that if teachers were to ask social workers to join them in the school to work together on problems with children they would welcome the opportunity to do so. When this was tried at two schools on an experimental basis as a result of suggestions from the action learning set (Part II, Chapter 6), everyone found the arrangement helpful. The advantages of working in a team in the school have been summarised in Part II, Chapter 8 (i). It looks as if the principal role of child guidance staff in schools would be in the understanding (diagnosis) of school problems, and helping schools and educationists to change and adapt. Social workers on the other hand would probably be the best help for teachers with individual children. In the absence of social workers in schools, if there were a social work agency specifically to deal with social problems of school children, teachers would know whom to contact. Social workers appointed to liaise between schools and courts would also help. Clearly communications between teachers and social workers could be improved with benefit to social services, the schools, the children and parents.

Supervision orders

The role of the social worker in supervision orders, a non-custodial way of dealing with delinquency, should be used to the full. Supervision orders are made by magistrates when it is thought that a child or his family needs active help and support to prevent him becoming, or continuing to be, delinquent. The probation service usually carries out these orders for 15 and 16 year olds. If the supervision order is given a low priority by social workers they are missing an opportunity to help the child in the community, to prevent him getting into further trouble so that custodial or care orders have to be considered. Teachers are critical of the inefficiency of supervision orders as currently often administered. Contact between child and social worker may be quite inadequate. In one case a twelve year old child of a single mother who was mentally ill, when asked if his social worker would help with a problem, replied that he had not seen her for eleven months.

The child in care

Residential care provided by the social services

We have discussed some of the problems associated with taking children away from their parents, and have mentioned the ill-effects of residential care (Part I, Chapter 3). As a preventive measure long-term residential care should be avoided if possible. Any form of residential care is inappropriate for many adolescents with problems, though not for all. The number of children in care has dropped appreciably over the last few years. As a consequence of this, of increased boarding out, and clearer policies on adoption and rehabilitation, the proportion of children in residential care has also dropped. Nevertheless, in a crisis, removal of a child to a residential home may be the essential preliminary to fuller assessment of needs and remedies. Some children have to be segregated from society because society cannot tolerate their behaviour. For others a good residential establishment is, as some ordinary schools are, a refuge from a damaging environment. A few places prove to be the haven the adolescent needs and are successful in helping him to lose his wish to be revenged on the adult world. They may cater for boarders or day pupils, and are valuable training establishments for staff and students. It is easier to bring about an almost magical change of personality in younger children, but some people achieve it with adolescents whether the establishment be hospital, school, post-school community or community home. The teenager, just as much as the primary school child, needs to know that he is loved and valued. Only then can he learn to love. Unfortunately many residential establishments give no more than custodial care, ultimately releasing an embittered young person who has learnt merely how to be a successful delinquent.

It would help to improve the calibre of residential care staff if they were trained and paid adequately. It is essential to attract to this work people who, at the least, will not inflict unauthorised violence on their charges or sexually abuse them — and who can manage them without using corporal punishment. (See Part III.)

Assessment

Assessment of the need for taking a child into care is often a complex process that may have to be spread over a period of time. It should be done at home if possible, as it usually is, for that is the child's natural milieu (Hoghughi, Dobson, Lyons, Muckley and Swainston, 1980). This helps to reduce the institutionalisation of children, and its cost. In East Sussex and in some other authorities workers in residential homes visit the children's own homes and work as a team with field workers, though this requires adequate trained staff. Assessment in a residential centre is necessary when the risk to the child at home is too great, if his home has collapsed, or if there is danger to the community from leaving him at large. Children of 14 and over who are known to be violent probably need to go to a regional residential centre. Staff can establish a relationship with a young person who is being assessed or is in the early stages of training only if they are in close contact with him. No teenager should, however, be assessed in a remand centre unless an unruly certificate has been issued by a social services department and these should be used sparingly. Currently the categories of children who can be dealt with in prison establishments (i.e., remand centres) are fast diminishing and it will not be long before no young person under 17 charged with any but the most horrendous offence will go into these centres. If there is no local assessment centre boys of 15-16 may find their way to a regional assessment centre (the old remand homes), possibly some distance away. Some of these have secure accommodation but a juvenile court order is needed for a child to stay in one normally for more than 72 hours.

Sometimes therefore a child may be assessed at home, sometimes in day care at an assessment centre, sometimes as a resident there, and rarely under more secure conditions. Assessment in fact includes two processes – firstly determining what are the child's special needs, and secondly finding how best to provide for them. The time taken for assessment will vary, the second part of the process being the more time consuming. The process of assessment has been examined by MIND (1975), and described in detail by Hoghughi *et al* (1980). It may be very expensive (see Introduction). Taylor *et al* (1979) have criticized the very inadequate process of 'assessment' provided by many assessment centres and the inordinate time some children stay in them (13 per cent over six months), often for purely custodial purposes.

Intermediate treatment

Intermediate treatment (IT) is one of the innovations introduced by the 1969 Children and Young Persons Act. The methods of treating disturbing children are changing and developing, and we need a wide variety of treatments; a reflection of advances in our knowledge of the subject and the complexity of the problem. The basis upon which IT works is that community resources, often underused, should be part of intermediate provision for a child between being at home in his own environment on supervision and being put on a care order that almost always uproots him. It is an alternative to custodial sentences and tries to stop the child treading a delinquent path. It provides a means to help the child to behave in a manner less damaging to himself and others, and to integrate him into society.

With the growing acceptance of the concept that the offender has suffered from excessive stresses in the past and is likely to be exposed to them in the future, has come a belief that an essential element of treatment is one or more activities likely to build up his self-esteem, to help him to lose or diminish the hostile and anti-social feelings which have actuated his behaviour and to gain satisfaction from giving service to others.

Organisation. While there needs to be a movement away from long-term residential provision for delinquent adolescents to non-residential local forms of IT, to achieve the desired results IT must be well organised and adequately financed (Leissner, Powley and Evans, 1977). Under the Criminal Justice Act 1982 local authorities now have a statutory duty to consult with other interested parties locally and to produce and publish schemes for IT. Government has made some money available to voluntary organisations to develop such schemes.

All IT schemes have to be agreed with the young person concerned. In court cases a magistrate must agree to an IT order being made with the supervision order. Normally it is made on a recommendation in the social enquiry report. To satisfy the Education Acts an educational input should be provided. Some authorities use IT to get truants back into school and many have recruited teachers to their IT staffs. Youth clubs can be used in the evenings. IT is more effective if the children's families can be incorporated. The element of discipline would be a requirement to complete a certain number of hours in IT, if possible in activities the child might like or benefit from. There is evidence that young people need, and will use, counselling services ('drop-in centres'), and these should be available, though not necessarily as part of the IT service. It may be noted that young persons of 16 and over, who are still at school, are a group under-represented in the CGC intake.

The social work group process in intermediate treatment. IT helps children who have difficulties in communicating with adults in authority.

189

The group process allows children to settle into a group of their peers without feeling as threatened as some do in a one-to-one relationship. Such measures are helpful when punishment has been counterproductive. Some children respond to group therapy and some to one-to-one relationships. From a relatively non-threatening start they are able to develop more meaningful relationships with a social worker and gradually become able to discuss their anxieties and difficulties. The social worker responds by relating to the positive attributes of the child. He finds that the child usually has a good perception of his own problem which may not be understood by people who do not listen to what he has to say.

Operation. Children may be referred for IT from a variety of sources, including courts, probation services and schools; and it may be provided for children in care who are below the age of criminal responsibility. Children and adolescents who come before the juvenile courts can be roughly divided into those few who are able to make good inter-personal relationships at a feeling level, those who show evidence of having some capacity for doing so, and those who seem unlikely to be able to do so. The first group almost always does well under supervision. The second and third groups need something more and can be recommended for IT as well as supervision. The third group will probably contain the most persistent offenders and may benefit least from an IT order. However, in many cases this should be tried before the upheaval of a residential care order.

Almost any project designed to engage young people in relationships with their peers and a responsible trained adult will qualify. Various possibilities may be considered:

a. Groups and projects run by an IT officer.

b. Detached youth workers.

c. Suitable voluntary work: juvenile community service orders are now available for young people aged 16 and above, operated by the probation service.

d. Alternatives to school for children who refuse to attend ordinary school.

e. Youth clubs: special arrangements would be needed so as not to compromise the non-authoritarian approach of the youth service.

The distinctive feature of IT is that it combines some disciplinary element, even if no more than the loss of a few hours of liberty, with elements that 'have regard to the young person's welfare'. Coupled with a supervision order IT can achieve its aims.

In summary IT (5) will mostly include:

1. Some element of mild discipline.

2. Some activities pleasurable and useful to the young person, with an accent on satisfaction to be gained from giving service.

3. Some provision for discussion of his problems and feelings either one-to-one with a qualified adult, or in a group of some sort.

Any or all may take place at, or be based on, a day centre or may have as a condition residence away from home. The child may spend up to 30 days in it in any one year, broken into periods from a few hours to several weeks; or he may go away from home for weekends, or whole weeks at a time. Alternatively a child may spend up to 90 days at one time in residence at some appropriate centre. These arrangements may be voluntarily extended, but they are the maxima that can be imposed. Return to the conditions in which hostile feelings and anti-social behaviour have developed, with likelihood of relapse, is one of the weak points of short-term residential care.

Many schemes try to work closely with parents both to help them and to gain their cooperation (Pearce and Ward, 1979). Others involve professionals and voluntary bodies in the community (6).

Some conclusions

1. Owing to the present shortage of resources and staff, social workers can give little attention to preventive work since they are obliged to give priority to crises. While new legislation may in the long run be the means of effecting economies, the social worker's immediate reaction may be frustration when, as is usual, there is a shortfall in resources to implement it.

2. It hinders preventive work when schools do not refer difficult children to social services (and other agencies) early in the development of their problems.

3. It will be difficult for social services to give greater help to schools until teachers and social workers understand better their complex attitudes to each other, and their respective roles and powers in dealing with difficult children. For this some time will have to be found for talking and working together. Insight as to how communications between these and other agencies such as the child guidance service might be developed and maintained, has been gained as the result of the action learning project already described.

4. When resources are insufficient to satisfy apparent needs two things may be done. The unsatisfied agents or agencies can discuss with those supplying the service what seems to be lacking so that the problem is more clearly defined: this is the start of the process of 'accountability' between agencies discussed in Part IV, Chapter 12. Secondly, to satisfy aims of agreed high priority, agencies can examine by a process of audit, as objectively and jointly as professional people should be able to do, how it might be possible to reorganise their work so as to make resources available for new tasks.

5. A part-time social worker should be permanently attached to every school to work with disruptive children and their teachers. These social workers would be part of the social services department for purposes of supervision, professional development and ultimate responsibility. Although outposted from their social work department they would nevertheless be an integral member of a team based either on the home, the school or both. For such liaison to work effectively schools would have to ensure close contact between social worker, classroom teachers and senior school staff. They should work in a team in the school with teachers, child psychologist, EWO and school counsellor — the 'essential basic team' for dealing with children's and teachers' problems (Part II, Chapter 8 (i)).

6. If social workers could work more closely with specialist voluntary agencies, clients' friends and neighbours, and caring community groups (National Institute for Social Work, 1982), it might well be that social work would be more effective, and more satisfying to those performing it.

Notes

1. There appears to be no universally accepted definition of casework. To some it appears to be little more than a form of counselling. Dame Eileen Younghusband (1968) has stated: 'Casework is a continuous professional relationship, a process of dynamic interaction between worker and client, consciously used for social treatment purposes, defined by a study of the particular person in his situation, the problems which most concern him and the ways in which he could be helped to meet these by the use of his own and the community's resources.'

   There are perceptive accounts of casework in *Good enough parenting*, a report (study 1) of a group on *Work with children and young people and implications for social work education*, published by the Central Council for Education and Training in Social Work (1978).

   In the Barclay Report (National Institute for Social Work, 1982) it is stated (p xiv): 'By *counselling* we mean the process (which has often been known as "social casework") of direct communication and interaction between clients and social workers, through which clients are helped to change, or to tolerate, some aspects of themselves or of their environment.'

2. Hardy J. (of the Department of Government, Brunel University) (letter) in *Guardian* 16/1/1979 — 'The Seebohm Committee paid very little attention to the structure appropriate for the provision of personal social services . . . the monolithic and hierarchical structure of local government seemed to be automatically accepted as the only pattern. Many people would say that the structure has not worked. Complex and delicate jobs are being undertaken by untrained and inexperienced workers . . . (There) is a waste of . . . many people coming into social work, who could be far better utilised in a simpler, smaller, . . . more human structure — maybe not even in local government. If the structure of social work organisations were to be examined now in relation to the task, this would be for the *first* time since the Curtis Report . . .'

3. *Preventive social work in primary schools: Coventry.* Centre for Information and Advice in Educational Disadvantage, undated.

4. Johnston S. School-based social workers in Haringey. *Ibid*, undated.

5. Further information may be obtained from the Intermediate Treatment Information Service at the National Youth Bureau, 17 Albion Street, Leicester LE1 6GD.

6. *Junction Project*. A partnership between Lambeth Social Services Department and the Save the Children Fund.

iv   Miscellaneous agencies and facilities

Provided largely by the Local Authority

The Bristol Social Project of Spencer, Tuxford and Dennis (1964) was a bold attempt to see the requirements of the family in the round. It set an example for others to follow. Authorities vary in what they provide. Most have some permanent play facilities and play centres which offer creative and imaginative activities. Adventure playgrounds are valuable for children out of school, especially in the holidays.

The youth service. A commonly held view that youth work 'keeps them off the streets' is unfortunate, for it suggests that normal young people have no need of the service. Generally speaking the methods of youth organisations enable young people to associate freely. The youth service aims to contribute to the personal and social education of the adolescent. It offers opportunities complementary to those of formal education, vocational training and parental influence, but in a non-compulsory setting with maximum scope for self-expression, self-determination and above all enjoyment. The youth worker encourages young people to contribute to what is provided, as part of the process of maturing, character development and the growth of a spirit of independence. Close working of the service with teachers would help to identify and provide for the needs of young people.

Some youth services publish a handbook of facilities available. Examples are described by Spencer et al (1964) and in the project 'Avenues Unlimited' in Tower Hamlets (1). Some secondary schools arrange for older pupils to have a week or so away from their homes, and encourage the children to do most of the planning for it. Ideally all inner city boroughs should have an 'outdoor pursuit centre' for 14-16 year olds.

Community centres. These offer a variety of activities for young people and may undertake projects to cater for local needs.

Parks and amenities. Play space is especially needed in areas with tower blocks and few open spaces. If socially acceptable forms of excitement and adventure are not available ingenious youth will find its own devices which may be antisocial, and costly to the community. 15-16 year olds like motorbikes, roller skates, getting together and showing off. So they want a place for a coke and a chat, and room outside for belting around. There is nowhere like this in most urban boroughs but there are always possibilities.

Community and voluntary help

In boroughs where they are available, residential home helps, peripatetic house mothers and rehousing are facilities to help families in difficulties. Coordinating committees of housing, finance, social services and health are used in some places to alleviate problems arising from chronic indebtedness associated with low income, rent arrears, infirmity and old age.

Some communities have compiled lists of agencies of use to professionals and individuals needing assistance with a wide range of problems (Haringey Association for the Advancement of State Education, 1974; MIND, Wandsworth, 1975; Ealing Community Health Council, 1984a and b).

The amount of crime amongst juveniles has made people think of alternative, more effective and less costly methods of dealing with it. The main object of the Hammersmith Teenage Project is to divert adolescents at risk from the juvenile justice system. Its essential feature is that the young person becomes a partner in a team that aims to provide a caring environment with opportunities to obtain satisfactions from living and working (Blaber, 1977; Whitlam, 1977; NACRO, 1978a). Significantly the project encountered difficulties because of failure in communications between relevant agencies.

Attempts are being made to reduce vandalism by involving young people in the construction and care of their local environment (Blaber, 1979; NACRO, 1981; Gilbert, 1981a and b). It is too early to say how effective these initiatives will be. There are many sensible schemes that could be run by Community Service Volunteers (2) and the National Association of Youth Clubs. Use of the local canal or river for canoeing and camping organised by some parks and amenities departments with voluntary bodies might be extended. Young people might use and enjoy local amenities more if they had a say in what was provided, and played an active part in its provision. For example Waterway Recovery Groups, all volunteers and self-managed, are active in various parts of the country restoring canals. There are enterprises like the Pirate Club in the London Borough of Camden, which provides adventure for young people on a London canal (3).

Family service units (FSUs). A mother who becomes over-extended trying to cope with family burdens, will be chronically tired, and may often be depressed, short-tempered and impatient with children's demands. Affection is less to the fore, anger and punishment more so, and the child responds with difficult behaviour. An agency that can relieve parents of some of their intolerable burdens, and by doing so give them the opportunity to be better parents will also help to make the children's behaviour more manageable. The essence of the work of family service units is the provision of friendship and practical help to families with multiple problems, particularly to mothers who seem inadequate but who may be suffering from depression or be overwhelmed by the struggle to cope with social, financial and marital complications. In Bowlby's words they help to 'mend the home'. Family service units are voluntary organisations. Help is provided by the well organised use of volunteers, often in conjunction with social workers, and through group work with local children, mothers with toddlers and so on. Referrals come through the local authority and other agencies – schools, GPs.

FSUs offer training facilities for social workers. They are funded by charitable grants with additional money from local authorities. The cost to the rates is trivial compared with the sums required for a child in an observation and reception centre.

Voluntary bodies. The provision of leisure activities for young people is often done well by voluntary groups who may have wide interests, and be flexible in the way they work. *But they have to be funded.* All sorts of bodies come voluntarily into existence and have led to the introduction of statutory services or allocations of money. The Wolfenden Report (Joseph Rowntree Memorial Trust and Carnegie UK Trust, 1977) found plenty of evidence of vigorous and widespread voluntary bodies. Examples are Community Service Volunteers (2), Inter-Action and International Voluntary Service. There is interest in working with offenders in educational settings, as in intermediate treatment, mainly as a means of rehabilitation and the prevention of recidivism (Marks, 1979). The value of voluntary work in relation to social work is dicussed in the Barclay Report of the National Institute for Social Work (1982). The London Borough of Ealing has pioneered a scheme, Unified Community Action (4), to integrate the initiatives and energies of official departments and voluntary bodies. The results are encouraging.

The police and magistrates

Brushes with the law. Magistrates in the juvenile court make decisions that label the young person delinquent and may determine the course of his life. They are perhaps too remote to become an object of hatred. The police have close contact with the delinquent before and after he is sentenced. Carrying out their duty they may appear to the child as enemies. The police are undoubtedly sorely tried at times, but aggressive reaction arouses similar responses in young people. It is against the police's own endeavours with their juvenile bureau, that some policemen seem gratuitously to adopt aggressive tactics (Gopsill, 1979; O'Halloran, 1981). It is plain from the report of the Policy Studies Institute (1983) that there is a great deal wrong with police relationships. Aggressive, provocative actions by the police amount to the use of fear ('terror') as a method of citizen control, surely anathema in a social democracy. To achieve their highest aim of crime prevention police must communicate with, and be in some measure accountable to, the community (Alderson, 1977-8; Moore, 1978).

Police relationships with schools. Some chief education officers are against direct links between police and teachers but in practice informal relationships develop between the police and some schools, which are found to be valuable. Many schools do not seem to know that when a young person is cautioned by the police at least one of the parents should accompany him to the police station. A juvenile may not be charged without the presence of a parent.

The role of the courts. Although the police get all their information to the court within 3-4 weeks, the case may not be finally dealt with for nine months. The school and the child suffer by repeated remands but magistrates are concerned not to proceed precipitately. Without full knowledge of the social circumstances less caring decisions will be made. Social reports take time to prepare and social workers may be overloaded. Many young persons *remanded in prison* are eventually acquitted or receive non-custodial sentences.

When sentencing magistrates have a somewhat limited number of courses open to them and their views may clash with those of social workers. In spite of evidence that segregation and punishment are unlikely to improve behaviour and may worsen it (West, 1982), magistrates may want to use them. It is at this stage that places providing a therapeutic environment are most likely to help. The number of children, girls as well as boys, sent to penal institutions has increased rapidly since 1969 and there has been a drop in the number of young offenders allowed to remain in their own homes while supervised by social workers. Police forces expand and social services contract. Institutions for young offenders have re-conviction rates of 70-80 per cent (Cornish and Clarke, 1975; NACRO, 1978b).

There is no evidence that 'short sharp shock treatment' of young offenders in detention reduces crime (NACRO, 1979). The Prison Officers Association is against it. Re-conviction rates with this form of 'treatment' at four detention centres remained at about 80 per cent. Nevertheless it is being extended to all 20 detention centres. Similar 'treatment' has even been suggested in a 'Catch 'em Young' scheme for primary school children aged 9 or 10, diagnosed by their teachers as having 'deep seated vicious streaks' or 'sly and vindictive natures'. Being persistently troublesome at school at this age is often followed by delinquency (West, 1982), but we should consider prevention and treatment in relation to causes, rather than just prescribe punishment. Few people are competent to make such accurate assessments of young people's natures as is implied in the above diagnostic categories. These schemes display negative and aggressive attitudes to children in trouble. Instead of alienating them why not try to reintegrate them into society? (See recommendations of the Association of Chief Officers of Probation; and of the Apex Trust). Young people will often listen to each other in peer groups and some are helping in schools (Martin, 1984). To exercise their preventive role why not let police work in juvenile liaison schemes in which the failure rate is of the order of only 20 per cent (Taylor, 1971) and the cost is much less?

Court liaison officers, where appointed, have helped teachers by briefing them about courts' actions. In Liverpool for example 'juvenile liaison committees' bring police, teachers, social workers and parents together. What a pity that the best provisions of the juvenile justice system in Scotland, well tried now for 14 years, cannot be used south of the border (Murray, 1982; Association of Directors of Social Services, 1985).

Information is available on children's and families' interests and rights (*British Medical Journal*, 1979; Family Rights Group, 1979).

Social and environmental development

Lewis Mumford (1940) analysed the cycle of growth and decay of the polis (town, city), and attributed decline mainly to its unbalanced use by interests unconnected with renewal. Without re-birth both young and old suffer culturally and psychologically, not least because of the way in which city life undermines independence. Mumford's analysis should stimulate councils and town planners to consider how the local environment might be improved. People need not only shops, offices and residences, but also such facilities for adults and *children* as to foster re-creation, refreshment and renewal; and 'socially acceptable excitement'. Society too must understand that it gets the politicians it deserves, and the policies it is prepared to pay for. Many environmental changes may, indeed can only, be brought about by initiatives from the community.

Councillors, and MPs too, are not elected simply to keep rates and taxes down, but to regulate in constructive manner the environment. This may cost money: it will certainly require the honest questioning of attitudes and shibboleths; and it will not be done without bold new initiatives.

Notes

1. *Avenues unlimited*. Tower Hamlets Youth and Community Project.

2. Community Service Volunteers: The National Volunteer Agency. Its principal object is to involve people in community service and to encourage social change and innovation. Its main task is with the young; involvement should enable them to help the community and to develop their own potential.

3. The Pirate Club, founded by Lord St Davids.

4. Information leaflet, 1982, from the chief education officer, London Borough of Ealing, Hadley House, 79-81 Uxbridge Road, Ealing, London W5 5SU.

Chapter 9 — The place of clients

While suitably trained people are clearly needed to carry out the multifarious tasks entailed in educating children, we may ask will there ever be enough people in the relevant professions to deal, on their own, with matters ranging from the formulation and maintenance of ethical principles, to standards of training and performance, and detailed provision of service? Do we really want a society that provides a specially trained person of some sort for each of our needs? Naturally we commend a caring society and what it means in terms of attitudes, laws, regulations, training and standards; but the best care concerns all of us as individuals, it is 'everybody's business'. We pay merely lip service to caring if we leave the practice of it entirely to the professions, or to an abstraction — 'society'. Professional activities cannot be conducted without reference to, or indeed participation by, the people for whom the service is designed, the 'clients'. Certainly this is increasingly clear in medicine, where doctors, at least technically, only 'advise', and the client's (patient's) wishes are what the profession is expected to try to meet.

The trend now is for clients — patients, parents, even school children — to want to play a more active role in what happens to them through participating in decisions about it. Parents, and pupils especially in their last two years at secondary school, are interested in the business of 'children growing up'. They should be brought into discussions on how to deal with teenage growing pains that are exercising schools, parents, children and society in general. Pupils and their families have a right to expect the society they live in to be caring, but they have a duty to make a personal contribution to it. Nothing fortifies the spirit so well to cope with one's own problems, Group Captain Cheshire has remarked, as helping someone else with his.

Relationships between schools and parents

Schools cannot stand alone in educating and bringing up children. Concepts of school-community inter-relationships can become practical realities only through closer and richer relations between teachers and parents. Opening up relationships brings help and support to the school (1). Parents and anyone in local industry, business or services can help the school. Unfortunately the authoritarian nature of the organisation of many secondary schools has put people off. Some teachers have been reluctant to accept the mild recommendations of the Taylor Report on school governance (DES, 1977; Where, 1978a) (2) (3).

Parents, although they are one of the two great pillars of the child's educational process, often expect the school to do most of the work; but the school may not appreciate a concerned or interested parent. Parents are so obviously important in the rearing of their children that they should be high on the list of outside agencies with whom the school should interact. It is the intention that parents and schools should share to a greater extent the upbringing of children (Secretary of State for Education and Science, 1985). A 'binding' relationship between teachers and parents would be useful though it may be difficult to match it with that between doctor and patient, where the patient is actively seeking help. Some teachers capture the situation by showing what the school has to offer as is done in the Cambridgeshire village colleges (4). Schools that have developed a collaborative method of working with parents through parent teacher associations, have derived enormous benefits in material facilities and in moral support, though PTAs are not always encouraged to give all they are capable of, and there are untapped reserves of parental goodwill.

With increasing complexity of social life and of specialisation at work it is unlikely that institutions serving human affairs, and schools are only there to serve children and parents, can fulfil their purposes without help from others. The Strathclyde experiment (Wilkinson, Grant and Williamson, 1978) showed how a partnership in education may be started. Many primary schools are open and friendly, and find parents a valuable resource. Useful information about, and discussion of, home-school relationships is to be found in publications of the Home and School Council (Goodacre, 1968; Lingard and Allard, 1972; Green, 1975; Wood and Simpkins, 1980).

Parents who are reluctant to visit school. In spite of all attempts to open up schools some parents will not readily visit although these are the ones teachers might most wish to meet. Ethnic minority mothers have been particularly diffident. School counsellors help in making contacts. Many 'reluctant parents' can with a little effort be incorporated into their child's educational experience. They may be enticed into school by devices like those at one first school where there is a parents' room in which coffee is provided each morning and a washing machine is available as a focus for 'non-directed' discussion. Many parents will come to 'parties' when they will not come to 'meetings'. Enrolling the hesitant parent is easier if the school is relatively small which is a good argument for keeping primary schools that way. Large secondary schools can be divided into groups. Opening doors like this, it may be said, is all very fine for clubbable parents but not so effective for those trying to overcome the effects of their own disadvantaged childhood. Nevertheless, wherever initiatives for open schools come from, trends spread and other parents gain confidence to follow.

Parents' contribution

Few things have changed more in recent decades than the relationship between teachers and parents. Fifty years ago the almost universal view among teachers was 'if only there were no parents.' Today there is generally a more cooperative attitude, though underlying hostility can often be observed. A high proportion of schools have parent-teacher associations, at whose meetings the staff explain the principles and aims of the school; demonstrate any new methods they may have adopted; and answer parents' queries and criticisms. Among the governors of a school it is mandatory that there should be at least one parent, and in some parts meetings are held from time to time for the parent governors of a group of schools to encourage them to make full use of their powers. It is proposed to increase the proportion of parents on schools' boards of governors though the suggestion that they should be in a majority (DES, 1984b) has generally not been well received and does not seem sensible (Sallis, 1984).

Parents can undertake fund raising and make suggestions about the objects for which money is to be raised. What parents especially appreciate are close relationships with the head and class teachers. Some schools invite parents to attend assembly on one day a week, some invite them to case conferences at which their child will be discussed, just as often when his progress has been unusually good as when he is in trouble. Parental acceptance of advice from the school on the future schooling of their children is dependent largely on the trust and confidence that exists between parents, heads and teachers. Parents may be willing and able to help the school with social functions, with out-of-school activities, games and clubs after school hours, going on outings with the children, helping to supervise and run projects for small groups and even help with the recruitment of teachers. In primary schools parents, usually mothers, can help in the class room. One head remarked that the voluntary helpers lessened the teachers' workload, and discipline improved. In a Somerset experiment when the children were taken for remedial reading by mothers or grandmothers in addition to the county's remedial teachers, not only reading ability but also attitudes and self-esteem improved markedly more than when children were taken by the remedial teachers alone.

Parents have a profounder influence on their children's education than many teachers realise (Tizard and Hughes, 1984). There are a number of organisations that promote clients' interests in schools and indicate methods of cooperation (Advisory Centre for Education (ACE), Confederation for the Advancement of State Education (CASE), National Association of Governors and Managers (NAGM), National Union of School Students (NUSS), Pre-School Playgroups Association (PPA)). At the other extreme there are still schools without parent-teacher or similar associations (5).

Parents may also enlarge a school's ambit by themselves becoming pupils. A successful project incorporating adults into the sixth form is in operation at Boundstone School, Sussex. A similar project has started in two high schools in the London Borough of Ealing. There should be more scope in schools for children and adults to work together in music, woodwork and all that may be put under the heading 'design'. There seems no reason why pupils and adults should not sit side by side following 'A' level courses.

Parents and other adults could offer their skills and experience for specific subjects, a facility seldom used by schools that is worth wider consideration. Parents could help teachers to prepare pupils for work after leaving school, and they could help the school to teach children about relationships in all kinds of settings. Unfortunately, for many teachers, closer contact with parents is still merely a means of changing parental behaviour. The teaching tradition is more to explain and influence than to listen and find out. Such use of parents and others should in fact extend teachers' professional role.

We have mentioned the value to some mothers in helping to run preschool playgroups (Part II, Chapter 5). As one mother said 'Playgroups are not only for children, they are for parents too.' That does not mean they cannot learn from, and make use of the services of professionals trained in the care of pre-school children. But in a playgroup the parents run the show, and have opportunities to learn from each other about rearing children. In a nursery class professionals are in charge, mothers are not in a direct learning situation, and if the professionals are unforthcoming parents may learn very little.

208

Pupils' contribution

Schools exist to foster virtuous circles.

— Plowden Report

(DES, 1966)

Throughout the ages education at school has been regarded as a part, even if an elementary part, of the intellectual life. In the last half century the rapid development of the physical and biological sciences and of technology, has made this truer than ever. The 20th century has also been the century of psychological and social science, and the emphasis now placed on the study of child development has brought into being a large number of 'child-centred' schools. This means, among other things, that children are enabled to use their curiosity on the human as well as the non-human environment; and so are able to contribute criticism and suggestions for the methods of teaching and the organisation of their schools. Even very young children show a capacity for organizing their working day.

Some schools hold daily or weekly meetings in which teachers can give their opinion on the group as a whole, the wise ones putting the emphasis on examples of intellectual or moral progress that they have noted since the previous meeting, and where any child may have his say so long as he keeps to established rules, such as not speaking out of turn and addressing his remarks to the chairman, who may be a child or an adult. It is interesting that this type of discussion is found in schools for mal-adjusted children and fascinating to observe how these 'psychologically disturbed and emotionally unstable' children may conduct their affairs with not much less decorum than some adult committees. A system of classroom meetings devised by Glasser (1975) drew all the children into the work of the class, and gave each a sense of control of his destiny, a factor thought to be strongly related to achievement. Glasser found some teachers resistant to the idea of class discussions, but when they accepted it, *and pupils and teacher sat in a circle*, they functioned successfully as 'working, problem-solving groups'.

As children grow up in secondary schools they are treated more as adults and may form close relationships with a wise member of the teaching staff. At one school a pupil committing an offence was invited, alone or with others, by his housemaster to coffee, when the general principles of social relationships were discussed and the particular event touched on. We should accept that young people are as good as most, and better than some, at telling a hawk from a handsaw. Their penetrating insight may perhaps be unnerving to the insecure. A splendid indictment by the students of the system of education they were subjected to at a county school (in the USA) is reported by Gross and Gross (1972).

There is only one way to induce people to act responsibly, and in this children are no different from adults: give them responsibility and maintain their interest. Helping to formulate school rules would encourage commitment; curricula relevant to pupils' aspirations would stimulate interest; feedback systems between pupils and teachers would enhance pupils' sense of control, fulfilment and self-esteem. When children have helped to look after others less fortunate, for example the old or the handicapped, they have done it well and benefited themselves. Some schools have school councils which influence pupil behaviour by peer pressure and, by involving the children, enable them to make a contribution to the wellbeing and running of their school. However, the National Union of School Students has found it an uphill task persuading heads to discuss their proposals.

Some authorities have appointed pupils to secondary school governing bodies, as was recommended by the Taylor Report (DES, 1977), though not by the subsequent White Paper (DES, 1978c) and in our experience this practice works well. Now it is proposed to abolish the office of pupil governor. At a boarding school for maladjusted children the head found that smoking among the pupils declined when they were encouraged to make a study of the smoking habits of boys in the school and their reasons for smoking (Shaw, 1965). It has been found possible to obtain the cooperation of even very disturbed children by letting them take part in decision making. Pickering (1979), a teacher of political studies in a comprehensive school hit the nail on the head:

> When writing about civil government over 300 years ago John Locke explained how vital it was that the government should have the consent of the Governed. Without such a consent Locke doubted whether anyone would feel obliged to accept the authority of the government as legitimate . . . We cannot rightfully expect that children who have been given no say in the affairs of their school, will suddenly adjust to, and participate in, the democratic process outside of the school.

There is a vast resource of pupil experience to be made manifest to teachers about their methods, the subjects they teach and their personalities. This has been indicated for the most part in only occasional limited studies. Teachers who have solicited, openly or anonymously, the

210

opinions of their pupils on their teaching methods and practice have often been amazed at the grasp of classroom realities shown by the pupils, and their insight into teaching difficulties. Pupils see things differently from the teacher who, if not defensive, can learn much from this fresh view. Many children see their teachers as unkind. In one study (Maizels, 1970) over one-third of ex-pupils believed their teachers had had favourites and nearly a quarter remembered them as sarcastic and moody. Nine per cent had found them frightening. Argyle (1967) found that when pupils' comments on teacher performance were conveyed to teachers, the teachers' behaviour improved. An elaborate study of over 2000 fifteen year old children in 27 secondary modern schools (Revans, 1973) elicited opinions about teachers that were distinct and homogeneous for pupil groups. Many of the responses indicated intensely hostile and aggressive feelings. One 15-year old has described, in her school newspaper, thoughtless and unruly behaviour at a teachers' conference at which she did a holiday cleaning job (Rawnsley, 1986).

Relationships between schools and community

By community we mean everyone who lives in the neighbourhood (in some cases catchment area) of the school. For teachers the most prominent clients are the pupils and their parents, but there are also the professionals and professional bodies from whom the school expects help, and there are volunteers. The village colleges in Cambridgeshire (4) were the pivot of the village, and the teacher in a French village is looked to as a leader concerned with every aspect of its social life.

The Plowden Report spoke approvingly of community schools, the present-day equivalent of the Cambridge village colleges whose buildings remain open for 5 or 6 hours after the end of the normal school day, either for children to pursue some special interest or for adults to come to further education classes. One obstacle to the setting up of village colleges is the closure of so many village schools. However, some big and well designed schools are in villages and it is tragically wasteful if they are used for only a few hours each day. The ideals and practicalities of community schools have been discussed by Yardley and Swain (1980). The Associations of Metropolitan Authorities, County Councils, and District Councils, have agreed on how dual use and joint provision of leisure buildings should become a reality (6). A first step would be for the school to act as a centre for certain social functions. This would imply more than people just using the premises outside school hours. In examining the neighbourhoods' wants and needs the school may have to question its own aims, methods and results, as Sybil Marshall (1963) did in a small village school (7). Alas, the capacity to question is not well developed in most secondary school teachers, a casualty of schools' single-minded preoccupation with text book knowledge.

A start could be made through current parents asking the community about its needs by questionnaire, house visits, letters to the local press and so on. Some of the parents and professional people connected with the school would certainly have ideas for practical initiatives and for cooperative effort with others. A team could be raised for a building project and could carry it through with a continuing monitoring process (Hale, 1974). The school could come to be seen as a 'community college'.

The ideal has been realised in some places at some times. Even where there is no lack of initiative and enthusiasm on the part of the teachers, difficulties may be put in their way by official policy. The alleged economies of large scale production have had a great influence on policies for schools (as it has for hospitals). Many small schools have been closed and links with parents broken. Larger schools will, of course, provide more, and more varied, activities for the children and may be relatively cheaper, but as far as we know comparisons of *social* cost-benefits have not been made between the small school which serves an all-age community in valuable ways, and a remote and more impersonal establishment which at best provides for children but not for their parents or the community at large.

Notes

1. In the medical field in the UK there are about 180 patients' associations. These are groups of people who have disabilities or illnesses of different kinds. They provide feedback to the medical profession and sometimes money and ideas for research. The relationship is far removed from confrontation. In the US on the other hand patients attempt, to a much greater degree, to influence medical care by recourse to the courts. This is extremely costly and a less effective form of learning.

2. The metropolitan education authorities strongly opposed the Taylor Report recommendations at a special conference to discuss them. — *Guardian* 14/12/1977.

3. 'The National Association of Schoolmasters/Union of Women Teachers has come out strongly against the Government's proposal to allow pupils over 16 to serve on school governing bodies.' — *Guardian* 9/11/1978, reporting publication of a pamphlet *Who runs our schools?* by the National Association of Schoolmasters/Union of Women Teachers.

4. The addresses of the Cambridge Village Colleges are available from the Cambridge Local Education Authority: The Cambridge Area Office, Gloucester Street, Cambridge CB3 0AP.

5. The National Confederation of Parent-Teacher Associations (NCPTA) produces pamphlets on the subject of parents working in schools, such as *Forming a home and school group*.

6. *Towards a wider use*. A report of an inter-association working party on joint provision and dual or multiple use of facilities for recreational use by the community. Association of County Councils, 1976.

7. When she had achieved success with children of all ages in the village the LEA closed the school.

Part III: Training and education of the professional: the learning process

Part III — Training and education of the professional: the learning process

This is not the occasion to consider professional training in depth. All we wish to do is to underscore the view that training can be used to help the professional worker to identify the child with disturbing behaviour at an early stage, to take part in measures to prevent it, and to help in the 'treatment' at whatever stage the problem 'appears'. Implicit in training would be the recognition of the part schools, that is largely teachers, may themselves play in the causation or aggravation of behaviour problems.

If the vulnerable child from the not 'good enough' family is unprotected damaging social consequences follow. An educational drive to achieve understanding of the physical and emotional development of children, and to realise warm adult/child relationships, needs directing at all who work in the child care services — house parents whose main concern is with children; social workers, one of whose tasks is to maintain contact with the parents of children in care; administrators whose work may bring them into little contact with people and to whom children and families tend to be names on papers; and teachers, general medical practitioners, paediatricians, educational psychologists, psychiatrists, nurses and health visitors. All should be trained to appreciate the child's emotional needs, his sense of loss and rejection if he is moved around to suit the wishes of adults (including his own parents), his need to gain and consolidate a sense of identity and membership of a family and, to put it at its most general, to see that in all decisions that are made about him, his welfare is paramount.

Professional training requires setting and maintaining high standards of work and achievement; and encouraging a habit of questioning attitudes and practices, however uncomfortable such an enquiring frame of mind may be to mentors or colleagues. Professionals, and their clients, deserve safeguards against unthinking conformity. Training should leave workers more ready to learn and not to see themselves as finished products — 'experts'. Innovations in training for those concerned with children of all ages, and for youth leaders, are seen by Poulton and James (1975) as necessary for professionals to learn how to work *with* clients as well as *for* them. In the DBIS group the point was made that all the well qualified people attending it had received what was generally regarded as 'appropriate' training for their work, yet it was often insufficient for dealing with problems they met. Is the later correction of training deficiencies to be fortuitous or part of planned in-service training?

The best managers, and this applies as much to professionals as to administrators, see that staff have an opportunity to learn from their own and others' experience, and ensure that suggestions accepted after full discussion are put into practice, the staff playing a central part in the action. Such sequences should not be one-off events, but part of an iterative process in which all staff learn from the effects of their actions, the exercise being repeated indefinitely in a cyclical form so that learning, and action (improvement and innovation) are continuing processes (Appendix 2), a valuable form of training. Participative management should be practised by all staff involved in child care.

Teachers

The prime purpose of schools as places of learning can be furthered by reducing impediments to learning, especially in children unable to learn. There will never be enough social workers, psychologists or psychiatrists to deal with all children's problems so teachers will have to help resolve them. Nothing can stop the effects of disturbing behaviour spilling across boundaries whether of the school, the family or the community. In a team of teachers, social workers, doctors and others necessary for the work, each must be ready to take on some of the functions of the others. In dealing with the general subject and the specific case, demarcation wrangles are as socially damaging in professional services as they are elsewhere.

If teachers were to do quite different work for a year or two before 'going back to school' to teach they would be likely to take a broader view of education and to develop a maturity that could help them to cater for children's enormously varying needs and responses. However, extended experience of work outside education still occurs for only a small minority of teachers (DES, 1982b). The profession gains from teachers returning after raising a family.

Many of the difficulties teachers have over disruptive children arise from inadequate training (Evans, 1981). They need to understand children's defence mechanisms such as projection and displacement, and the causes of disturbing behaviour even when they are using methods of behaviour modification. Although colleges of education are required to cover child development, psychology and classroom practice, subjects that are usually taught by qualified psychologists with much teaching experience, they may not be taught in sufficient depth and there may not always be enough emphasis on the practical problems of handling disruptive children. Some colleges do educate trainees about 'growing up' children, and teach them classroom practice. A few listen carefully to what their student teachers have to say about their experiences.

An action research study by Lewis (1974) brought out the value for teacher training of close *working* relationships between student teachers, lecturers and school teachers. Feedback from students was a means of learning for mentors. A few colleges run courses in depth on children with special needs, children with behaviour difficulties in ordinary schools and on conflict management in the classroom; and give their students practical experience in social adjustment (withdrawal) units. Wragg and Sutton (1979) produced a handbook on class management. Others are doing similar work (McGuiness, 1977) (1). Most books on bringing up children — in home or school — are concerned with one, and sometimes several, aspects of the child or the therapy — the need for encouragement, to avoid failure, to preserve dignity, to modify behaviour, or to examine the relevance of the curriculum as a means of motivation. Publications on pupil and classroom management were referred to in Part II, Chapter 6. Teachers must use their judgement to choose which methods suit them and their pupils. They may get help in this from other teachers and from educational psychologists. Training in new practices should be offered, using small groups, for both trainee and qualified teachers (Gordon and Burch, 1974; Glasser, 1975). How much of what is known about the causes of disruptive behaviour in children and how to correct it, is filtering through to teacher training establishments, and on to those in training, and indeed to experienced teachers?

School staff are at fault if they tell newly qualified teachers to forget any new-fangled nonsense they may have learnt at college and indicate their belief in the use of coercive methods of teaching. A school's dependence on a tradition of punishment may make it difficult for even an experienced teacher coming from a different school culture to avoid classroom disruption. Some training colleges and university departments may fail to help teachers in training because their methods are too idealistic and out of touch with the culture that trainees are going to enter. It is unacceptable for people to qualify as teachers with little regard to their ability actually to teach and manage a classroom of children.

It is becoming accepted that teacher training should be at least partly in the hands of experienced teachers who are actively teaching in schools, and that this part of the training should take place mainly in schools. However, there is still the problem of ensuring that those who train teachers are themselves good teachers. 'Sitting next to Nellie' will not help if Nellie is a poor teacher. The DES (1983b) is concerned about the absence of rigorous standards for teaching, and about the quality of teachers turned out by training establishments. Who teaches teachers' teachers? And who monitors their competence? About a quarter of newly trained teachers are poorly equipped with teaching skills, three in ten are not provided in their first post with conditions likely to promote their professional development; and many receive scant support from heads and fellow staff. Many in primary and secondary schools are asked to teach subjects for which they lack appropriate academic training (DES, 1982b). It is difficult to see how standards of training and work can be raised and maintained until some body is formed analogous to the General Medical Council which oversees the curriculum and training of medical students, and the fitness of doctors to practise. Though such a development has often been mooted, teachers seem unready for it (DES, 1983b). Pressure is mounting from the DES for teacher assessment.

Inadequacy in pastoral work may be rectified by in-service training. If teachers have not enough time for the work more should be appointed. None of this will help unless the teaching profession accepts a counselling role and for this they need some social work skills. So integral to the teacher's work is pastoral care that we believe those who have no aptitude for it should not be selected for training. The role of the child care support services does not feature much in teacher training (FitzHerbert, 1982). Social workers need an understanding of teaching if they are to help teachers with disruptive children. The time available to teachers to learn simple social work skills would be limited. Eventually, as already happens in some colleges, this could be incorporated in all teacher training curricula. As we have suggested (Part II, Chapter 8 (iii)) closer working together of teachers and social workers would help them to learn about each other's work and difficulties, and how they could assist each other. The need for an apprenticeship type of training for teachers now seems cardinal. In law, medicine and engineering the trainee is introduced to the rough and tumble of client contact while still supported by the more experienced. This gives the newly qualified professional greater confidence to deal with the intricacies of the client-face. There is a trend in this direction. Teacher training does not stop when newly qualified teachers begin their first job. They are on probation for at least a year. Is the word probation threatening? Doctors in their pre-registration year are not regarded as probationers and virtually never fail to be accepted into the profession. Junior doctors work under one or two chiefs and have the guidance of other doctors (called registrars), and of ward sisters. They are normally never left solely in charge of patients.

The induction of inexperienced teachers needs a thoughtful process. Probationers should be given the less difficult classes. There is a place too for trying to find out from the pupils the impact of the teacher and his methods (Part II, Chapter 9). The use of video play-back has been found of value in training doctors (Fletcher, 1979). It was used in one study of the management of a group of difficult young children (Jones CO, 1977).

There is much evidence both of the need and of the effectiveness of support even for quite experienced teachers, since many are faced with social and behavioural events they have not been trained to deal with. Jackson (1976) and Lawrence *et al* (1984) describe people finding themselves acting as counsellors when doing research in schools, an indication of need. A supportive consultative system that helps teachers to look for alternative approaches and trains them in case analysis with their difficult pupils, as happens in special schools, could be initiated by a qualified adviser, as advocated in the Warnock Report (DES, 1978b) and by publications on disruptive pupils (DES, 1978a and d; Galloway, 1985a). Groups of teachers, meeting with appropriate counsellors, gain insight into the reasons for children's, parents' and their own behaviour. Such groups offer teachers support that by itself may be sufficient to enable them to tackle behaviour and learning problems with more confidence (Hanko, 1981, 1982, 1985; Salzberger-Wittenberg, Henry and Osborne, 1983).

In-service training requires supply teachers to take the place of those undergoing it. Teachers themselves now want in-service training to be school-based by *serving* teachers. After all, whoever heard of post-graduate training in clinical medicine by anyone except doctors practising full-time in their profession? However, such training will only be successful if teachers and schools conducting it are of high standard, and there must be machinery to ensure this. It need not be costly.

There has been little tradition for schoolteachers to do research on their own or others' work. Its value for raising standards of practice and teaching, notably in medicine, are an example for school teachers and those who train them. The results of research that is done should be evaluated in schools (Wragg, 1982). Research is of greater value when practitioners (teachers in schools) play an active part in it, best of all when they initiate it, carry it through, evaluate it and apply it. It can be a powerful form of in-service training (Lawrence *et al*, 1984).

Teachers who are going to take on largely administrative roles, such as headships or work in the education office, should receive training in modern methods of management. Do educational administrators even need to have been teachers? It might be argued that working in an authoritarian organisation (most schools) is not conducive to accepting ideas of management that emphasize (though not yet in many parts of British life) provision for the needs and wishes of staff in order to get the best response from them. Managers in education will perform more effectively if they use *teachers'* experience and expertise to find solutions to problems of teaching and pupil management, and if professionals have some control over their working lives. Whoever administers ('manages') a school, training and experience in participative forms of management will facilitate teachers' work (Revans, 1981a). The Local Government Training Board has incorporated action learning into its management development skills programme and the MSC uses it.

Child psychiatrists

The child psychiatrist is a doctor with a long and arduous training. Courses in academic psychology have been introduced though most students do not find these help their understanding of the emotional problems of patients they meet in clinical practice. Some medical schools have experimented by combining clinical and general scientific teaching to enable the student to become aware from the start of the nature of the doctor's work.

Once qualified, the junior doctor has a year of in-service training as a 'pre-registration doctor' which should, among other things, draw on his human sympathy and increase his understanding of complex human relationships. Newly qualified doctors have a great deal of clinical medicine to learn. Their responsiveness to early clinical experiences depends on their personalities and on the awareness of, and sympathy for, patients' social and emotional problems shown by the consultants they work under. To find a doctor with an unsympathetic personality who is not interested in treating patients 'in the round', raises questions about methods of selection as well as the training of medical students. Unfortunately the selection process may be operated by senior doctors with the same defects.

At some stage after qualification some doctors will be attracted to enter training for the specialty of psychiatry. They will undertake further training, starting with general psychology, neuro-anatomy and neuro-physiology, followed by theoretical training and practical experience with patients suffering from severe mental disorders. This may be supplemented by a personal psychoanalysis. The time spent in mental hospitals and/or neurosis centres should be of value in helping the young doctor to understand the complexities of the human mind and the many possibilities of malfunctioning. If the doctor then goes on to child psychiatry he embarks on a subject with ramifications into many branches of medical knowledge — general medicine, neurology, paediatrics, social medicine, epidemiology and genetics. His training could be broadened and enriched by a study of the humanities. Many child psychiatrists will add to this some specialised training in psychotherapy. Such training will generally carry the child psychiatrist into his late thirties, but throughout it he is unlikely to be introduced to problems of behaviour experienced by schools.

Educational psychologists

These are almost invariably people who have started their professional careers as teachers. They do a 3-year undergraduate course in psychology plus at least one postgraduate year in educational psychology at a university. The educational psychologist has therefore a long training. He is likely to be acceptable to school staff because he was first a teacher. He either works in and from a child guidance clinic, or more independently as part of the school psychological service. In many cases the director of the CGC is an educational psychologist who will have administrative functions such as other professionals take on in their later careers. But he will receive no special training for this. If educational psychologists are to work more closely with schools, as has been suggested, managerial training might help to promote deeper relationships with agencies they interact with.

Social workers

Adequate training of professional people needs appropriate resources — time, money and competent staff. A study commissioned by the DHSS indicated that understaffing and inexperience among social workers and health visitors were responsible for some of the shortcomings found during the examination of 18 cases of child abuse, of which 17 died. But when the report of the study appeared (DHSS, 1982), the Secretary of State offered no action, reportedly merely saying that the publication might help to prevent other children suffering the same fate (Hencke, 1982b). Parliament enacts more and more legislation giving social services more and more work while their resources are cut. Lack of concern for prevention and early treatment of social problems sows the seeds of future trouble.

It has been a perennial complaint of directors of social services that the people who are appointed to their first post, although knowledgeable about social and political theories, are not trained to do social work. Although trainees get some practical placements during their course, and a few are fortunate to work in hospitals, a child guidance clinic or a family service unit, the majority do not take responsibility until their first post. Social work training emphasizes intervention in crises, and intensive casework. Doubts have been voiced about the academic standards of some social work training courses, about the calibre of some entrants, about examination standards and about the number of incompetent social work practitioners being turned out. Even today some recruits to social services departments have had no training at all.

Neither time nor resources permit of more than a smattering of training in all the many and varied social work tasks. If students are taught mainly about crises, they are likely to see crises as their most important task. This leads to a narrowing of social workers' professional development and expectations, other agencies seeing them only as 'firemen'; and the value of prevention is under-emphasized.

After training, social workers may find the reality of the job different from what they had been led to expect. Since the reorganisation of social services that followed the Seebohm Report (Home Office, 1968), social workers are expected to be 'generic', that is they should be able to carry out many kinds of tasks for each of which in the past there was a specific training and an expertise acquired through an apprenticeship. There is a trend once more towards some degree of specialisation, but each worker in the department can be called on to undertake statutory duties which must be given priority, and to spend time as 'duty officer' in which he may be faced with crises for which he has had little preparation. Reduction of staff in social services departments is making it more difficult to foster specialisation. Social workers in the CGC and in special schools have usually had special training and experience in psychiatry.

Nearly all social workers' practical training takes place while in post. In their early years the work load will be limited by inexperience and by time spent on courses. Juniors are closely supervised and are best taught by seniors still doing practical casework. We suggest that an opportunity to learn about the work and exigencies of allied professions should be incorporated into under- and post-graduate social science academic courses through attachment to different disciplines. The British Association of Social Workers supports the concept of interdisciplinary training for teachers and social workers (*Select Committee on Violence in the Family*, 1977) (2).

In view of the manifest inability of many social workers to take decisions, mentioned in Part I, Chapter 3 (DHSS, 1985; Vernon and Fruin, 1986), and the increasing demands made upon social services departments, the kind of training given to social workers should be urgently developed and extended. As the DHSS seems aware of these deficiencies and workloads we hope that plans to reduce funds for social work training by 17 per cent will be shelved. The CCETSW wants the minimum training for qualification in social work to last for three years.

Residential child care staff

There are some 14000 staff employed full-time in residential homes for children in England and Wales, 80 per cent of them with no formal training (Page, 1977; National Institute for Social Work, 1982). Now that a larger proportion of field social workers are professionally qualified, local authorities are recruiting qualified field workers straight from college and universities and using their secondment resources to get the residential and day care staff trained who already work for them.

Whether because of lack of training or for other reasons, residential staff who have close contact with the children and do a great deal for and with them, nevertheless play little part in the management of the homes they work in. Incorporation into the management structure of those who actually do the sensitive work of caring day by day for the children should improve the standard of care and morale of staff (Coghill *et al*, 1977). They should join in at least weekly discussions with professional people about all aspects of the children's care.

The Gatsby Project was set up to enlarge the availability of training, on a flexible pattern, for those engaged in the residential care of children and young persons (3).

Education welfare officers, school welfare workers, health visitors, midwives, doctors
(especially GPs, paediatricians, psychiatrists and obstetricians)

It may seem strange to put together such diverse kinds of worker, but all in different ways should be aware of people's social needs and be versed in the art of communication if they are to serve their clients effectively. All need to know about the causes and effects of emotional and neurotic disorders in children, and how to treat and prevent them. We suggest that all these workers should at some stage in their training be brought together, along with teachers and social workers, to study child development, child psychology and human relationships. Such study in the company of others with similar concerns would be particularly valuable for medical students whose selection hinges heavily on their 'A' levels, who are segregated from other students when their clinical training starts, and many of whom resent having to learn about social and psychological aspects of malfunctioning, which they see as irrelevant to 'medicine'. Yet the number of children suffering from them presenting to the district hospital paediatrician far outweighs those with organic diseases.

Medical schools do not encourage contact of students with behavioural sciences even when such departments exist in the same university (Fletcher, 1979). A senior medical registrar who took part in a study of hospital communications was criticised by his professor of medicine who thought the exercise a waste of time as it would interfere with his 'proper' training to be a consultant, and jeopardise his career. He obtained a consultant post without difficulty and used what he had learnt from this study to such effect that his work was greatly appreciated by his colleagues. Fletcher (1979) has examined deficiencies in training doctors to develop the 'social' arts of interviewing patients and communicating with them in ways most meaningful to the *patients*. In teaching and medicine it is in the field of relationships and communications that most clients' complaints arise about the service they receive.

More use of mixed discussion groups in training would help to open students' eyes to many social and psychological problems and the need for joint action to solve them. The London Medical Group has shown the way since 1963. It arranges a very large number of discussion groups involving students from many different disciplines. There are now similar groups in nearly all the medical schools in the UK. Together they comprise the Society for the Study of Medical Ethics, an educational charity. Contacts between professions should continue throughout practising life. At present they tend to be limited to individual initiative and sporadic conferences run by such bodies as the medical Royal Colleges, the Royal Society of Medicine and the Ciba Foundation. The concept of a 'common core' of training for a wide variety of professionals is gaining ground and experimental courses are in being (Jeffrey, Kolvin, Robson, Scott and Tweddle, 1979).

Judges, magistrates and police

It is evident from the behaviour of some police, magistrates and judges that they too have much to learn about the social and psychological causes of unacceptable behaviour and about good ways of dealing with it preventively and therapeutically. If they work in isolation from professions such as teaching, social work and medicine, they will not render society as much help as it deserves.

Volunteers

Volunteers are drawn from all walks of life. The 'training' of the volunteer worker could really start in the fifth and sixth forms of the secondary school. There his social attitudes may be developed and his motivation sparked. Volunteers may attend special induction courses in their chosen field such as those arranged by Dame Geraldine Aves in the DHSS, by the Blackfriars Settlement, the former London Care Committee and by LEAs (for example for school governors).

Notes

1. The college of St Hild and St Bede, Durham University, includes in curriculum courses units which deal specifically with the treatment of disruptive pupils. These units involve:

- An analysis of the social psychology of adolescence,

- An introduction to group dynamics,

- An opportunity for students to test out student-teacher responses to ill-discipline in simulation exercises,

- Critical analysis of the responses made, using closed circuit TV playback facilities,

- An opportunity to visit, observe and help in a local centre for disruptive pupils,

- Close contact with, and support from staff in such units and in local comprehensive schools.

The last feature is thought to be crucial. It allows students to develop constructive perceptions of what schools are like in the real world and gives school staff an opportunity to share and help allay the apprehension of young teachers.

2. *First Report.* Vol. II, p 232, para 27.

3. Nicholas Stacey, Director of Social Services for Kent, took the initiative with others to set up a research and development project to examine the need for training for those engaged in the residential care of children and young persons (not only those cared for by social services). The Project was funded by the Gatsby Charitable Foundation. The proposal is for an Open University course.

Part IV — Ideals, purposes and impediments in the care of children

Chapter 10 — Introduction

In Part IV we examine three systems of training and practice that directly affect the care and upbringing of children and so their behaviour. They are related: the development of any of them depends upon good practice in the others.

The education and training for capability that the child receives, and the values he adopts, will profoundly affect his behaviour, his ability to derive satisfaction from life, and his capacity to serve others. Communications and the subsidiary items under this heading; and trust between professionals, and between them and their clients, are cardinal elements in the rearing of children. These are the indispensable processes for people to develop so that they, and the society they compose, will not be overwhelmed by events.

Chapter 11 — Education: its nature and purpose

Education proper?

Much Madness is divinest Sense —
To a discerning Eye —
Much Sense — the starkest Madness —
'Tis the Majority
In this, as All prevail —
Assent and you are sane —
Demur — you're straightway dangerous —
And handled with a Chain —

— Emily Dickinson c 1862 (Johnson, 1975).

The function of education has never been to free
the mind and the spirit of man, but to bind them . . .

— Jules Henry (1972).

It is the innovators of new ideas, not the discoverers
of new scientific facts, who feel the wrath of
conservative society.

— W J Dempster (1978).

What one man takes as loyalty to the past another
sees as treachery to the future.

— Reg Revans. *Analects about action* (1982 c).

This is a large subject and we seek to illuminate only a small, though
vital, part of it. Our purpose is to emphasize that 'education' which does
not help young people to fulfil their legitimate desires will lead to
expressions of resentment through behaviour that teachers find
'disruptive' (Revans, 1982e). There are many definitions of education.
The Shorter OED includes the words 'preparation for the work of life'. It
may be better to say merely preparation for life, which after all consists of
more than work, and the young need preparation for many things —
living without work being one of them (Handy, 1984).

White (1982) claims that his is the first book-length study of priorities in
educational aims. For him the basic purpose of education is to help the
pupil to become a morally autonomous person. Whereas other accounts
of educated man have made possession of *knowledge* his chief characteristic, White makes virtues more central. Before the 19th century there
were very few people who held views contrary to those of the society
around them. There were a few mathematicians who were allowed to let

their reason guide them, probably because they were concerned with a branch of knowledge which meant little to people in general. But when people formed opinions that affected the beliefs and thoughts of others they were abominated and sometimes paid with their lives. No one regarded Pythagoras in this light, yet Socrates was executed. Kepler was not attacked but Galileo was. Newton and Leibnitz were honoured in the 17th century but Darwin was execrated in the 19th. In our day *Principia mathematica* got Bertrand Russell his Fellowship at Trinity College, Cambridge, but his public announcement that 'Killing people is wrong' lost it for him. Anthropologists have shown that there is a close relationship between adult cultural attitudes and patterns of child rearing.

There seem to be three strands in a child's education: first that which he provides for himself, using his native curiosity to explore the environment, and his capacity for observing and imitating the behaviour of others; second, what is told to him about beliefs, knowledge and behaviour; and third, what is imparted by those trained and qualified to give 'systematic instruction' of various sorts. All three contribute to the individual's readiness for later life. The child by his unaided efforts learns a great deal about his 'environment' and may develop skill in manipulating some part of it. He is putting himself on the road to a career which may require anything from a very simple skill to the complexities made possible by the highest activities of the brain. At the same time he is finding out about human nature; that some people are nice, some are nasty, many are both; how they react, how to bring out the best or worst in them. The amateur instructors — parents, neighbours, people in frequent contact with the child, 'transmit culture'. In a primitive society, knowledge, beliefs and behaviour are handed down from generation to generation. Most of the people of the world owe their education to what they have learnt for themselves and what has been imparted to them by those with whom they have close contact. However, most societies have an elite who have also been educated by 'professionals': those who have studied some branch of knowledge in depth and in more recent years have also been taught the art of conveying it to others, that is the technique of teaching. In this country it was only five years after schooling for all children became compulsory that teacher training colleges were set up, in 1885; not very impressive at the time, but now important establishments of higher education. What they impart to their students is something of various branches of knowledge, of one or more special skills, a technique of thinking, as yet insufficiently developed, and increasingly an understanding of the problems and troubles of those whom they will later teach.

'Education' has become 'professionalised': we have Local Education Authorities, education officers and at the top of the pyramid the Department of Education and Science (DES), none of which pay much attention to the 'informal' strands of education. Hitherto professional educators, concentrating on teaching what they 'know', have been amongst the slowest to learn what is needed to cope with change and so they have been unable to guide their clients, learners of all ages, towards the field of action. We are not able to use to the best advantage opportunities made possible by new technology and operational practice. Too often they serve as pitfalls rather than launching pads because scientific advances are put to uses not based on value systems derived from social needs, and our society contains many examples of confused and contradictory values. Re-examination of one's own and society's aims, and the methods to attain them, will be more rewarding if people are imbued with a sense of values (White's 'virtues' maybe) that arise from awareness of the needs of others. Such values would help the development of a sense of service in young people growing to adulthood.

Various aspects of schooling have been radically analysed by such as Illich (1971, 1974), Reimer (1971), Gross and Gross (1972), Postman and Weingartner (1972), Goodman (1974) and Lister (1974a). Their iconoclastic approach is as relevant to the needs of children growing up in a world where they are ignoramuses, misfits or too conformist, as to attempts we should be making to change that world. However, it is not necessary to follow deschoolers to the end of their argument — and they may be at their weakest when suggesting alternative modes of education. It is sufficient to suggest that teachers make a start at improving their service to children, especially in secondary schools, by examining the degree to which they encourage 'learning' rather than just 'education' or 'training'.

Holt (1969) believed that the concept of 'curriculum' needed radical re-examination. The lives of the more academic children in secondary schools are dominated by the curricula demanded by examination boards and institutions of tertiary education. Their heavy hand has ensured a disproportionate emphasis in schools and universities on learning what can be regurgitated in forms of examination that can readily 'assess' the candidate's 'proficiency'. Not only has education become formalised administratively, its content has been restricted largely to an acquisition of facts, figures, thoughts, opinions — already known or expressed in books, tapes, films and people's memories — 'programmed knowledge' by 'systematic instruction' by 'professionals' with 'special knowledge' of their 'subjects'. Such knowledge is certainly essential for the proper conduct of the world's business, but it is not sufficient alone (Revans, 1984a).

239

If the pupil sees little relationship between what he is being taught and his aspirations he will be bored if not rebellious. Hemming (1980) described how disruptive behaviour was eliminated by arranging curricula acceptable to the children. Galletly (1978) has discussed the value to the school's operations when real attempts were made to include children in decision making. Revans (1980) has shown how the objectives of classroom learning should be to demonstrate to pupils and teachers the excitement of creating a learning forum out of any participant group, helping to close the gap between learning and doing.

Children who get high marks for answers to factual questions in science examinations may get low ones for questions testing their ability to solve problems new to them. Holt (1969) remarks that the true test of intelligence is not how much we know how to do, but how we behave when we don't know what to do in new, strange and perplexing situations.

Young children's propensity for enquiry and experiment (Montessori, 1965) (1) is too often later quenched and independent thinking discouraged. Relatively few people, as they grow older, retain early questioning proclivities which may even be seen as deviant behaviour. Colleagues who question the status quo may be criticized for 'rocking the boat'.

Social and family customs, and traditional knowledge taught by family and school, act as a cement to make societies cohesive, and to instil values. They set patterns of adult thought and behaviour. It may reasonably be asked, what is the point of training if it is not to 'stick'? The paradox is that training which 'sticks' but later becomes inappropriate for life is nevertheless what we are 'stuck' with. We live in a world that is the scene of rapid technological, social and political change. If we do not adapt at a rate roughly commensurate with the rate of change we are in trouble. Facts and experience, though valuable raw materials, will not by themselves be sufficient to help us to change our attitudes, behaviour and actions at a speed to safeguard our quality of life, or even our survival. The key is for schooling to preserve through to adulthood the child's natural propensity for enquiry, so that he will be able to look afresh at intractable problems and make good use of opportunities. For most people these difficult and complex tasks will only be possible in a supportive milieu with well-functioning communication systems. People have to learn how to set these up and that should start at school. Then services and industry may begin to provide conditions that would enable people to make the best use of their knowledge and experience.

Schools, like the rest of us, are faced with a multitude of today's and tomorrow's problems that they have difficulty in solving at a rate that will satisfy the educational and social needs of their children. The DES sees as a purpose of education 'to help pupils to develop lively, enquiring minds, the ability to question and argue rationally . . .' (Secretary of State for Education and Science, 1985). Teachers may need support when their success in this results in pupils turning their critical faculties on what goes on in their schools. Failing to develop the academic child's capacity to think for himself, to be creative, and to learn how to deal with problems and make use of opportunities in work and life is bad enough, but it is disastrous for the academic 'failures' who are pushed out of school into the world with no qualifications except perhaps a distaste for authority. 'Failure in a success-oriented culture is hard to take' (Holt, 1969).

Showing how to use knowledge for promoting technological and social adaptation helps teachers as much as taught, for in the kind of education we are talking about the acts of teaching and learning are intertwined. Most learning is a social process, done best when motives are derived from personal or social imperatives, and the learner also teaches the educator (Frese, 1974; Revans, 1984b). It is a measure of how far we are from this simple elysium that our universities are staffed with dons who still seem to believe that knowledge for its own sake is the principal end of education, and its highest form. An Oxbridge don informed us of his pride in avoiding learning how to wire up an electric plug. There is a generational gap not only of years, but also of ideas, perceptions and ideals.

In order to reduce dependency and give him some control over his life the school child might engage in discussions about the constructive use and protection of the environment; and about ways in which newspapers, TV and other forms of media communication could improve his understanding of events that affect him and his family and friends. He could be helped to learn, in discussion with peers, teachers and others how to deal with his own process of growing up — how to resist blandishments and how to make relationships and to understand others' attitudes and problems. It takes time and experience to form opinions about the use of tobacco, alcohol or drugs, and about other activities such as sex that the young person may feel unready for. He needs to gain insight into means used by authority and the media to at best manipulate opinion and at worst to misinform; and to think about ways of reducing international tensions that make our world so fraught with danger and anxiety. Every secondary school should be a warm, friendly, purposeful, accepting place in which the primary aim is to teach self-confidence, self-respect, cooperation and respect for others (Hemming, 1982, 1983). Examinations are not the best way of helping children to grow up into self-reliant, confident, thoughtful, questioning adults.

Changes in schooling and curricula are slow because of entrenched beliefs in places of higher education about the meaning and purpose of knowledge. The Royal Society of Arts began its campaign for 'Education for Capability' in 1979. A group from a wide spectrum in society published its 'Manifesto for Change' in the *Times* in 1981. In succeeding publications HMI have criticized aspects of education in our schools. Methods that put the teacher in a secondary role, and use each particular here-and-now rather than the standard book, as the learning medium, are seen as a threat to our academies (Revans, 1981b). The attention being directed to these matters by Hemming (1980), Hargeaves (1982), the Royal Society of Arts and others, deserves support.

We suggest that to be fulfilled the moral autonomy of White (1982) must be matched by some degree of physical autonomy, certainly so far as may be practised without discomfort to others. Yet dependency is a feature of our age. It may indeed be fostered, though for very different reasons, by both 'right' and 'left' ideologies, and by professional groups. Dependency is reduced when people discern that those they have relationships with — parents, spouses and colleagues at work, or who are in 'authority' — teachers, supervisors, managers and other professional people — are ready to listen to what they have to say and, the ultimate accolade, sometimes act upon it. Only then will the buds of young personalities begin to swell and bloom. So we do not believe that White goes far enough. Children must be helped to *practise* social virtues.

Demands, duties and rewards

Vulnerability is apparent in many professionals who are insufficiently trained, from schooldays onward, to cope with the responsibilities and trauma of innovation, of high standards of work and of providing service for others; and who are not versed in setting up supportive communication systems and learning how to use them. A competitive society is not predisposed to notions of compassion and of drawing upon others' help.

Interaction with the environment may act as a challenge, a demand upon the individual. It should be part of the educational process to encourage young people to respond positively to challenges for they are part of character training for life after school, not as in dependency, occasions simply for commiseration. HMI have criticized schools for not demanding enough of pupils (DES, 1980). The child has to learn that rights have to be earned or paid for, and that duties are the obverse of rights on the coin of life (Pence, 1983). Willingness to accept responsibilities, and to discharge corresponding duties, implies accepting 'ownership' of a problem.

To 'own' a problem, with an appropriate set of social values, is the first step to constructive action upon it by an individual or group. Learning is most effective when the outcome is relevant action, which then leads to further learning. The process is helped, and likely to be more effective, if it takes place in the company of others ('comrades in adversity') facing problems and challenges. It can be greatly facilitated by participative, supportive methods such as action learning.

We should not underestimate the task of bringing about changes in methods of teaching in an educational culture dominated by authority and dependence. But there are enough ideas about to give impetus to observing and measuring more exactly causes and effects in social affairs so as to alter the course of the educational stream and put it in spate.

Notes

1. Dr Maria Montesorri (1870-1952) believed that one of the teacher's principal roles was to observe: 'The teacher must understand and *feel* her position of *observer*: the *activity* must lie in the *phenomenon*.' (p 87). '. . . the fundamental guide must be the *method of observation*, in which is included and understood the liberty of the child.' (p 108). (Emphases in the original.)

Chapter 12 – Communications

> When complaints are freely heard, deeply consi-
> dered, and speedily reformed, then is the utmost
> bound of civil liberty attained that wise men look
> for.   — Milton: Areopagitica.

When human affairs are in disorder, and perceptions of diagnosis and therapy clouded, the first step to clarity is to examine the facts relevant to the confronting problems; needs must be understood and expressed, and systems formulated for assistance. Free communications are integral to all these processes. The school problem that brought the DBIS group into being was unresolved because of failures in communication between agencies connected with it. The subject is so important in dealing with such delicate matters as behaviour that we give special, though brief, attention to some aspects of it.

Communications are much more than the physical act of transmitting information, whether by speech, writing or mechanical means. They embrace non-verbal cues offered by people during interaction, the messages people perceive from the way others behave towards them, and how people react to what others say or do. Communications are not an end in themselves; they are a tool, a process, for a variety of purposes in life and work, and they are a basic element in building relationships.

Examples of failure in communications

Failures in communication cause frustration and anger in people who are trying to maintain high standards in their work for clients. Seemingly trivial instances of maladroit communications negate the communicator's intention, and may betoken a dismissive if not arrogant attitude. Mal-communications carry their own messages. The head of a primary school had a meeting about a child with a social worker. The social worker did most of the talking and after three quarters of an hour no advance was made in solving the *school's* problems connected with the child. The head of a secondary school was astonished to hear from the police juvenile bureau that his school had one of the highest rates of children being taken to court in the borough. During a conversation with a secondary school teacher about pupil disaffection James Hemming's book *The betrayal of youth* (1980) was mentioned. The teacher had not heard of it and construed the title to mean that children were letting down their schools — the opposite of the author's case.

Social workers may decide to take a child into care without sufficient regard to the fact that he might have to leave his school which had become a valuable anchor for him, indeed perhaps his only one. Teachers have gone to court to try to prevent this and they should be included in preliminary discussions. Failure of social workers' communication systems has been examined by Lask and Lask (1981). Residential staff in children's homes work not only in isolation from the community but also from their colleagues. 'They (management) never come near us unless something goes wrong' was a common complaint made by these workers involved in the National Children's Bureau 'Who Cares?' project (Page, 1977). The project demonstrated how little was known of children's feelings about being in care until they were asked. Then 'The young people readily identified the stresses of daily life for staff and children alike' (Page, 1977). Our experience of listening to nurses talking about their hospital when starting their training has been mentioned: 'Sister' they said, 'has her problems too'. When young people are so perceptive, why are managers so unresponsive to human needs?

The form of the working party set up by Ealing Borough Council (see Introduction) was such that the day-to-day problems of disruptive behaviour in schools could not be suitably illuminated because of the remoteness of its members from the chalkface. Thus some actions, however well-intentioned, may block the very enlightenment that is sought. Davies (1976) saw how much teachers could learn from each other if they discussed their work and methods together. In a comprehensive secondary school he found that the art department had successfully practised team-teaching whilst the rest of the school knew virtually nothing of what it was doing.

If, as happens, teachers criticize the work of another agency in intemperate terms, probably getting some of their facts wrong, and if staff of the criticized agency reply simply attacking the teachers as ignorant busybodies (as also happens), little advance is made in understanding the causes of friction. Yet social services, child guidance staff and educational administrators are well equipped to enquire into the causes of teachers' anxiety that is at the bottom of their 'disruptive behaviour'. Inappropriate ripostes are a form of labelling; they help no one, least of all the child; no one learns anything useful; only attitudes harden. Such experiences underline the need for inter-agency accountability.

In a study of specialist fostering (Shaw and Hipgrave, 1983) foster parents said that their major problems stemmed not from the behaviour of the foster children but from the vagaries of social workers and of agency policies and procedures. Social workers thought that their human relations skills were most severely tested not by clients, but by the agencies within which they worked and others with which they negotiated. The foster parent group was seen as a 'threat' by some area social workers not directly involved in it, who regarded its solidarity as dangerous to social work authority.

Information should be freely available, but small economies hinder preventive social reform: there is delay in publishing figures for children in care; the work of the Office of Population Censuses and Surveys is being restricted; the Children's Committee and the Centre for Educational Disadvantage are no more; the annual publication of information about the numbers of people in poverty has been suspended.

Sybil Marshall (1963) said in her account of her school: 'It seemed to me that the first objective was to close the gap between spoken and written English. School life had a tradition that talking was what you did out of school, and writing what you did inside. My pupils were at first as loath to talk inside as they would have been to write in the playground, and had no idea that talking and writing and reading bore any relation to each other. The freedom given to them soon loosened their tongues . . . As the children . . . talked freely . . . they began to realise that a good discussion was as exciting as any other sort of contest . . . Discussions ranged far and wide over many different subjects, but nearly always came round, in the end, to questions of religion, ethics and morals.'

Causes of poor communications

Anxiety. It is accepted that a mild degree of anxiety commonly improves the ability to learn and act, and sharpens performance. Greater degrees may inhibit learning and delay or distort action. The reasons for anxiety, and the environment in which it arises, may also determine not only its degree, but how it influences behaviour. One of us (NFC) found that the nurse in charge of the sick staff ward at his hospital had stopped visiting for a nurse with a cold after two nurse friends had been found sitting on her bed. The hospital was short of nurses and the staff nurse thought of two more being off sick with colds caught from the patient. She abruptly sent them off and told them not to visit again. The two visitors learnt that the staff nurse was unsympathetic to junior nurses, but not that as nurses who were offering their services to dependent people (patients) they should protect their health. The staff nurse came to see that her anxiety, arising from proper thoughts about maintaining patient care, had prevented her from helping the three student nurses to learn that their behaviour might interfere with their aims as nurses. The visitors might

249

even have been allowed, without risk, to put their heads round the patient's door once a day to say hello to their friend. They might then have gone off in a more positive state of mind about senior nurses and the hospital as a place of work. Here the senior nurse's behaviour was influenced by the training she had received in an authoritarian institution (a hospital) and by consciousness of the need to accept the discipline of her role as a professional worker in that institution.

Bruner (1968) has remarked that the ability of problem solvers to use information correctively is known to vary as a function of their internal state, for example their degree of anxiety. Insecurity and anxiety may cause people to doubt the validity of questions, or even to discourage them (Revans, 1971). Laslett and Smith (1984) describe how easily teachers become anxious and how they may communicate this to pupils, causing undesired pupil behaviour. They and Kyriacou (1980) suggest methods for reducing anxiety in teachers.

Labelling. Knowledge about ourselves, the effects upon others of what we do at work, how we appear to others, how our own and others' attitudes may be changed, can come only through feedback — that is what we glean, implicitly or explicitly from others and from our own examination of events we take part in. If we attach a derogatory epithet to a child we are telling him our feelings about him and this may appear to him almost an act of violence. It is a form of malcommunication.

Examples of labelling may be culled from any school classroom or hospital ward, when pupils or teachers, student nurses or doctors attempt to relieve their anxiety or frustration. But the negative nature of labelling ensures that the stigmatized learns only to dislike, even to hate the critic. It can act as a form of rejection. Classroom teachers' dismissive attitudes to the work of remedial teachers, school counsellors, teachers in withdrawal units and in special schools amount to a form of labelling and spoil relationships and communications.

Labelling has dangerous social implications. We relieve our feelings about Peter Sutcliffe, the Yorkshire murderer of women, by calling him the 'Ripper'. No serious study of his childhood history appears to have been reported, to help us to understand why he behaved as he did. We have learnt little from this wretched episode about how to prevent other people from behaving in the same way. What do we really care about the safety of women?

Hierarchy. It is a matter of common observation that in a hierarchy there is a general flow of information, opinion and orders downwards from superiors to subordinates. It is an integral part of the structure, as Revans (1973) remarked: 'I know of no organisation theory postulating that the first condition for survival (let alone growth) is a capacity to learn; and that, since learning is a social process, the first institutional need is for a communication system that maximises the feedback from subordinate to superior. Most organisation theories have much to say upon the need for managerial control (a form of institutional coercion), but little, if anything, about managerial learning. Since writers on these subjects are, whether managers or academics, generally those who have managed to get on in life, this may not be surprising.' Obviously we cannot do without hierarchies in organisations in which there are wide differences in experience and expertise among staff; but those moving up the hierarchy should remain sensitively aware of the inhibiting effects of notions of 'managerial prerogative' and 'status' on *communications from lower levels*, and ensure that these are not stifled but encouraged. Many professional decisions affecting people's lives and health will be the responsibility of senior people, but such decisions will be all the more correct and effective if formulated after taking into account views of others concerned, particularly those directly involved in client interaction.

Hierarchies encourage people to distance themselves from others and to encourage attitudes which make communication less easy. Teachers' authoritarianism, engendered by the school structure, so affects children as to limit their capacity to learn, and pupils' attitudes to teachers and schools when they themselves become parents are so wary, that co-operation over *their* children's education is less than wholehearted.

Professionalism. The basis of good professional practice is to get clear who is the client and to define the degree and method of accountability to him. Freidson (1970) and Wilding (1982) have discussed attributes of professionalism, particularly the tendency to depersonalize the client. Dahrendorf (1984) points out that 'the other side of "privileges and protection" (for professionals) is always responsibility.' The teacher, by concentrating on his *teaching* may (like the doctor or nurse focussing too intently on the patient's physical state) ignore the emotional and social needs of child and parent, with unlooked for effects on his own work, and the child's behaviour.

There are many strands in professional work, some good when they relate to the maintenance of standards of work and integrity, some more doubtful that relate to power. Lord Horder claimed that only the doctor knew what good doctoring was, but the patient and his relatives may have ideas too. It is unhelpful for the teacher, in deciding what is best for his pupils, to leave out of account the feelings and wishes of parents and children. Such behaviour may 'disrupt' the lives of pupils. Some teachers avoid responsibility by simply denying that teaching is a profession.

Many definitions of a profession have been attempted. They should surely include the concept of service to the client. Its proper development would entail such converse between professional and client as to indicate a willingness on the professional's part to learn about himself and the effects of his work. Then the client might even be said to serve the professional, rather different from the use of status to protect him.

What can be done to improve communications?

> A moment of communication is a moment of reciprocal exchange. — Clare Winnicott (1968)

Ways of improving communications are often implicit in descriptions of their failures. In describing difficulties in communications we have made some suggestions for overcoming them. We refer the reader to other work on the subject (Fletcher, 1973, 1979, 1980; Byrne and Long, 1976; McLachlan, 1979) and to studies in which one of us (NFC) participated (Wieland and Leigh, 1971; Revans, 1972, 1976; Wieland, 1981). It is clear that communication systems will inevitably be complex and many faceted if they are to be effective and will necessitate hard work and soul searching by participants in the enterprise to make them so. Responsive relationships are a prerequisite for success. We must look to teachers to work constructively with remedial teachers, teachers in special schools, educational psychologists, social workers and other professionals, so as to provide themselves with the help necessary for dealing with children's behaviour problems and special needs.

However excellent the individual agencies that deal with children's disturbing behaviour, schools will get little relief unless those agencies work together, and relief comes quickest when they communicate directly with each other, as was found for example in a study of services for the mentally handicapped (Revans and Baquer, 1972; Baquer and Revans, 1973; Paine, 1974). These are the requirements for dealing with truancy and behavioural problems in schools (DES, 1978a). A liaison officer can provide a useful link between courts and other agencies (1). The value of coordination (communication) between services was emphasized by the Minister of State at the DHSS in his evidence to the *Select Committee on Violence in the Family* (1977) (2).

Not much is known about schools as communities though some light has been cast on them by Hargreaves (1967), Revans (1973, 1980), Davies (1976) and Mortimore (1978). Communications within and between schools and within the teaching profession would bear examination and development.

Young people respond when drawn into systems designed to enlarge communications, for example in play using Inter-Action games (Caldwell, 1972), or in the classroom (Glasser, 1975); or when asked to recount their personal experiences in care, at school or in higher education. Adults, like young persons, have much to learn from others' experiences as well as their own. Professionals' satisfaction from their work, and the quality of service they render, is dependent upon how they respond to the needs of their clients.

Consultation. The best administrators and managers develop consultation as a means of cultivating good communications and relationships. To be effective consultation is more than just asking someone for his opinion, or of giving people information, though these may be indispensable elements. People's views must be sought as part of a process of action — putting right something that is amiss, or starting an initiative. To ask for advice or opinions only to ignore them, or to request them at such short notice that a sensible reply is impossible — as is not infrequent in education and health services, is to depress morale. The art of listening is part of consultation — '. . . the way people's opinions are listened to and dealt with or ignored; the way their feelings are ruffled or respected . . .' (Dr Russell Barton, 1972, on what he calls 'people time').

Attitudes, relationships and adaptation. 'All too often, structures and organisational features can seem to take on a life of their own, which results in the people who work within a particular structure having so much work to do to keep the structure stable that the *purpose* of the structure is never doubted.' (Shaw and Hipgrave, 1983). Any change threatening a state of 'equilibrium' is met with forces to restore the *status quo* (Argyle, 1967), and there may be no easy way to circumvent them. Professionals with pride in their work may be vulnerable to suggestions that they might do their work differently. However valid the reasons for new methods, their mere mention may be taken as criticism, and some find this hard to bear. It does not make much difference whence the pressure for development comes. Bruner (1968) distinguished between coping and defending. 'Coping respects the requirements of problems we encounter while still respecting our integrity. Defending is a strategy whose objective is avoiding or escaping from problems for which we

253

believe there is no solution that does not violate our integrity of functioning.' He admitted that in real life there was always a mixture of coping and defending.

The un-met need for support for the 'wounded healer' in the social services may affect the quality of work (Oliver, 1983). The principle of accountability between interacting professionals and agencies that we have discussed, would encourage people to look beyond their own immediate work arena. Articles in newspapers criticizing those who look after children in care may elicit a flood of defensive replies (3). Some may be justified, but the point is missed. It is that we expect too much of children who have been rejected at home and are trying to cope with being in care — a greater burden in fact than we know their rejecting parents (themselves rejected as children) can cope with.

It is the impression that administrators have little appreciation of personal qualities or of the importance of team work. They can find a replacement for a much valued secretary in the same way as a replacement for a chair. Interdisciplinary communications will not develop adequately unless those appointed to be the chief officers concerned with the care of children wish to have a genuine understanding of children and of the many factors that promote or harm their welfare.

In considering the development of children's relationships we must remember the effect upon them of national and international tensions which, though they have always been with us, seem now to be more intense and extensive. Man's technological advances in the 'arts' of war and the horrific destructive power of his weapons; the tensions arising in societies because of racialism, sexism, economic stringency, unemployment and issues of law and order; and the clash of ideologies — are all causing divisions within societies and between them. In order to reduce young people's anxieties about the adult world they are entering why not encourage those in secondary schools' fifth and sixth forms and in higher education to examine the reasons for conflict between ideologies and people, and for individual and group combative responses, and introduce them to ideas about how to find non-aggressive ways to deal with conflict? The staff of special schools for maladjusted children who have learned how to manage aggressive behaviour could help with this. Such exercises would help professions to be more client oriented. They would begin to equip adults to make constructive use of their increasing leisure, for example in youth work and child care, and to run a social democracy that was more participative for more people. It would probably be the best way to make inroads into delinquency and crime statistics. None of this can be done without the informed participation of teachers.

The study and understanding of relationships is a complex and as yet rather uncharted sea of human experience. Dyadic relationships have received some attention (Argyle, 1967; Hinde, 1979; Duck, 1986). 'Peace studies' in schools, which are starting down some of these roads, have come in for criticism from those who see them as a menace to national stability. Politicians too can be defensive.

Young people brought up to question constructively received knowledge and establishment attitudes might become more independent minded and able to change their own attitudes and beliefs in the face of here-and-now imperatives. Exploration of attitudes formed by nurses in their work illustrated the complexities of the subject (Boorer, 1970). For further treatment of attitudes the reader is referred to a comprehensive collection of papers by Warren and Jahoda (1973).

Team work. The Shorter OED defines a team rather narrowly and we have suggested that the concept should be broadened. Though professional people may have disagreements, they have a common aim in their work for the service of clients. We have mentioned what we believe to be the merits of team working and the basic 'core team' for child care, in Part II, Chapter 8 (i) and Part II, Chapter 8 (iii). To get commitment from members of a team the purposes and aims of the work must be defined and accepted. Teams work better if supportive methods of working, as in action learning, are built in to reduce natural defensiveness and encourage acceptance of change. Not all members of a team might need to be present at every discussion. Important elements in team work are the learning that takes place through pondering individual members' problems with mutual respect and sharing of knowledge and experience; and the likelihood of agreement about action (Coghill, 1981).

Communications are facilitated by the use of teams, though there are pitfalls (Cortazzi, 1973). Professionals are busy people with many responsibilities and they do not like to waste time. So team meetings should be as seldom as is compatible with objectives, should be purposefully and expeditiously conducted, and decisions promptly carried out. Otherwise teams won't 'work'. The working of multi-disciplinary teams was examined in a King's Fund project (Batchelor and McFarlane, 1980). Payne (1982) has written about team work, mainly in the social services. Knight and Bowers (1984) mention points to make teams work well.

The Court Report (DHSS, 1976b) recognised the importance of a child-centred service, with the same inter-disciplinary team of health workers covering all aspects of the child's health and medical needs from birth and through the school years. The Committee concluded that a great deal could be done with existing resources.

Management. People with special knowledge are valuable resources and make essential contributions to the work not only of their own organisations but also to that of other agencies. However, while involvement of a social worker or a member of the CG team, as 'experts' may be necessary to solve a school problem, they cannot do it alone. Their advice and help ('input'), though necessary, will seldom be sufficient. Teachers, other school and agency staff, and parents, all perhaps 'experts' in the sense that they have special knowledge and experience, must also be committed to solving the problem. Good solutions are most likely when everyone concerned gets together to examine the matter, for it is then that each learns with and from the others. Feedback from clients and professionals is a useful management aid.

The inherent difficulty experienced by a superior in learning from a subordinate may be at least partially overcome by training (Part IV, Chapter 11) and by the use of groups or teams for specific purposes. To achieve such learning those in authority need support — managing directors, headteachers, hospital consultants or senior nurses, but the nature of the system tends to preclude both insight and support. Supportive management should be able to turn contretemps into learning exercises so that confrontations are diffused and their recurrence prevented. 'User groups', a form of inter-professional accountability, can reduce friction between departments and agencies. They may be one-off or on-going occasions for those who render or receive a service, colleagues or clients, to find out if provision is adequate or needs revision. Comments may be made on requests thought to be unreasonable, or on the best use of what is available. To get the best from a service the seeker must decide what he really wants and how to ask for it, initial processes that may be facilitated by discussion with those to be asked for help. Counselling is a form of communication that managers seldom consider. It can be valuable for people at all levels. Experiences with action learning have shown how people like managing directors and hospital consultants can learn with and from each other in homogeneous or heterogeneous groups, once they are persuaded to come together. Such benefits are available to teachers.

Why not offer budgets, to be spent after discussion by all parties in the school or the residential home, so that everyone concerned is incorporated into decision making and the cared-for feel the money is to some extent theirs to spend?

All that has been said about the anxieties of hospital workers, and the need for thoughtful questioning of attitudes and practices by all who care for patients (Revans, 1964), applies equally to schools and teachers, and to social workers, CG staff and educational administrators. Thought-ful management has a role in getting unaware professional people to see how these factors influence the development of communications, relationships and decision making.

Notes

1. The London Borough of Hounslow employed a court liaison officer in its Social Services Department. He acted as a coordinator, and organised joint visits, for example of magistrates, CG staff, social workers and others, to institutions such as assessment centres, residential homes and other places run by the local authority for children. He arranged meetings between social workers and magistrates.

2. *First Report*, Vol. II, p 421, para 825.

3. For example as happened after the publication of the article by Sally Vincent in the *Observer* of 22/4/1979 quoted in Part I, Chapter 3.

Chapter 13 — Confidence and confidentiality

In our society we recognise that people have a right to keep matters of health, family and personal affairs private if they wish. In the church, medicine and the law there is a long tradition of confidentiality. Its basis is confidence that unless he agrees information given by the client shall go no further than the professional and the team of which he may be a part, except for certain statutory requirements (Parkes, 1982), even if the intention is to be helpful to the client. Information obtained by social workers about their clients is treated similarly. We believe that requirements for the child in school differ little from those for sick people.

This sounds simple enough but what we think or do may affect others, who also have rights. What is the doctor to tell the spouse of his patient who is found to have venereal disease? What should the social worker do who discovers his client is an arsonist? In such predicaments the client may be urged to talk with relatives, friends or even the police though such exhortations may not be followed. School counsellors may be reluctant to share information about a child with teacher colleagues or even the head. Social workers may keep from teachers information about a child or his family for it is not only its confidential nature that is important but what the recipient does with it. If social workers believe that teachers will use information to label a child so making his life more difficult, they will be reluctant to tell teachers much. Then teachers will feel let down by social workers, so increasing the mistrust that is a main cause of faulty communications between them in the first place.

Do parents, or children, know about school record cards? Some parents may be worried about what is written on them. They may not want teachers to know about their private selves, partly because of a memory of teachers as figures of authority. Yet a head and his staff may need to look up information to help a child. How much 'confidential' information obtained from a parent who has trusted him, should a head give to a social worker whom he hardly knows? When a pupil's behaviour is unacceptable the school may not be well informed about his medical or psychological history, and know little more of the family social circumstances than it can discover for itself. One child we know of had had numerous surgical operations about which the school appeared to know nothing.

Doubts about what a school will do with personal information about a child reflects upon the school, the teachers and the system. Professionals sufficiently confident about each other's caring attitudes may exchange information about a child and his family with frankness. Such confidence would lead to parental acquiescence in educational exchanges, for example, between head, governors and the authority, to avoid ordering suspension while they learn about the psychological and social circumstances of the pupil. Doubt about how information is to be used, leading to its being withheld, may impede care of the client. Working as a team, with accountability between professionals and agencies, helps people to use information in a professional manner.

Even non-forthcoming parents may discuss their problems with their GP or health visitor, and this may be the first and only intimation of the existence of a distressed child. The singularity of the matter is that usually no one, neither parents, child nor professional, can solve these problems alone and if for whatever reason other professionals are excluded then the problems are likely to remain unsolved, so that the child and perhaps his teacher continue to suffer.

There are not infrequently gaps in the information passed by CG staff to teachers, though sometimes the teacher knows far more about the family. The great problem is the time that it takes to build up the relationship in which information, or even suspicions, can be shared. Once two people begin to discuss a situation, they can often get off the horns of their dilemma without betraying their informant(s).

There may be particular difficulties when children have psychological troubles. There are things that the child is not supposed to know or, if he knows, is supposed not to tell. Some of these he will want to tell his psychotherapist, for instance his own illegitimacy, the extra-marital relationship of one of his parents, incestuous behaviour of a parent or relative to the patient or to a sibling, father's criminal activities or mother's shoplifting. These, and even less serious family secrets, may shed light on the origins of the child's problems. All the report to the school may mention are 'difficulties in the background', leaving the head and other teachers with little information and much frustration. It is a true doctor's dilemma. If the child tells him that the baby of the family (or the subnormal child) is being physically battered, it is the therapist's duty to suggest that the appropriate agency should investigate. The therapist need not imply that his information is true or give the source of it, but children are as good as adults at putting two and two together and, if the end result is a prison sentence for father, the child will feel that his trust has been betrayed and that he himself has been treacherous. Similarly, if the child reveals his own delinquencies, the parents and probably the school ought to know, but if the therapist has promised not to tell . . .? Promises should be kept if possible, but the child can be urged to tell his parents and the school, perhaps mentioning that he has told the therapist.

If a child psychiatrist wants to communicate with a teacher this must be cleared with the child and his parents, and it must be certain that the teacher will act in a professional manner. There may be such doubt that the psychiatrist plays his cards close to his chest. Teachers have it largely in their own hands to get themselves out of this dilemma by which their work is made more complicated and they get less help with their difficult children. We have argued that if parents have confidence in the 'school care team' they may be readier to talk to its members. Dismissive attitudes of professionals towards each other do not conduce to confidence between them. Trust between teachers and CG staff should grow with greater contact between schools and helping agencies.

A lively debate is developing concerning the client's 'right to know' about what is placed in files about him (NUT, 1984). Answers to the delicate questions raised in this debate can best emerge from informed, perceptive and trusting dialogue between professionals and clients.

The complex dilemmas and contradictions of confidence and confidentiality will become clearer with continuing discussion and appraisal of the issues involved — the client's desire for privacy, and the professional's need for relevant information in order to act responsibly. Above all the possession of information should never be used to harm the client.

We end by emphasizing that the need for confidentiality, with the insoluble dilemmas it brings, would arise less often if our care of children were such that their behaviour was less of a problem. Prevention is best.

Appendix 1

Activities, bodies, initiatives — voluntary, charitable or government funded, local or national — concerned to help people with family and related difficulties

Adoption Resource Exchange, 11 Southwark Street, London SE1 1RQ.

Advisory Centre for Education (ACE), 18 Victoria Park Square, London E2 9PB.

Aide à Toute Ditresse (ATD), British Secretariat, 48 Addington Square, London SE5 7LB.

Apex Trust, 31 Clapham Road, London SW9 0JE.

Association for Improvements in the Maternity Services (AIMS), 21 Franklin Gardens, Hitchin, Herts SG4 0NE.

Association of British Adoption Agencies, 4 Southampton Row, London WC1B 4AA.

Association of Chief Officers of Probation, 20-30 Lawefield Lane, Wakefield, West Yorkshire WF2 8SP.

Association of County Councils, Eaton House, 66A Eaton Square, London SW1W 9BH.

Association of Directors of Social Services, Social Services Department, County Hall, Taunton, Somerset TA1 4DY.

Association of Workers for Maladjusted Children. Monographs are obtainable from the Treasurer, 71 South Road, Portishead, Bristol BS20 9DY. The Association publishes a journal — *Maladjustment and Therapeutic Education.*

Blackfriars Settlement, 44 Nelson Square, London SE1 0QA.

Boundstone School, Sompting, Lancing, West Sussex BN15 9QZ.

British Association for the Study and Prevention of Child Abuse and Neglect (BASPCAN), Jacob Bright Children's Centre, Whitworth Road, Rochdale, Lancs OL12 6EP.

British Association of Social Workers, 16 Kent Street, Birmingham B5 6RD.

Central Council for Education and Training in Social Work, Derbyshire House, St Chad's Street, London WC1H 8AD.

Centre for Information and Advice on Educational Disadvantage, 11 Anson Road, Manchester M14 5BY. (Closed in 1980 in Government economies.)

Chartered Institute of Public Finance and Accountancy, 2/3 Robert Street, London WC2N 6BH.

Child Poverty Action Group, 1 Macklin Street, London WC2B 5NH. Publishes *Poverty; and Welfare Rights Bulletin.*

Children's Legal Centre, 20 Compton Terrace, London N1 2UN. Publishes *Childright.*

Childwatch, 60 Beck Road, Everthorpe, South Cave, Brough, North Humberside HU15 2JJ.

Community Service Volunteers, National Volunteer Agency, 237 Pentonville Road, London N1 9NJ.

Confederation for the Advancement of State Education (CASE), Mrs Y Peacock, 10 Parkfield Street, Rowhedge, Colchester, Essex CO5 7EL.

Cranfield Institute of Technology, Cranfield, Bedford MK43 0AL.

CRY-SIS, BM CRY-SIS, London WC1N 3XX. Phone: 01-404 5011.

DES, Elizabeth House, York Road, London SE1 7PH.

DHSS, Alexander Fleming House, Elephant and Castle, London SE1 6BY.

Disability Alliance, 21 Star Street, London W2 1QB.

Disfigurement Guidance Centre, Clydesdale Bank Buildings, 152 High Street, Newburgh, Cupar, Fife KY14 6DY, Scotland. Publishes the *Bulletin of the Society of Skin Camouflage and Disfigurement Therapy.*

Ealing Community Health Council, 119 Uxbridge Road, Hanwell, London W7 3ST.

Equal Opportunities Commission, Overseas House, Quay Street, Manchester M3 3HN.

Fabian Society, 11 Dartmouth Street, London SW1H 9BN.

Family Rights Group, 6-9 Manor Gardens, Holloway Road, London N7 6LA.

Family Service Units (Headquarters), 207 Old Marylebone Road, London NW1 5QP.

Family Welfare Association, 501-505 Kingsland Road, Dalston, London E8 4AU.

Gingerbread, 35 Wellington Street, London WC2E 7BN.

Gloucestershire Association for Family Life, 2 College Street, Gloucester GL1 2NE.

Grubb Institute of Behavioural Studies, Cloudesley Street, London N1 0HU.

Haringey Association for the Advancement of State Education, 28 Lanchester Road, London N6 4TA; or 74 Mountview Road, London N4 4JR.

Health Education Council, 78 New Oxford Street, London WC1A 1AH.

Help! I need somebody, Kimpton's Bookshop, 205 Great Portland Street, London W1N 6LR.

Home and School Council, 17 Jacksons Lane, Billericay, Essex CM11 1AH.

Huddersfield District Health Authority, St Luke's House, Blackmoorfoot Road, Crosland Moor, Huddersfield HD4 5RH.

Incest Crisis Line, 32 Newbury Close, Northolt, Middx. UB5 4JF. Phones: 01-422 5100; 01-890 4732. Information available about regional centres.

Inner London Education Authority (ILEA) Educational Home Visiting Project, Deptford Green School, Edward Street, London SE14 6LQ.

Inter-Action, The Centre for Social Enterprise, 15 Wilkin Street, London NW5 3NG.

International Foundation for Action Learning, 28 The Grove, Ealing, London W5 5LH.

International Voluntary Service, 53 Regent Road, Leicester LE1 6YL.

Junction Project, Northcote House, 37 Royal Street, London SE1 7LL.

Kidscape, 82 Brook Street, London W1Y 1YG. Phone: 01-493 9845.

King Edward's Hospital Fund for London, 14 Palace Court, London W2 4HT.

King's Fund Hospital Centre, 126 Albert Street, London NW1 7NF.

Local Government Training Board, 8 The Arndale Centre, Luton, Beds LU1 2TS.

London Medical Group, Tavistock House North, Tavistock Square, London WC1H 9LG.

Manpower Services Commission, Corporate Services Division, Moorfoot, Sheffield S1 4PQ.

Maternity Alliance, 12 Park Crescent, London W1N 4EQ.

Mental Health Foundation, 10 Hallam Street, London W1N 6DH.

MIND: Wandsworth, 3 Brodrick Road, London SW17 7DZ.

Mutual Aid Centre, 18 Victoria Park Square, London E2 9PF. Publish *Hello, can I help you?* 1980.

National Association for Care and Resettlement of Offenders (NACRO), 169 Clapham Road, London SW9 0PU.

National Association for Mental Health (MIND), 22 Harley Street, London W1N 2ED.

National Association for the Welfare of Children in Hospital (NAWCH), Exton House, 7 Exton Street, London SE1 8UE.

National Association of Governors and Managers (NAGM), 81 Rustlings Road, Sheffield S11 7AB.

National Association of Young People in Care (NAYPIC), Salem House, 28A Manor Row, Bradford BD1 4QU.

National Association of Youth Clubs, Keswick House, 30 Peacock Lane, Leicester LE1 5NY.

National Childbirth Trust, 9 Queensborough Terrace, London W2 3TB.

National Children's Bureau, 8 Wakley Street, London EC1V 7QE. Publishes *Concern*.

National Children's Centre, A division of the National Educational Research and Development Trust, Longroyd Bridge, Huddersfield, West Yorkshire HD1 3LF. Phone: 0484-41733. They have a list of voluntary groups who will help parents at risk.

National Children's Home, 85 Highbury Park, London N5 1UD. Publishes *Children Today*.

National Confederation of Parent-Teacher Associations, 43 Stonebridge Road, Northfleet, Gravesend, Kent DA11 9DS.

National Council for Civil Liberties, 186 Kings Cross Road, London WC1X 9DE.

National Council for One Parent Families, 255 Kentish Town Road, London NW5 2LX.

National Council for Special Education, 1 Wood Street, Stratford-upon-Avon CV37 6JE.

National Council for Voluntary Organisations, 26 Bedford Square, London WC1B 3HU. Publishes a *Directory of Voluntary Organisations*.

National Foundation for Educational Research, The Mere, Upton Park, Slough, Berks SL1 2DQ.

National Information for Parents of Prematures: Education, Resources and Support (NIPPERS), c/o Sam Segal Perinatal Unit, St Mary's Hospital, Praed Street, Paddington, London W2 1NY.

National Institute for Social Work (NISW), Mary Ward House, 5 Tavistock Place, London WC1H 9SS.

National Perinatal Epidemiology Unit, Research Institute, Churchill Hospital, Oxford OX3 7LJ.

National Society for the Prevention of Cruelty to Children, 67 Saffron Hill, London EC1N 8RS. The National Advisory Centre, NSPCC, offers advice and consultation. Phone: 01-242 1626.

National Union of School Students (NUSS), 3 Endsleigh Street, London WC1H 0DU.

National Union of Teachers (NUT), Hamilton House, Mabledon Place, London WC1H 9BD.

National Women's Aid Federation, 52-54 Featherstone Street, London EC1Y 8RT. Phone: 01-251 6429.

Nuffield Provincial Hospital's Trust, 3 Prince Albert Road, London NW1 7SP.

Office of Population Censuses and Surveys (OPCS), St. Catherine's House, 10 Kingsway, London WC2B 6JP.

Parents Anonymous, 6 Manor Gardens, Islington, London N7 6LA. Phones: 01-263 5672 (office); 01-263 8918.

Parents for Children, 222 Camden High Street, London NW1 8QR.

Parents Magazine, 116 Newgate Street, London EC1A 7AE.

Patients' Association, Room 33, 18 Charing Cross Road, London WC2H 0HR. Publishes a directory of national organisations concerned with various diseases and handicaps.

Personal Social Services Council, Brook House, 2-16 Torrington Place, London WC1E 7HN.

Pirate Club, Pirate Castle, Oval Road, London NW1 7EA.

Policy Studies Institute, 1/2 Castle Lane, London SW1E 6DR.

Pre-School Playgroups Association (PPA), Alfred House, Aveline Street, London SE11 5DJ; or 7 Royal Terrace, Glasgow G3 7NT.

Right to Comprehensive Education (formerly the Campaign for Comprehensive Education), 4 Hammersmith Terrace, London W6 9TS. Publishes *Comprehensive Education*.

Royal Society for the Encouragement of Arts, Manufactures and Commerce, John Adam Street, London WC2N 6EZ.

Save the Children Fund, Mary Datchelor House, 17 Grove Lane, London SE5 8RD.

School Curriculum Development Committee (incorporating the Secondary Examination Council — formerly the Schools Council), Newcombe House, 45 Notting Hill Gate, London W11 3JB.

Schools Council — see School Curriculum Development Committee.

Scope Family Centre, 26 Teme Crescent, Millbrook, Southampton SO1 9DF.

Scottish Health Education Unit, Woodburn House, Canaan Lane, Edinburgh EH10 4SG.

Society for the Study of Medical Ethics, Tavistock House North, Tavistock Square, London WC1H 9LG. Publishes the *Journal of Medical Ethics*.

Society of Teachers Opposed to Physical Punishment (STOPP), 18 Victoria Park Square, London E2 9PB.

Spastics Society, 12 Park Crescent, London W1N 4EQ.

Study Commission on the Family, 231 Baker Street, London NW1 6XL.

Tavistock Institute of Human Relations, 120 Belsize Lane, London NW3 5BA.

Tower Hamlets Youth and Community Project, 162A Brick Lane, London E1 6RU.

Waterway Recovery Groups, 15 Nuns Orchard, Histon, Cambridge CB4 4EW. (WRG Ltd is a wholly-owned subsidiary of the Inland Waterways Association).

Appendix 2

Action learning

The outcome of work depends upon the ability of those engaged in it to learn from their experiences while doing it. Learning will occur when workers ask questions such as: What are the problems and opportunities confronting us and our organisation? How shall we define them, and decide what has to be done about them? What system of values shall guide us? What are the impediments to progress? What action can we take to achieve better performance?

Enterprises have within them all or most of the resources needed to solve their problems and to make use of their opportunities. The basis of action learning is to get people to relate action to learning, and learning to action, by dealing with their own and each other's everyday problems and opportunities. To achieve this end people are brought together, for example in an action learning project set, so that they learn with and from each other in a mutually supportive questioning process. This helps to make clear what are the real problems, reduces defensiveness and promotes changes in attitudes and relationships, and results in practical plans for progress.

Action learning produces its best results when those in the enterprise, especially the senior managers, are committed to making it work, and by setting up a sensitive and active communications network within their own organisation.

Learning and action take place sequentially and together by interchange in the group (managerial development), and by interplay between participants and their colleagues in the enterprise (institutional learning: organisational development).

The beginning of institutional learning (after Revans)

Seen in terms of logistics (the organisational steps that must necessarily be contrived to get action learning moving once it has been agreed to introduce a programme, or assembly of projects over the same period), the primary support is offered by the set. In this the participants ('fellows'), from different organisations, or different parts of the same organisation, meet regularly, each with a project, or an aspect of the same project,

271

different from the remainder. This is where the fellows debate, analyse and work out their particular problems, and the solutions to them. But since each project demands diagnosis and treatment in a real world that is necessarily outside the set, and since this real world, which in fact is the organisation which employs the fellow, is staffed with persons with whom the participant also has to work and to learn, it is necessary to secure some order in that world. The pattern of organisation so set up must also aim at action and learning, no less than does the set of particip-ants, although each participant may structure his/her pattern differently from any other. The pattern of discussion and debate that develops between the fellow and his colleagues at work in the real world has been named the 'structure d'acceuil' (literally 'framework of reception'); it is quite distinct from the project set. Some people prefer to use the term network, with its connotations of support, awareness and commitment to a task.

See also Revans (1983b).

References

Abercrombie MLJ. *The anatomy of judgement.* London: Hutchinson, 1960.

Advisory Centre for Education (ACE). *A case for alternative schools within the maintained system.* London: ACE, 1979.

Alderson J. *Communal policing. Part one: From resources to ideas.* Ditchley Conference on Preventive Policy, 1977. *Part two: A fundamental approach.* Paper presented to the Magistrates Association, Nottingham, 1978. Published by the Devon and Cornwall Constabulary, Force Headquarters, Middlemoor, Exeter.

Aplin G, Pugh G. (Eds) *Perspectives on preschool home visiting.* London: National Children's Bureau, 1983.

Argyle M. *The psychology of interpersonal behaviour.* London: Penguin, 1967.

Association of Directors of Social Services. *Children still in trouble.* A report of a study group. Chairman: Jillings J. 1985.

Badger B. Behavioural surveys — some cautionary notes. *Malad Therap Educ* 1985; *3*(2): 4.

Baldwin J, Wells H. (eds) *Active tutorial work.* Books 1-5. Oxford: Blackwell/ Lancashire County Council, 1979.

Baldwin JA, Oliver JE. Epidemiology and family characteristics of severely-abused children. *Br J Prev Soc Med* 1975; *29*: 205.

Baldwin JA, Thorpe D, Brown T. Comments on recent government white paper on young offenders. British Association of Social Workers, 6/1/1981.

Baquer A, Revans RW. *'But surely, that is their job'.* A study in practical cooperation through action learning. ALP International Publications, 1973, obtainable from the International Foundation for Action Learning (IFAL).

Barker P. *Basic child psychiatry.* 4th edn. London: Granada, 1983.

Bartlett G. *Cooperative care: a school counsellor's experience of liaison between school and welfare agencies.* Centre for Information and Advice on Educational Disadvantage, 1974.

Barton EM. Threat of war in minds of children (letter). *Lancet* 1985; 1: 226.

Barton R. In *Hospitals: communication, choice and change — the hospital internal communications project seen from within.* Ed Revans RW. p79. London: Tavistock, 1972.

Batchelor I, McFarlane J. *Multi-disciplinary clinical teams.* London: King's Fund Project Paper no RC 12, 1980.

Bazalgette J. *School life and work life: a study of transition in the inner city.* London: published for the Grubb Institute by Hutchinson, 1978.

Bedfordshire County Council. *The effects on schools of recent changes in financial and staffing policies,* 1982. Report of the Chief Education Officer, County Hall, Bedford, MK42 9AP.

Belson P. *The pattern of visiting today.* London: National Association for the Welfare of Children in Hospital, 1976.

Belson WA. *TV violence and the adolescent boy.* Farnborough, Hants: Saxon House, 1978.

Benians RC. Failed fostering placements. *Adoption and Fostering* 1980; *101*: 3 and 50.

Benians R. Preserving parental contact: a factor in promoting healthy growth and development in children. In *Fostering parental contact.* Family Rights Group, 1982.

Beswick K. Prevention and violence (letter). *Br Med J* 1979; *2*: 1085.

Bidder J. What you thought about birth in Britain. Report on nearly 4000 replies to a questionnaire distributed to readers in 1980. *Parents Magazine* no 61, p21, Apr 1981.

Blaber A. *Hammersmith teenage project: a report on 2½ years' experience.* London: NACRO, 1977.

Blaber A. *The Exeter community policing consultative group.* London: NACRO, 1979.

Blishen E. *The school that I'd like.* London: Penguin, 1969.

Bolton EJ. Disruptive pupils. In *Disruptive pupils.* Report of a seminar on the needs of disruptive pupils in secondary schools, 1980. Ed Evans M. London: Schools Council, 1981.

Boorer D. *A question of attitudes* (second series). London: The King's Fund Hospital Centre reprint no 519, 1970.

Boseley S. Threats made by pupils to 25 pc of teachers. *Guardian* 27/3/1986.

Bower EM. *Early identification of emotionally handicapped children in school.* 2nd edn. Springfield, Ill: Charles Thomas, 1969.

Bowlby J. *Maternal care and mental health.* Geneva: World Health Organisation, Monograph Series no 2, 1951.

Bowlby J. *Attachment and loss.* Vol 1: *Attachment.* First published 1969. London: Penguin, 1978. Vol 2: *Separation: anxiety and anger.* London: Penguin, 1978.

Boyd C, Sellers L. *The British way of birth.* London: Pan Books, 1982.

Brimblecombe FSW, Richards MPM, Robertson NRC. Introduction. In *Separation and special care baby units.* Eds Brimblecombe FSW, Richards MPM, Robertson NRC. Clinics in Developmental Medicine no 68 London: Spastics International Medical Publications, Heinemann, 1978.

British Medical Association. Report to the DHSS on violence in the family. *Br Med J* 1977; 4: 1496.

British Medical Journal. Violence and television 1976; *2*: 856.

British Medical Journal. Care proceedings: the child's interests. 1979; *2*: 1570.

British Medical Journal. Recognising child abuse. 1980; *280*: 881.

Brown G, Davidson S. Social class, psychiatric disorder of mother, and accidents to children. *Lancet* 1978; 1: 378.

Bruner JS. *Toward a theory of instruction.* New York: Norton, 1968 (First published 1966).

Bull R. The psychological significance of facial deformity. In *Love and attraction*. (Eds) Cook M, Wilson E. London: Academic Press, 1978.

Bull R, Stevens J. Effect of unsightly teeth on helping behaviour. *Perceptual and Motor Skills* 1980; 51: 438.

Burland JR. What is maladjustment? A behaviourist without blinkers attempts an answer. *Malad Therap Educ* 1983; 1(2): 15.

Button L. *Discovery and experience*. Oxford: Oxford University Press, 1971.

Button L. *Developmental group work with adolescents*. London: Hodder and Stoughton, 1974.

Button L. *Group tutoring for the form teacher. 1 Lower secondary school. 2 Upper secondary school*. London: Hodder and Stoughton, 1981, 1982.

Byrne PS, Long BEL. *Doctors talking to patients*. London: HMSO, 1976.

Caldwell W. Ed, who is our friend, plays games with us. *Remedial Education* 1972; 7: 26.

Carter F. Your service: whose advantage? In *Reconstructing educational psychology*. (ed) Gilham B. London: Croom Helm, 1978.

Caspari I. *Troublesome children in class*. London: Routledge and Kegan Paul, 1976.

Cave CWE. Comment. *London Educational Review* 1973; 2: 41.

Cawson P. *Community homes: a study of residential staff*. London: HMSO, 1978.

Central Council for Education and Training in Social Work. *Good enough parenting*. A report (study 1) of a group on *Work with children and young people and implications for social work education*, 1978.

Chalmers I, Oakley A, MacFarlane A. Perinatal health services: an immodest proposal. *Br Med J* 1980; 280: 842.

Chandos J. *Boys together: English public schools 1800-1864*. London: Hutchinson, 1984.

Chazan M, Moore T, Williams P, Wright J. *The practice of educational psychology*. London: Longman, 1974.

Child Guidance Special Interest Group. *The child guidance service*. Report of the 1969 survey undertaken by psychiatric social workers. Birmingham: British Association of Social Workers, 1975.

Child Poverty Action Group. The Finer report. *Poverty* no 31, Winter/Spring 1975.

Children's Legal Centre. *Locked up in care*. A report on the use of secure accommodation for young people in care, 1982.

Clayton S. *Maternity care: some patients' views*. Report of a survey carried out under the aegis of the Newcastle Community Health Council in Newcastle-upon-Tyne hospitals. Lancaster University, 1979.

Clegg A. *About our schools*. Oxford: Basil Blackwell, 1980.

Clegg A, Megson B. *Children in distress*. London: Penguin Education Specials, 2nd edn, 1973. (Preface to 1st edn, 1968.)

Cline T. More help for schools — a critical look at child guidance. *Therapeutic Education* 1980; 8(1): 3.

Coakley D, Woodford-Williams E. Effects of burglary and vandalism on the health of old people. *Lancet* 1979; 2: 1066.

Cobbett E. *Stay-away parents — how to draw them in*. A Home and School Council Publication, 1975.

Coghill NF. Development in the health services: action studies, participation and involvement. In *Action learning in hospitals: diagnosis and therapy*. Ed Revans RW. London: McGraw Hill, 1976.

Coghill NF. Consultants rule OK? The changing pattern of medical hierarchy. *Jour Med Ethics* 1981; 7: 28.

Coghill NF, Mohey E, Steffens EM, Stewart JS. Workers' participation and control in hospitals: the relevance of management. Second International Conference on Participation, Workers' Control and Self-Management, Paris, Sept 1977. Liste des communications in *Autogestion et Socialisme* 41-42, juin-septembre 1978, p252. Available from IFAL.

Colley M. Another kind of handicap. *New Society* 1976; 35: 327.

Colley M. A junior day school for maladjusted children in a large urban borough. *Malad Therap Educ* 1984; 2(1): 34.

Collingwood C, Alberman E. Separation at birth and the mother-child relationship. *Develop Med Child Neurol* 1979; 21: 608.

Connolly C. *Enemies of promise*. London: Routledge, 1938.

Cook IRW. The making of a murderer. *Observer* 30/11/1975.

Cornish DB, Clarke RVG. *Residential treatment and its effects on delinquency*. Home Office Research Study no 32. London: HMSO, 1975.

Cortazzi D. *Illuminative incident analysis: a technique for team building*. ALP International Publications, 1973. Available from IFAL.

Coyne A-M. *Schoolgirl mothers*. Research Report no 2. Health Education Council, 1986.

Creighton S. *Child victims of physical abuse*. London: NSPCC, 1976.

Creighton SJ. Child abuse deaths. Information briefing no 5, NSPCC, 1985.

Cross J. The real life of the community. *New Growth* 1981; 1(1): 3.

Cunningham I. Getting out of school. *Guardian* 7/2/1978.

Curren D. Psychiatry limited. *J Ment Sci* 1952; 98: 373.

Dahrendorf R. In defence of the English professions. *J Roy Soc Med* 1984; 77: 178.

Daines R. Withdrawal units and the psychology of problem behaviour. In *Problem behaviour in the secondary school*. Ed Gilham B. London: Croom Helm, 1981.

Dartington T, Henry G, Lyth IM. *The psychological welfare of young children making long stays in hospital*. CASR Document 1200. London: The Tavistock Institute of Human Relations, 1976.

Davies DP, Herbert S, Haxby V, McNeish AS. When should pre-term babies be sent home from neonatal units? *Lancet* 1979; 1: 914.

Davies H. *The Creighton report: a year in the life of a comprehensive high school*. London: Hamish Hamilton, 1976.

Dawson RL. *Special provision for disturbed pupils: a survey*. Schools Council Research Studies. London: Macmillan Education, 1980.

de Chateau P. Effects of hospital practices on synchrony in the development of the infant-parent relationship. *Sem perinatol* 1979; 3: 45.

de Chateau P, Holmberg H, Jakobson K, Winberg J. A study of factors promoting and inhibiting lactation. *Dev Med Child Neurol* 1977; 19: 575.

de Chateau P, Holmberg H, Winberg J. Left-side preference in holding and carrying newborn infants — Mothers holding and carrying during the first week of life. *Acta Paediatr Scand* 1978; 67: 169.

Dempster WJ. Towards a new understanding of John Hunter. *Lancet* 1978; 1: 316.

Department of Education and Science (DES). *Children and their primary schools*. A report of the Central Advisory Council for Education (England). Chairwoman: Lady Plowden. London: HMSO, 1966.

DES. *Psychologists in education services*. Report of a working party. Chairman: A Summerfield. London: HMSO, 1968.

DES. *A new partnership for our schools*. Report of a committee of enquiry. Chairman: Tom Taylor CBE. London: HMSO, 1977.

DES. HMI Report on *Truancy and behavioural problems in some urban schools*. London: DES, 1978a.

DES. *Special educational needs*. Report of the Committee of Enquiry into the Education of Handicapped Children and Young People. Chairwoman: Mrs HM Warnock. Cmnd 7212. London: HMSO, 1978b.

DES. *The composition of school governing bodies*. Cmnd 7430. London: HMSO, 1978c.

DES. *Behavioural units: a survey of special units for pupils with behavioural problems*. London: DES, 1978d.

DES. *Aspects of secondary education in England*. A survey by HMI of schools. London: HMSO, 1979.

DES. HMI Report. *Educational provision by the Inner London Education Authority*. London: DES, 1980.

DES. HMI *Report on the effects on the education service in England of local authority expenditure policies — financial year 1980-81*. London: DES, 1981.

DES. HMI *Report on the effects of local authority expenditure policies on the education service in England — 1981*. London: DES, 1982a.

DES. *The new teacher in school*. HMI Series: Matters for Discussion 15. London: DES, 1982b.

DES. *Statistical Bulletin, 17/83*. London: DES, 1983a.

DES. *Teaching quality*. Cmnd 8836. London: HMSO, 1983b.

DES. *Education observed*. A review of the first six months of published reports by HMI. London: DES, 1984a.

DES. Green paper. *Parental influence at school*. Cmnd 9242. London: HMSO, 1984b.

DES. *Training for jobs*. Cmnd 9135. London: HMSO, 1984c.

DES. *Report by HMI on the effects of local authority expenditure policies on education provision in England — 1983*. London: DES, 1984d.

DES. *Report by HMI on the effects of local authority policies on education provision in England — 1984*. London: DES, 1985.

DES. Crime prevention in schools: building-related aspects. A discussion paper. London: DES, 1986a.

DES. *Report by HMI on the effects of local authority expenditure policies on education provision in England — 1985*. London: DES, 1986b.

Department of Health and Social Security (DHSS). *The battered baby*. London: HMSO, 1970.

DHSS. *Report of the committee on one-parent families*. Chairman: The Hon. Sir Morris Finer. Cmnd 5629. London: HMSO, 1974.

DHSS. *Priorities for health and personal social services in England*. London: HMSO, 1976a.

DHSS. *Fit for the future*. Report of the Committee on Child Health Services. Chairman: Prof SDM Court. Cmnd 6684. London: HMSO, 1976b.

DHSS (and DES). *Coordination of services for children under 5*. Local Authority Social Services Letter (78) 1, Jan 1978a.

DHSS. *The management of community homes with education on the premises*. London: DHSS, 1978b.

DHSS. *The reduction of perinatal mortality and morbidity: a discussion document*. The Children's Committee. London: DHSS, 1979.

DHSS. *Reply to the second report from the Social Services Committee on perinatal and neonatal mortality*. Cmnd 8084. London: HMSO, 1980a.

DHSS. *Inequalities in health*. Report of a research working group. Chairman: Sir Douglas Black. London: DHSS, 1980b.

DHSS. *Legal and professional aspects of the use of secure accommodation for children in care*. Report of an internal working party. Chairman: Prof N Tutt. London: DHSS, 1981.

DHSS. *Child abuse: a study on inquiry reports: 1973-81*. London: HMSO, 1982.

DHSS. *Children in care in England and Wales, 1982*. London: HMSO, 1984.

DHSS. *Social work decisions in child care: recent research findings and their implications*. London: HMSO, 1985.

DHSS. *Child abuse: working together*. *A guide to arrangements for inter-agency co-operation for the protection of children*. London: DHSS, 1986.

Derbyshire F, Davies DP, Bacco A. Discharge of pre-term babies from neonatal units. *Br Med J* 1982; *284*: 233.

Derrick D. *Social work support team, Grange County Comprehensive School, Ellesmere Port*. Centre for Information and Advice on Educational Disadvantage, 1977.

Dessent T. Personal view: three interviews. In *Reconstructing educational psychology*. (Ed) Gilham B. London: Croom Helm, 1978.

Dessent T. Special schools and the mainstream — 'The resource stretch'. In *Management and the special school*. (Ed) Bowers T. London: Croom Helm, 1984.

Diamond LJ, Jaudes PK. Child abuse in a cerebral-palsied population. *Dev Med Child Neurol* 1983; *25*: 169.

Dinkmeyer D, Dreikurs R. *Encouraging children to learn: the encouragement process*. Englewood Cliffs: Prentice-Hall, 1963.

Dobinson C. Trainers' bench. *Guardian* 25/3/1975.

Docherty SC. (Ed) *The book of the child: pregnancy to 4 years old*. Scottish Health Education Unit, 2nd edn, 1980.

Dominian J. *Marriage — making or breaking?* London: Family Doctor Publications (BMA House, Tavistock Square, London WC1H 9JP), 1981.

Douglas JWB. *The home and the school: a study of ability and attainment in the primary schools.* London: MacGibbon and Kee, 1964.

Douglas JWB, Kiernan KE, Wadsworth MEJ. Illness and behaviour: a longitudinal study of health and behaviour. *Proc Roy Soc Med* 1977; *70*: 530.

Dowling S. Inverting the inverse care law — a challenge for the 80s. Paediatric Conference, Royal College of Physicians, London, 1980.

Dreikurs R. *Psychology in the classroom: a manual for teachers.* 2nd edn. New York: Harper and Row, 1968.

Dreikurs R, Cassel P. *Discipline without tears.* 2nd edn. New York: Hawthorn/Dutton, 1972.

Dreikurs R, Grey L. *Logical consequences.* New York: Meredith Press, 1968.

Duck S. *Human relationships: an introduction to social psychology.* London: Sage, 1986.

Dunn J, Kendrick C. The arrival of a sibling: changes in patterns of interaction between mother and first-born child. *J Child Psychol Psychiat* 1980; *21*: 119.

Dyke S. Getting better makes it worse: some obstacles to improvement in children with emotional and behavioural difficulties. *Malad Therap Educ* 1985; *3(3)*: 30.

Ealing Community Health Council. *Good practices in mental health in Ealing.* 1984a.

Ealing Community Health Council. *The good health guide.* 1984b.

Ellis M. Personal view. *Br Med J* 1986; *292*: 268.

Ellis S. The work of the DO5 schools support team. *Malad Therap Educ* 1985; *3(2)*: 27.

Equal Opportunities Commission. *Parenthood in the balance.* 1982.

Evans M. (Ed) *Disruptive pupils.* Report of a seminar on the needs of disruptive pupils in secondary schools, 1980. London: Schools Council, 1981.

Family Rights Group. *A guide to care proceedings,* 1979.

Ferri E. *Growing up in a one parent family.* National Children's Bureau. Published by the National Foundation for Educational Research, London, 1976.

Field F. (Ed) *Education and the urban crisis.* London: Routledge and Kegan Paul, 1977.

Finlayson DS, Loughran JL. Pupils' perceptions in high and low delinquency schools. *Educational Research* 1976; *18*: 138.

FitzHerbert K. *Child care service and the teacher.* London: Temple-Smith, 1977.

FitzHerbert K. Communication with teachers in the health surveillance of school children. *Paediatrics* 1982; *7*: 100.

Fletcher CM. *Communication in medicine.* Rock Carling Monograph. London: Nuffield Provincial Hospitals Trust/Oxford University Press, 1973.

Fletcher C. Towards better practice and teaching of communication between doctors and patients. In *Mixed communications.* Ed McLachlan G. Oxford: Oxford University Press for the Nuffield Provincial Hospitals Trust, 1979.

Fletcher C. Listening and talking to patients. *Br Med J* 1980; *281*: 845; 931; 994; 1056.

Floud J, Halsey AH, Martin FM. *Social class and educational opportunity.* (Ed) Floud J. London: Heinemann, 1956.

Franklin AW. (Ed) *The challenge of child abuse.* Proceedings of a conference at the Royal Society of Medicine, 1976. London: Academic Press, 1977.

Fraser E. *Home environment and the school.* London: London University Press, 1959.

Freidson E. *Professional dominance: the social structure of medical care.* New York: Atherton Press, 1970.

Frese HH. Permanent education — dream or nightmare? In *Deschooling.* (Ed) Lister I. London: Cambridge University Press, 1974.

Fry M. (Ed) *Child care and the growth of love.* Abridged version of *Maternal care and mental health* by Bowlby J, with additional chapters by Ainsworth MDS. 2nd edn. London: Penguin, 1965.

Galletly I. Democratic decision making in schools. *Where* 142, Oct 1978.

Galloway D. *Schools, pupils and special educational needs.* London: Croom Helm, 1985a.

Galloway D. Meeting special educational needs in the ordinary school? Or creating them? *Malad Therap Educ* 1985b; 3(3): 3.

Galloway D, Ball T, Blomfield D, Seyd R. *Schools and disruptive pupils.* London: Longman, 1982.

Galway J. What pupils think of special units. *Comprehensive Education* Issue 39, Winter 1979.

Gary R. *La vie devant soi.* Mercure de France, 1975.

Gilbert RV. Report on staff-tenant integration 1980-81. In *Action learning and the inner city.* (Ed) Revans RW. IFAL, 1981a.

Gilbert RV. *Youth, vandalism, antisocial behaviour and security in Flemington and Kensington high rise estates.* Housing Commission of the State Government of Victoria, Australia. IFAL, 1981b.

Gilham B. (Ed) *Reconstructing educational psychology.* London: Croom Helm, 1978.

Gilham B. Rethinking the problem. In *Problem behaviour in the secondary school.* (Ed) Gilham B. London: Croom Helm, 1981.

Glasser W. *Schools without failure.* New York: Harper Colophon, 1975 (first published 1969).

Goffman E. *Stigma: notes on the management of spoiled identity.* London: Penguin, 1963.

Goldacre P. Children of violence. *Times Educational Supplement* 30/12/1977.

Goodacre E. *Home and school relationships: a list of references with notes for parents, teachers and teachers in training.* A Home and School Council Publication, 1968.

Goodman P. Mini-schools: a prescription for the reading problem. In *Deschooling.* Ed Lister I. London: Cambridge University Press, 1974.

Gopsill T. Why young people dislike the police. *Observer* 1/7/1979.

Gordon RR. Predlcting child abuse. *Br Med J* 1977; 1: 841.

Gordon T, Burch N. *Teacher effectiveness training.* New York: Wyden, 1974.

Grafton T, Smith L, Vegoda M, Whitfield R, Bamford C, Comber S. *Preparation for parenthood in the secondary school curriculum.* A research project report prepared for the DES, 1983. Department of Educational Enquiry, University of Aston in Birmingham.

Gray F, Graubard PS, Rosenberg H. Little brother is changing you. In *Discipline and learning: an enquiry into student-teacher relationships.* Washington DC, USA: A National Education Association Publication, 1975.

Green L. *School reports and other information for parents.* A Home and School Council Publication, 1975.

Greig C. Personal view. *Br Med J* 1981; *282*: 561.

Griffiths T. Maladjustment in the comprehensive school. *Malad Therap Educ* 1983; 1(2): 41.

Gross, R, Gross B. (Eds) *Radical school reform.* London: Penguin, 1972.

Grubb Institute of Behavioural Studies. *Transition to working life in practice.* 1981. Report and assessment of a research and action project with unemployed young people, 1979-81.

Grunsell R. *Born to be invisible: the story of a school for truants.* London: Macmillan Education, 1978.

Guardian. Denning puts people first. 29/11/1977.

Gulliford R. *Special educational needs.* London: Routledge and Kegan Paul, 1971.

Gunter M. The mother's view of herself. In *Breast-feeding and the mother* (Ciba Foundation Symposium 45). Amsterdam: Elsevier/Excerpta Medica/North Holland, 1976.

Hale J. *Pools for schools.* A Home and School Council Publication, 1974.

Halsey AH. Democracy for education? *New Society* 1981; 56: 346.

Halsey AH, Heath AF, Ridge JM. *Origins and destinations: family, class and education in modern Britain.* Oxford: Clarendon Press, 1980.

Hamblin DH. The teacher and pastoral care. Oxford: Blackwell, 1978.

Handy C. *The future of work.* Oxford: Blackwell, 1984.

Hanko G. Staff support and training groups for teachers. *New Growth* 1981; 1(1): 23.

Hanko G. *Staff support and training groups for teachers dealing with disturbed and disturbing children in ordinary classrooms.* Supplement no 20. Forum for the Advancement of Educational Therapy. Dec 1982.

Hanko G. Special needs in ordinary classrooms: an approach to teacher support and pupil care in primary and secondary schools. Oxford: Basil Blackwell, 1985.

Hargreaves DH. *Social relations in a secondary school.* London: Routledge and Kegan Paul, 1967.

Hargreaves D. Deviance: the interactionist approach. In *Reconstructing educational psychology.* (Ed) Gilham B. London: Croom Helm, 1978.

Hargreaves DH. *The challenge for the comprehensive school: culture curriculum and community.* London: Routledge and Kegan Paul, 1982.

Haringey Association for the Advancement of State Education. *An A-Z of education in Haringey,* 1974.

Hart T. *Safe on a seesaw: a book of children.* London: Quartet, 1977.

281

Hazel N. *A bridge to independence: the Kent Family Placement Project*. Oxford: Basil Blackwell, 1981.

Help! I need somebody. A directory of associations and charities and self-help groups, 1980 (see Appendix 1).

Hemming J. *The betrayal of youth: secondary education must be changed*. London: Marion Boyars, 1980.

Hemming J. Exams that fail the pupils (letter). *Guardian* 22/6/1981.

Hemming J. The battle against barbarity (letter). *Guardian* 27/1/1982.

Hemming J. The long, long haul from sadism to erotica (letter). *Guardian* 20/10/1983.

Hencke D. Cells for children brings Whitehall conflict. *Guardian* 6/7/1982 (1982a).

Hencke D. Children who died from abuse 'failed by inexperienced staff'. *Guardian* 28/9/1982 (1982b).

Henry J. In suburban classrooms. In *Radical school reform*. Eds Gross R, Gross B. London: Penguin, 1972.

Hersov L. School refusal. *Br Med J* 1972; *3*: 102.

Hersov L, Berg L. (Eds) *Out of school*. London: Wiley, 1981.

Hewitt P. Facing facts (letter). *Guardian* 16/12/1980.

Highfield ME, Pinsent A. *A survey of rewards and punishments in schools*. London: NFER/Newnes Educational Publishing, 1952.

Hill JC. *Teaching and the unconscious mind*. New York: International Universities Press, 1971.

Hinde RA. *Towards understanding relationships*. London: Academic Press, 1979.

Hiskins E. Personal view. *Br Med J* 1982; *285*: 204.

Hoghughi M, Dobson C, Lyons J, Muckley A, Swainston M. *Assessing problem children: issues and practice*. London: Burnett/Deutsch, 1980.

Holman P. Child psychiatry and the social setting. *Brit J Psychiatry* 1967; *113*: 1165.

Holman PG. Maladjustment: its treatment and prevention. *J Assoc Workers Malad Child* 1973; 1(1): 2.

Holman P, Libretto G. The on-site unit. *Comprehensive Education*, Issue 39, p10, Winter 1979.

Holman R. *Inequality in child care*. Poverty Pamphlet no 26, 1976, London: Child Poverty Action Group.

Holmes E. Educational intervention for pre-school children in day or residential care: the children, the class and the teacher. *Therapeutic Education* 1980; 8(2): 3.

Holmes E. The effectiveness of educational intervention for preschool children in day and residential care. *New Growth* 1982; 2(1): 17.

Holmes G. *The idiot teacher: a book about Prestolee School and its headmaster EF O'Neill*. Nottingham: Spokesman Books, 1977 (first published in 1952).

Holt J. *How children fail*. London: Penguin, 1969 (first published in 1965).

Home Office. *Report of the Committee on the Care of Children*. Chairwoman: Dame Myra Curtis CBE. Cmnd 6922. London: HMSO, 1946.

Home Office. *Report of the Committee on Local Authority and Allied Personal Social Services*. Chairman: F Seebohm. Cmnd 3703. London: HMSO, 1968.

Home Office; Welsh Office; DHSS. *Young offenders.* Cmnd 8045. London: HMSO, 1980.

Honey JR deS. *Tom Brown's universe.* London: Millington Books, 1977.

Humphrey N, Lifton RJ. (Eds) *In a dark time.* London: Faber, 1984.

Hunt JE. Crying baby advisory/relief service. Paediatric Conference, Royal College of Physicians, 1980. Details available from Huddersfield District Health Authority.

Illich ID. *Deschooling society.* London: Calder and Boyars, 1971.

Illich I. Schooling: the ritual of progress. In *Deschooling.* (Ed) Lister I. London: Cambridge University Press, 1974.

Jackson A. *Heading for what?* Counselling and Career Development Unit, Department of Psychology, Leeds University, 1976.

Jackson ADM. 'Wednesday's children': a review of child abuse. *J Roy Soc Med* 1982; 75: 83.

Jay P. *No one to laugh at you: the ILEA home based teacher scheme.* Fabian Occasional Paper 7, 1973. London: Fabian Society.

Jayne E. *Deptford educational home visiting project, 1976.* ILEA Educational Home Visiting Project.

Jeffrey LIH, Kolvin I, Robson MR, Scott D McI, Tweddle EG. Generic training in the psychological management of children and adolescents. *J Assoc Workers Malad Child* 1979; 7(1): 32.

Johnson TH. (Ed) *The complete poems of Emily Dickinson.* London: Faber, 1975.

Jones A. Adolescent behaviour and teacher stress. In *Behaviour problems in the comprehensive school.* Eds Upton G, Gobell A. Cardiff: Faculty of Education, University College, 1980.

Jones CO. Disruption and disturbance: observations on the management of a group of junior school-age children. *Concern* no 25, autumn 1977, p7.

Jones M. *Social psychiatry.* London: Tavistock, 1952; published in the USA as *The therapeutic community.* New York: Basic Books, 1953.

Jones M. *Social psychiatry in the community, in hospitals and in prisons.* Springfield, Ill: Chas C Thomas, 1962.

Jones M. *Beyond the therapeutic community.* London: Yale University Press, 1968.

Jones N. The Brislington project at Bristol. *Special Education* 1971; 60(2): 174.

Jones N, McKeown J, Noel N, Kerridge J, Du Plat-Taylor K. *Day units for children with emotional and behavioural difficulties.* AWMCTE, Monograph no 1. Ed Rodway A. 1981. (Available from Visser JG, Dept of Education, University College, PO Box 78, Cardiff CF1 1XL).

Jones NB, Ferreira MCR, Brown MF, MacDonald L. Aggression, crying and physical contact in one-to-three-year old children. *Aggressive Behaviour* 1979; 5: 121.

Jones NJ. Special adjustment units in comprehensive schools. I: Needs and resources. II: Structure and function. *Therapeutic Education* 1973; 1(2): 23.

Jones NJ. Special adjustment units in comprehensive schools. III: Selection of children. *Therapeutic Education* 1974; 2(2): 21.

Jones NJ. Special adjustment units in comprehensive schools. *Therapeutic Education* 77; 5(2): 12.

Jones-Davies C, Cave R. (Eds) *The disruptive pupil in the secondary school.* London: Ward Lock Educational, 1976.

Joseph Rowntree Memorial Trust and Carnegie UK Trust. *The future of voluntary organisations.* Report of a committee set up by these Trusts. Chairman: Sir John Wolfendon. London: Croom Helm, 1977.

Keeley B. *The effect of preschool provision on the mothers of young children.* MSc Thesis. Department of Social Policy, Cranfield Institute of Technology, 1981.

Kempe RS, Kempe CH. *Child abuse.* London: Fontana/Open Books, 1978.

Kempe CH, Silverman FN, Steele BF, Droegemueller W, Silver HK. The battered child syndrome. *Jour Amer Med Assoc* 1962; *181*: 17.

Kendrick C, Dunn J. Caring for a second baby: effects on interaction between mother and firstborn. *Dev Psychology* 1980; *16*: 303.

Kennell JH. Are we in the midst of a revolution? *Am J Dis Child* 1980; *134*: 303.

Kitzinger S. *Women as mothers.* London: Fontana, 1978.

Klaus MH, Jerrauld R, Kreger NC, McAlpine W, Steffa M, Kennell JH. Maternal attachment: importance of the first postpartum days. *N Engl J Med* 1972; *286*: 460.

Klaus M, Kennell JH. Parent-to-infant attachment. In *Recent advances in paediatrics.* Ed Hull D. London: Churchill Livingstone, 1976a.

Klaus MH, Kennell JH. *Maternal-infant bonding.* Saint Louis, USA: CV Mosby, 1976b.

Kloska A, Ramasut A. Teacher stress. *Malad Therap Educ* 1985; *3*(2): 19.

Knight R, Bowers T. Developing effective teams. In *Management and the special school.* (Ed) Bowers T. London: Croom Helm, 1984.

Kolvin I, Garside RF, Nicol AR. Maladjusted pupils in ordinary schools. *Special Education: Forward Trends* 1976; *3*: 15.

Kolvin I, Garside RF, Nicol AR, Macmillan A, Wolstenholme F, Leitch IM. *Help starts here: the maladjusted child in the ordinary school.* London: Tavistock, 1981.

Kyriacou C. High Anxiety. *Times Educational Supplement* 6/6/1980.

Kyriacou C, Sutcliffe J. Teacher stress: prevalence, sources and symptoms. *Br J Educ Psychol* 1978; *48*: 159.

Lancet. One parent families. 1978; *2*: 1112.

Lancet. Separation and special care baby units. 1979; *1*: 590.

Lask J, Lask B. *Child psychiatry and social work.* London: Tavistock, 1981.

Laslett R. *The needs of maladjusted children.* A paper for the AWMC/CCETSW, 1976.

Laslett R. Disruptive and violent pupils: the facts and the fallacies. *Educational Review* 1977a; *29*: 152.

Laslett R. *The disruptive child in the secondary school.* Report of a conference arranged by the London branch of the AWMC, 1977b.

Laslett R. *Educating maladjusted children.* St Albans: Crosby Lockwood Staples, 1977c.

Laslett R. A children's court for bullies. *Special Education: Forward Trends* 1982a; *9*: 9.

Laslett R. *Maldajusted children in the ordinary school.* National Council for Special Education, 1982b.

Laslett R. *Changing perceptions of maladjusted children 1945-1981.* AWMC Monograph no 2, 1983.

Laslett R, Smith C. *Effective classroom management: a teacher's guide.* London: Croom Helm, 1984.

Lawrence J, Steed D, Young P. *Disruptive children — disruptive schools?* London: Croom Helm, 1984.

Lealman GT, Haigh D, Phillips JM, Stone J, Ord-Smith C. Prediction and prevention of child abuse — an empty hope? *Lancet* 1983; 1: 1423.

Leifer AD, Leiderman PH, Barnett CR, Williams JA. Effects of mother-infant separation on maternal attachment behaviour. *Child Dev* 1972; 43: 1203.

Leissner A, Powley T, Evans D. *Intermediate treatment.* A National Children's Bureau action research report on community youth work, 1977.

Lewis A. Medicine and the affections of the mind. Harveian Oration, 1963. *Br Med J* 1963; 2: 1549.

Lewis I. *Supervision and student learning in relation to school experience: a summary report of an action-research study.* University of Bristol, 1974.

Lingard A, Allard J. *Parent/teacher relations in secondary schools.* A Home and School Council Publication, 1972.

Lister I. The challenge of deschooling. In *Deschooling.* (Ed) Lister I. London: Cambridge University Press, 1974a.

Lister I. Should schools survive? In *Deschooling.* (Ed) Lister I. London: Cambridge University Press, 1974b.

London Borough of Ealing Council. *Interim report of the joint working party on juvenile delinquency, school attendance and truancy,* 1977.

Loring J, Holland M. *The prevention of cerebral palsy: the basic facts.* London: The Spastics Society, 1978.

Lozoff B, Brittenham GM, Trause MA, Kennell JH, Klaus MH. The mother-newborn relationship: limits of adaptability. *J Paediat* 1977; 91: 1.

Lynch M, Ounsted C. Residential therapy — a place of safety. In *Child abuse and neglect. The family and the community.* (Eds) Helfer RE, Kempe CH. Cambridge: Ballinger, 1976.

Lynch M, Roberts J. Predicting child abuse: signs of bonding failure in the maternity hospital. *Br Med J* 1977; 1: 624.

Lynch MA, Roberts J. *Consequences of child abuse.* London: Academic Press, 1982.

Lynch M, Steinberg D, Ounsted C. Family unit in a children's psychiatric hospital. *Br Med J* 1975; 2: 127.

McGuiness JB. Classroom rebels and their causes (letter). *Education Guardian* 12/4/1977.

McLachlan G. (Ed) *Mixed communications.* London: Nuffield Provincial Hospitals Trust/Oxford University Press, 1979.

Macmillan A, Kolvin I. Behaviour modification in educational settings: a guide for teachers. *J Assoc Workers Malad Child* 1977; 5(1): 2.

Maizels J. How school-leavers rate teachers. *New Society* 1970; 16: 535.

Manifesto for change. Times Educational Supplement 30/1/1981.

Mant A. *The rise and fall of the British manager.* London: Macmillan, 1977.

Marks H. *Education for offenders: provision and needs.* London: NACRO, 1979.

Marland M. *The craft of the classroom: a survival guide.* London: Heinemann, 1976.

Marsden D. *Politicians, equality and comprehensives.* Fabian Tract 411. London: Fabian Society, 1971.

Marshall S. *An experiment in education.* London: Cambridge University Press, 1963.

Martin W. How the young offenders in the prisons can help those on the football terraces. (Letter) *Guardian* 9/3/1984.

MIND. *Assessment of children and their families.* Report of a working party. Chairman: Peter Righton. 1975.

MIND: Wandsworth. *Mental health services for Wandsworth,* 1975.

Ministry of Education. *Special educational treatment.* Pamphlet no 5. London: HMSO, 1946.

Ministry of Education. *Report of the Committee on Maladjusted Children.* Chairman: JEA Underwood. London; HMSO, 1955.

Ministry of Education. *Half our future.* A report of the Central Advisory Council for Education (England). Chairman: J Newsom. London: HMSO, 1963.

Montessori M. *The Montessori method.* Translated from the Italian by George AE. Massachusetts: Bentley, 1965 (first published in 1912).

Moore M. *From crime statistics to social policy.* Cranfield Conference on the Prevention of Crime in Europe, 1978. Published by the Devon and Cornwall Constabulary, Force Headquarters, Middlemoor, Exeter.

Morris JN. Social inequalities undiminished. *Lancet* 1979; *1*: 87.

Morris JN, Power MJ. Schools and delinquency (letter). *Times* 25/5/1972.

Mortimore P. Schools as institutions. *Educational Research* 1978; *20*: 61.

Mortimore P. Underachievement: a framework for debate. *Secondary Education* 1982; *12*: 3.

Mortimore P, Davies J, Varlaam A, West A, Devine P, Mazza J. *Behaviour problems in schools: an evaluation of support centres.* London: Croom Helm, 1983.

Moss SZ. How children feel about being placed away from home. In *Disturbed children.* (Ed) Tod RJN. London: Longmans, 1968.

Mumford L. *The culture of cities.* London: Secker and Warburg, 1940.

Murray K. Juvenile justice in Scotland. *New Growth* 1982; *2*(1): 2.

National Association for the Care and Resettlement of Offenders (NACRO). *The Hammersmith teenage project.* London: NACRO 1978a.

NACRO. *New approaches to juvenile crime. Sending young offenders away.* Briefing paper no 1. London: NACRO, 1978b.

NACRO. *New approaches to juvenile crime. Detention centres: regimes and reconviction rates.* London: NACRO, 1979.

NACRO. *New approaches to juvenile crime. Family placement and professional fostering schemes.* Briefing paper no 4. London: NACRO, 1980.

NACRO. *Vandalism: an approach through consultation — Cunningham Road improvement scheme.* London: NACRO, 1981.

National Children's Bureau. *Educational home visiting: some local authority and voluntary schemes.* 1977. Also: *Highlight no 29 — Educational home visiting.* 1977.

National Children's Home. *Children today,* 1983.

National Council for One Parent Families. Annual reports, 1977-80.

National Council for One Parent Families (NCOPF). *Pregnant at school.* Report of a joint working party (with the Community Development Trust) on pregnant school girls and schoolgirl mothers. London: NCOPF, 1979.

National Health Service Health Advisory Service. *Bridges over troubled waters: a report on services for disturbed adolescents.* London: DHSS (Leaflets), PO Box 21, Stanmore, Middlesex HA7 1AY; 1986.

National Institute for Social Work (NISW). *Social workers: their role and tasks.* Report of a working party set up in 1980 at the request of the Secretary of State for Social Services. Chairman: PM Barclay. London: published for the NISW by Bedford Square Press/NCVO, 1982.

National Union of Teachers. *Confidentiality and school records: a discussion document.* London: NUT, 1984.

Newman O. *Defensible space: people and design in the violent city.* London: Architectural Press, 1972.

Niblett R. *Report on the second phase of the 'Who cares?' project (1977-79).* London: National Children's Bureau, 1980.

Oakley A. Observations by a consumer. In *The reduction of perinatal mortality and morbidity.* Report of a conference held by the Children's Committee. Chairman: Prof F Brimblecombe CBE. London: DHSS, 1979.

Oakley A. *Women confined: towards a sociology of child birth.* Oxford: Martin Robertson, 1980.

Office of Population Censuses and Surveys. *Monitor* Ref DH3 82/5 Dec 1982.

Office of Population Censuses and Surveys. *Monitor* Ref DH3 83/2 Oct 1983.

O'Halloran T. Protests at police raid on school. *New Statesman* 27/3/1981.

O'Leary KD, O'Leary SG. (Eds) *Classroom management: the successful use of behaviour modification.* Oxford: Pergamon Press, 1972.

Oliver JE. Dead children from problem families in NE Wiltshire. *Br Med J* 1983; *286:* 115.

Oliver S. Taking care into account. *Guardian* 17/8/1983.

Ounsted C, Roberts JC, Gordon M, Milligan B. Fourth goal of perinatal medicine. *Br Med J* 1982; *284:* 879.

Page J. Discussion (p35) in *The reduction of perinatal mortality and morbidity.* Report of a conference held by the Children's Committee. Chairman: Prof F Brimblecombe CBE. London: DHSS, 1979.

Page R. *Proposal for a development project with children in residential care.* London: National Children's Bureau, 1976.

Page R. Who cares? *Concern* (Journal of the National Children's Bureau) no 26, Winter 1977-78, p17.

Page R, Clarke GA. (Eds) *Who cares? Young people in care speak out.* London: National Children's Bureau, 1977.

Paine L. *Coordination of services for the mentally handicapped.* London: King Edward's Hospital Fund for London, 1974.

Parkes R. The duty of confidence. *Br Med J* 1982; *285*: 1442.

Payne M. *Working in teams.* London: Macmillan, 1982.

Pearce J, Ward D. School-based intermediate treatment. *Therapeutic Education* 1979; *7*(1): 3.

Pedler M. (Ed) *Action learning in practice.* Aldershot: Gower, 1983.

Pedley R. *Comprehensive education: a new approach.* London: Gollancz, 1956.

Pedley R. *The comprehensive school.* London: Penguin, 1963.

Pence G. Rights. In *Medical ethics.* (Eds) Abrams N, Buckner MD. Cambridge, Massachusetts: MIT Press, 1983.

Perinpanayagam KS. Dynamic approach to adolescence; treatment. *Br Med J* 1978; *1*: 563.

Pickering C. The case for a pupils' democracy (letter). *Guardian* 16/10/1979.

Policy Studies Institute. *Police and people in London,* 1983.

Popay J. Happier healthier families? (Study Commission on the Family). *Lancet* 1980; *2*: 1240.

Porter R. (Ed) *Child sexual abuse within the family.* The Ciba Foundation. London: Tavistock, 1984.

Postman N, Weingartner C. What's worth knowing? In *Radical school reform.* (Eds) Gross R, Gross B, London: Penguin, 1972 (first published 1969).

Poulton GA, James T. *Pre-school learning in the community: strategies for change.* London: Routledge and Kegan Paul, 1975.

Power MJ, Benn RT, Morris JN. Neighbourhood, school and juveniles before the courts. *Brit J Criminol* 1972; *12*: 111.

Pringle MK. *The roots of violence and vandalism.* London: The National Children's Bureau, 1973.

Prioleau L, Murdoch M, Brody B. An analysis of psychotherapy versus placebo studies. *Behavioural and Brain Sciences* 1983; *6*: 275.

Pugh G. Educational home visiting schemes. *Where* 132, Oct 1977.

Pugh G. (Ed) *Preparation for parenthood.* London: National Children's Bureau, 1980.

Querido A. The problem family in the Netherlands. *Med Officer* 1946; *75*: 193.

Rabinowitz A. Schools for children or children for schools? *New Growth* 1981a; *1*(2): 3.

Rabinowitz A. The range of solutions: a critical analysis. In *Problem behaviour in the secondary school.* Ed Gilham B. London: Croom Helm, 1981b.

Rae M, Hewitt P, Hugill B. *First rights: a guide to legal rights for young people.* London: National Council for Civil Liberties, 1979.

Rawnsley A. Sir, you're such a yob. *Guardian* 16/5/1986.

Redl F. The concept of the life space interview. In *Conflict in the classroom: the education of emotionally disturbed children.* (Eds) Long NJ, Morse WC, Newman RG. 4th edn. Belmont, Calif: Wadsworth, 1980a.

Redl F. The concept of punishment. In *Conflict in the classroom: the education of emotionally disturbed children*. (Eds) Long NJ, Morse WC, Newman RG. 4th edn. Belmont, Calif: Wadsworth, 1980b.

Rée H. A childhoodful of prejudice about comprehensive schools (letter). *Guardian* 16/1/1981.

Reed BD. Across the great divide: preparing school leavers for working life. *Youth in society*, Feb 1980, no 39, p20.

Reed B, Bazalgete J, Armstrong D, Hutton J, Quine C. *Becoming adult*. London: Grubb Institute of Behavioural Studies, 1982.

Reeves C. Maladjustment: psychodynamic theory and the role of therapeutic education in a residential setting. *Malad Therap Educ* 1983; 1(2): 25.

Reeves MP. *Round about a pound a week*. London: Virago, 1979. (First published in 1913).

Reimer E. *School is dead*. London: Penguin, 1971.

Revans RW. *Standards for morale: cause and effect in hospitals*. London: Nuffield Provincial Hospitals Trust/Oxford University Press, 1964 p98. Reprinted in *Action learning in hospitals: diagnosis and therapy*. (Ed) Revans RW. London: McGraw Hill, 1976, p80.

Revans RW. Involvement in school. *New Society* 1965; 6: 9.

Revans RW. Introduction. In *Changing hospitals: a report on the hospital internal communications project*. (Eds) Wieland GF, Leigh H. London: Tavistock, 1971.

Revans RW. (Ed) *Hospitals: communication, choice and change. The hospital internal communications project seen from within*. London: Tavistock, 1972.

Revans RW. *Childhood and maturity*. Part I. IFAL, 1973.

Revans RW. (Ed). *Action learning in hospitals: diagnosis and therapy*. London: McGraw Hill, 1976.

Revans RW. The school as a community. In *Action learning: new techniques for management*. London: Blond and Briggs, 1980.

Revans RW. Worker participation as action learning. *Economic and Industrial Democracy* 1981a; 2: 521.

Revans RW. *Education for change and survival*. IFAL, 1981b.

Revans RW. *The origins and growth of action learning*. Bromley: Chartwell-Bratt, 1982a.

Revans RW. The teaching company. In *The origins and growth of action learning*. Bromley: Chartwell-Bratt, 1982b.

Revans RW. The anatomy of achievement. In *The origins and growth of action learning*. Bromley: Chartwell-Bratt, 1982c.

Revans RW. The psychology of the deliberated random. In *The origins and growth of action learning*. Bromley: Chartwell-Bratt, 1982d.

Revans RW. Alienation and resistance. In *The origins and growth of action learning*. Bromley: Chartwell-Bratt, 1982e.

Revans RW. *The ABC of action learning*. 2nd edn. Bromley: Chartwell-Bratt, 1983a.

Revans RW. *Action learning past and present*. IFAL, 1984a.

Revans RW. *The universality of action learning*. IFAL, 1984b.

Revans RW, Baquer A. *'I thought they were supposed to be doing that.'* A com parative study of co-ordination of services for the mentally handicapped in seven local authorities, June 1969 to September 1972. THC 72/735. London: The King's Fund Hospital Centre, 1972.

Richards M. One parent families (letter). *Lancet* 1979; 1: 46.

Richards MPM. Possible effects of early separation on later development of children — a review. In *Separation and special care baby units.* (Eds) Brimblecombe FSW, Richards MPM, Robertson NRC. Clinics in Developmental Medicine no 68. London: Spastics International Medical Publications, Heinemann, 1978.

Rist EC. Student social class and teacher expectations: the self-fulfilling prophecy in ghetto education. *Harvard Educational Review* 1970; 40: 411.

Roberts J, Lynch MA, Golding J. Postneonatal mortality in children from abusing families. *Br Med J* 1980; 281: 102.

Robertson J. *Effective classroom control.* London: Hodder and Stoughton, 1981.

Robson KM, Kumar R. Delayed onset of maternal affection after childbirth. *Brit J Psychiat* 1980; 136: 347.

Rodway A. (Ed) *Day units for children with emotional behavioural difficulties.* Monograph 1. Association of Workers for Maladjusted Children and Therapeutic Education, 1981.

Roe M. Medical and psychological concepts of problem behaviour. In *Reconstructing educational psychology.* Ed Gilham B. London: Croom Helm, 1978.

Ross GS. Parental responses to infants in intensive care: the separation issue re-evaluated. *Clin Perinatol* 1980; 7: 47.

Rowe J, Lambert L. *Children who wait.* London: Association of British Adoption Agencies, 1973.

Rumsey N, Bull R, Gahagan D. The effect of facial disfigurement on the proxemic behaviour of the general public. *J Applied Social Psychology* 1982; 12: 137.

Rutter M. A children's behaviour questionnaire for completion by teachers: preliminary findings. *J Child Psychol Psychiat* 1967; 8: 1.

Rutter M. *Helping troubled children.* London: Penguin, 1975.

Rutter M. *Changing youth in a changing society: patterns of adolescent development and disorder.* London: The Nuffield Provincial Hospitals' Trust, 1979a.

Rutter M. Separation experiences: a new look at an old topic. *J Paediatrics* 1979b; 95: 147.

Rutter M. *Maternal deprivation reassessed.* 2nd edn. London: Penguin, 1981.

Rutter M, Madge N. *Cycles of disadvantage: a review of research.* London: Heinemann, 1976.

Rutter M, Maughan B, Mortimore P, Ouston J, Smith A. *Fifteen thousand hours: secondary schools and their effects on children.* London: Open Books, 1979.

St John-Brooks C. *Who controls training?* Fabian Tract 506. London: Fabian Society, 1985.

Sallis J. How parent power put paid to partnership. *Guardian* 29/5/1984.

Salzberger-Wittenberg I, Henry G, Osborne E. *The emotional experience of learning and teaching.* London: Routledge and Kegan Paul, 1983.

Sampson O. *Child guidance: its history, provenance and future.* (Ed) Pumfrey PD. London: British Psychological Society, 1980.

Sclare AB. The foetal alcohol syndrome. In *Women and alcohol.* (Ed) Camberwell Council on Alcoholism. London: Tavistock, 1980.

Scope Family Centre. Annual report, 1979-80.

Scott T. Assaults in schools (letter). *New Statesman* 10/12/1982.

Seacome M. *A short history 1962-1982.* The Gloucestershire Association for Family Life, 1982.

Secretary of State for Education and Science, and the Secretary of State for Wales. *Better schools.* Cmnd 9469. London: HMSO, 1985.

Select Committee on Violence in the Family: First Report. Violence to children. Vol I Report. Vol II Evidence. Vol III Appendices. London: HMSO, 1977.

Shaw M, Hipgrave T. *Specialist fostering: child care policy and practice.* London: Batsford, 1983.

Shaw OL. *Maladjusted boys.* London: Allen and Unwin, 1965.

Shimmin S, McNally J, Liff S. Pressures on women engaged in factory work. *Employment Gazette* 1981; 89: 344.

Shuttleworth R. Wheels within wheels: a systems approach to maladjustment. *Malad Therap Educ* 1983; 1(2); 32.

Silberman ML. Behavioural expression of teachers' attitudes towards elementary school students. *Jour Educat Psychology* 1969; 60: 402.

Sills JA, Handley JE. Snap-happy parents (letter). *Br Med J* 1978; 1: 368.

Skinner BF. *Science and human behaviour.* London: Collier-Macmillan, 1953.

Skinner BF. *Contingencies of reinforcement: a theoretical analysis.* New York: Appleton-Century-Crofts, 1969.

Smith G. *Educational priority. Vol 4: The West Riding project.* Report of a research project sponsored by the DES and the Social Science Research Council. London: HMSO, 1975.

Smith R. Poverty in the cradle. *Br Med J* 1985; 290: 1340.

Smith SM. (Ed) *The maltreatment of children.* Lancaster: MTP Press, 1978.

Smythe T. The VIPs caught in the NHS crossfire (letter). *Guardian* 28/10/1985.

Social Services Committee. *Perinatal and neonatal mortality.* Second Report, 1979-80, Vol 1. Chairwoman: Mrs Renee Short MP. London: HMSO, 1980.

Social Services Inspectorate, DHSS. *Inspection of the supervision of social workers in the assessment and monitoring of cases of child abuse when children, subject to a court order, have been returned home.* London: DHSS, 1986.

Sosa R, Kennell J, Klaus M, Robertson S, Urrutia J. The effect of a supporting companion on perinatal problems, length of labour, and mother-infant interaction. *New Engl J Med* 1980; 303: 597.

Sosa R, Kennell JH, Klaus M, Urrutia JJ. The effect of early mother-infant contact on breast feeding, infection and growth. In *Breast-feeding and the mother* (Ciba Found Symp 45). Amsterdam: Elsevier/Excerpta Medica/North Holland, 1976.

Spencer J, Tuxford J, Dennis N. *Stress and release in an urban estate: a study in action research.* London: Tavistock, 1964.

Stone J, Taylor F. *Vandalism in schools.* Child Care Department, The Save the Children Fund, 1977.

Stott D. *Studies of troublesome children*. London: Tavistock, 1966.

Streissguth AP, Clarren SK, Jones KL. Natural history of the fetal alcohol syndrome: a 10-year follow-up of eleven patients. *Lancet* 1985; *2*: 85.

Sutton A. The psychologist's professionalism and the right to psychology. In *Reconstructing educational psychology*. (Ed) Gilham B. London: Croom Helm, 1978.

Tafari N, Sterky G. Early discharge of low birthweight infants in a developing country. *Environ Child Health* 1974; *20*: 73.

Tate T, Breslin F. Worse than prisoners: the scandalous treatment of children in care. *New Statesman* p12, 2/12/83.

Tattum D. *Disruptive pupils in schools and units*. Chichester: Wiley, 1982.

Taylor L, Lacey R, Bracken D. *In whose best interests? The unjust treatment of children in courts and institutions*. London: The Cobden Trust/MIND, 1979.

Taylor M. *Study of the juvenile liaison scheme in West Ham 1961-1965*. Home Office Research Study no 8. London: HMSO, 1971.

Thomas Coram Research Unit. *Health Visitor* 1975; *48*: 298.

Thompson D, Webb P, Pudney M. (Eds) *Someone to talk to directory*. London: Mental Health Foundation/Routledge and Kegan Paul, 1985.

Thomson WAR. Doctors and sexual disorders. *J Roy Soc Med* 1981; *74*: 390.

Tizard B. *The care of young children: implications of recent research*. Thomas Coram Research Unit; Working and Occasional Papers no 1. London: London Institute of Education, 20 Bedford Way, WC1H 0AL; 1986.

Tizard B, Hughes M. *Young children learning: talking and thinking at home and at school*. London: Fontana, 1984.

Tizard J. Maladjusted children and the child guidance service. *London Educational Review* 1973; *2*: 22.

Topping K. *Educational systems for disruptive adolescents*. London: Croom Helm, 1983.

Tutt N. Juvenile justice in a mess (letter). From the Centre of Youth, Crime and Community, Fylde College, Lancaster University. *Guardian* 2/11/1979.

Tutt N. Maladjustment — a sociological perspective. *Malad Therap Educ* 1983; 1(2): 7.

Tutt N. The punishment depends on the country, not the crime. *Guardian* 11/12/1985.

Upton G, Gobell A. (Eds) *Behaviour problems in the comprehensive school*. Cardiff: Faculty of Education, University College, 1980.

Valman HB. Mother-infant bonding. *Br Med J* 1980; *280*: 308.

Vernon J, Fruin D. *In care: a study of social work decision making*. London: National Children's Bureau, 1986.

Vincent S. How the nightmares are kept in order: a visit to a custom-built home. *Observer* 22/4/1979.

Ward E. *Father-daughter rape*. London: Women's Press, 1984.

Warren N, Jahoda M. (Eds) *Attitudes: selected readings*. 2nd edn. London: Penguin, 1973.

Watkins R, Derrick D. (Eds) *Co-operative care: practice and information profiles*. Centre for Information and Advice on Educational Disadvantage, 1977.

Watts, Janet. Children of despair. *Observer* 25/3/1984.

Watts, John. *The Countesthorpe experience*. London: Allen and Unwin, 1977.

Welsh Office. *Sixth form education in the schools of Wales*. London: HMSO, 1978.

West DJ. *Delinquency: its roots, careers and prospects*. London: Heinemann, 1982.

Wheldall K. (Ed) *The behaviourist in the classroom: aspects of applied behavioural analysis in British educational contexts*. Educational Review Offset Publications no 1, Faculty of Education, University of Birmingham, PO Box 363, Birmingham B15 2TT, 1981.

Wheldall K, Merrett F. Reducing troublesome classroom behaviour in the secondary school. *Malad Therap Educ* 1985; 3(2): 37.

Where April 1972, p121.

Where 124. Home link: the parents' home-visiting project. Jan 1977.

Where 140. Taylor bashing unions. July/Aug 1978a.

Where 141. Changing attitudes to one parent families. Sept 1978b, p231.

White J. *The aims of education restated*. London: Routledge and Kegan Paul, 1982.

Whitlam MR. The Hammersmith project — new hope for teenagers at risk. *Social Work Today* 1977; 9: 7.

Wieland GF. The hospital internal communications (HIC) project. In *Improving health care management: organization development and organization change*. Ed Wieland GF. Ann Arbor, Michigan: Health Administration Press, 1981.

Wieland GF, Leigh H. (Eds) *Changing hospitals: a report on the hospital internal communications project*. London: Tavistock, 1971.

Wild NJ. Sexual abuse of children in Leeds. *Br Med J* 1986; 292: 1113.

Wilding P. *Professional power and social welfare*. London: Routledge and Kegan Paul, 1982.

Wilkinson G. Psychotherapy in the NHS. *Lancet* 1984; 2: 988.

Wilkinson JE, Grant D, Williamson DJ. *Strathclyde experiment in education: Govan project*. Glasgow University, Department of Education; Strathclyde Regional Council, Department of Education, 1978.

Williams M. Rising suns; a report on rebellion and violence in Japanese high schools. *Guardian* 22/2/1983.

Wills D. *The Barns experiment*. London: Allen and Unwin, 1945.

Wills WD. *Throw away thy rod: living with difficult children*. London: Gollancz, 1960.

Wilson M, Evans M. Special units for the disturbed or disruptive. *Contact* (ILEA) 1979; 7(23): 20.

Wilson M, Evans M. *Education of disturbed pupils*. Schools Council Working Paper 65. London: Methuen Educational, 1980.

Winnicott C. Communicating with children. In *Disturbed children*. (Ed) Tod RJN. London: Longmans, 1968.

Winnicott DW. *The child and the outside world: studies in developing relationships*. London: Tavistock, 1957.

Winnicott DW. *The maturational process and the facilitating environment*. London: Hogarth Press, 1965.

Wirth AG. Exploring linkages between Dewey's educational philosophy and industrial organisation. *Economic and Industrial Democracy* 1981; 2: 121.

Wolfgang CH, Glickman CD. *Solving discipline problems: strategies for classroom teachers*. London: Allyn and Bacon, 1980.

Wood A, Simpkins L. *Involving parents in the curriculum*. A Home and School Council Publication, 1980.

Wragg EC. An assortment of hats to suit the occasion. *Guardian* 19/12/1978.

Wragg EC. *A review of research in teacher education*. London: NFER/Nelson, 1982.

Wragg EC, Sutton C. *Class management and control: a teaching practice handbook*. 1979. Available from: The Coordinator, Teacher Education Project, University Park, Nottingham University, Nottingham NG2 7RD.

Yardley A. Swain H. *Community schools in practice*. A Home and School Council Publication, 1980.

Young M. Getting parents into schools. *Observer* 29/10/1967.

Younghusband E. The nature of social work. In *A reader in social administration*. (Ed) Lochhead AVS. London: Constable, 1968.

Index

About the authors . . .

Portia G Holman MA, MD Cantab, FRCP, FRCPsych, DPM

The late Dr Holman's experience includes being President of the Association of Workers for Maladjusted Children (which she helped to found), Senior Psychiatrist at the Elizabeth Garrett Anderson Hospital and Director of the Ealing Child Guidance Clinic. Among her special characteristics was a penetrating yet sympathetic understanding of the troubles of children in School and their teachers, and of the difficulties of cooperation between professional groups.

Nelson F Coghill MA, MB Cantab, FRCP

Dr Coghill, now retired, was a physician at the West Middlesex Hospital. He has been well acquainted with a wide variety of clinical subjects and was one-time President of the British Society of Gastroenterology. He also studied the operational management of matters affecting all grades of hospital worker in the care of patients. For some 35 years he was a School Governor and has been Chairman of the Governors of a Special School for Maladjusted Children. For many years he has worked for an educational charity (The International Foundation for Action Learning — which he helped to found) whose purpose is to improve management by linking action to experimental learning.